TO: GF
"GROWING WITH GRACE"

RHYTHM FOR SALE

BY DR. GRANT HARPER REID

MAY GOD BLESS YOU. ENJOY THE READ.
            LOVE - GRANT

Copyright © 2013 by Grant Harper Reid
All rights reserved.

ISBN-13: 978-0615678283
ISBN-10: 0615678289
LCCN: 2012914071
CreateSpace Independent Publishing Platform
North Charleston, South Carolina

No part of this book may be reproduced or transmitted in any form or by any means, electronic or mechanical, including photocopying, recording or by any information storage and retrieval system, without permission in writing from the Author.

Registered with the Library of Congress Office of Copyright.

For God and Family

CONTENTS

INTRODUCTION vii

Chapter ONE *(1888 to 1923)*
    THE EARLY YEARS: *MEDICINE SHOWS & SILENT MOVIES* 1
    HARPER & BLANKS WITH LOVE 10
    COLORED DARLINGS OF LONDON? 21
    HARPER MOVED TO HARLEM & DID THE LINCOLN
    THEATRE 36

Chapter TWO *(1923 to the Early 1930's)*
    HARPER Did CONNIE'S INN 41
    HARPER Did the LAFAYETTE THEATRE 56
    HARPER Did the NEST CLUB 69
    HARPER Did the COTTON CLUB 70
    HARPER Did the HOLLYWOOD INN / KENTUCKY CLUB 77
    HARPER Did SMALL'S PARADISE 85

Chapter THREE *(1924 to 1928)*
    TAKE ME UP TO *THE ONLY HARLEM RENAISSANCE* 87
    THE GREAT (WHITE) *LEONARD HARPER* WAY 92
    LEONARD HARPER & FLORENCE MILLS 107
    LEONARD HARPER CHATTERED 111
    HARPER DID THE SAVOY BALLROOM 113
    HARPER DID NEW JERSEY 117

Chapter FOUR *(1928 to 1929)*
    HARPER'S *HOT CHOCOLATES'* 119
    THE CONCEPT, THE CHALLENGE AND THE CHANCE 122
    THREE TALENTED TAN-SKINNED CREATORS 130
    AN UNDYING BROADWAY INSCRIPTION 141

Chapter FIVE (*1929 to 1935*)
   'HOT HARLEM' GOT FROSTY 163
   HOLLYWOOD HERE WE COME—NOT! 173
   HARPER ROMANCED YOUNG FANNIE PENNINGTON 179
   HARPER "DUFFED" HARLEM FOR CHICAGO 184
   RHYTHM FOR SALE 189
   CHICAGO RHYTHM 194

Chapter SIX (*1935 to 1937*)
   UNSEEN PRODUCER/DIRECTOR 201
   HARPER DID THE UBANGI CLUB…TOO 205
   FANNIE AND POCKET-SIZED HARRIET JEAN HARPER 209
   MOTHER HARPER RELOCATED TO HARLEM JEAN
   HARPER LEFT FOR DOWN SOUTH WHILE- FANNIE'S
   ON THE GO 212
   THOSE FABULOUS HARPERETTES 217
   THE WORLD FAMOUS APOLLO THEATRE…Y'ALL 219

Chapter SEVEN (*1937 to 1942*)
   HARPER DID THE *DOWNTOWN* HARLEM UPROAR HOUSE ..225
   EV'RY SHOW'S GOTTA HAVE A FINALE 233
   HARPERETTES WALKED OUT OF THE APOLLO
   THEATRE 236
   HARPER DID THE ELK'S RENDEZVOUS (1941-1942) 240

Chapter EIGHT (*1942 to 1943*)
   WANTED: GLAMOROUS GIRLS 243
   HARPER DID MURRAINS 245
   STILL *CHOCK FULL OF RHYTHM* 248
   EXILED ON SEVENTH AVENUE 252
   1943 HARPER'S DEATH 255
   THE AFTERMATH 259

HARPER APOLLO THEATRE SIGNATURE SHOWCASE 263
AUTHORS NOTES 281
PHOTOGRAPHS & ILLUSTRATIONS 295
BIBLIOGRAPHICAL LISTINGS 297
ACKNOWLEDGMENTS 301
INDEX 303

INTRODUCTION

I went into the Countee Cullen library to browse about, and as I was exiting I happened to glance upon the librarian's table and spotted a book titled: *The Harlem Renaissance: A Historical Dictionary For The Era* edited by Bruce Kellner. My inquisitiveness obligated me to peek inside the covers and see if this Harlem Renaissance tome had any information about my grandfather Leonard Harper.

Harper's first name was spelled incorrectly as Leon, and at first I didn't think it was my grandfather. I asked the librarian what the Reference: "BB" denoted at the bottom of the paragraph, and I was told to walk around the corner to the Schomburg Center for Research in Black Culture and ask them for the book *Blacks In Blackface* by Henry T. Sampson. I rushed to the Schomburg Center and was able to find and unearth so much material about my grandfather that it took me years to fully complete my research. The discovery of my family heritage by way of my grandfather was like striking a treasure chest of precious metals.

Ms. Edwina Evelyn, who performed in some of Harper's shows in the "good old days" with her dance team duo Salt and Pepper, advised me to, "Check all of the old African-American newspapers because they all wrote about your grandfather back then." That little piece of information, which Ms. Evelyn shared, demonstrated to be my most valuable instrumental exploratory key.

I hungered to learn everything I could about Harper and the world within which he revolved. Harper's life and times had a distinctive spirit that coincided with every incident and accomplishment that was 'owned' by a particular station in time and history.

CHAPTER ONE
(1888 to 1923)

THE EARLY YEARS: *MEDICINE SHOWS & SILENT MOVIES*

Leonard Harper was born on April 9, 1889 to Sarah and William Harper in Birmingham, Alabama. When Harper turned four, he and his younger brother Eugene danced and performed for pennies, meals, and used clothing. They were known as pickaninnies.

Harper and his buddies made crude musical instruments from large animal jawbones, sticks of wood and metal buckets. The Harper boys inherited many of their best show business tips from their dad William, who was a professional thespian and Coon Shouter. William Harper was of a special lot of old time theatrical performers whose essence was rooted in the master showmanship of survival.

Coon Shouter's sang songs with titles such as *I Wish My Color Would Fade Away*, *An Educated Coon Is Best of All* by Scott Lawrence consisting of lyrics like "You talk about your swell coons. Well they don't count with me. It takes a coon with education. He's the one you see. Now my babe he is cultured. He's been through college too. He uses words I can't pronounce. That's what my babe, do."

One such theatrical show that William Harper starred in was titled *Doings in Coontown*. Young Leonard Harper was so deeply influenced by his father William's theatrical skills he often fantasized about performing with him before large audiences. Mother Sarah Harper, who regularly took Harper and his brother Gene to the country Baptist

Church every Sunday also had a strong dramatic influence on her boys. Young Harper sang as a church soloist. He had the extra gift of bearing an exquisite, soulful, high pitched singing voice. But his sweet little syrup sounding vocals from God altered early on, as he grew, and his male hormones developed and set in. This fast maturation of his voice forced him to concentrate and adjust his unique brand of dancing and comedic theatrical skills.

At the age of four, Leonard Harper dashed away from home accompanied by little Gene, to dance in medicine shows for pennies, using only their fast feet as their instruments. These kids, were born with an enormous amount of dexterity in their movements, and danced sometimes just for the appreciative smiles from audience members.

William Harper died when Leonard was just ten years old and everything in Harper's world became different. He tearfully vowed at his daddy's gravesite to take care of his mother and brother for his father. Harper had to fast become the little man of the family. His brother Gene no longer danced with him and Sarah found it difficult to make ends meet without her husband's income. Harper was forced into show business fulltime to support his family. He joined up with Al Shear's Show and quickly moved on to dance with the Cheatham Brothers at the Old Traction Park in Birmingham.

Under Bill Cheatham, Harper learned and refined the art of Soft Shoe from one of the greatest Soft Shoe dancers ever in a plantation show. Harper was taught how to dance not only atop of those little platforms but underneath them, to their side and around them, while never missing, a *clickity-clickity stomping* beat. Bill Cheatham's protégé at ten years old, was now a first-class dancer who could tap rings around most of the adults and veteran masters. In other words, young Harper be *boggity-boggity*.

Harper sported hobnailed boots', taps made from old broken off nails. These poor boy's tap shoes enhanced the sound of his banging footsteps that went along with the high speed physical movements of his routines. With fast acrobatic and spasmodic hand, arm and leg itches, Harper jerked, trying to find that inner scratch that jumped from one part of his body to the other, causing his muscles to go aflutter in his early version of the *hebbie jebbies.*

On July 2, 1910 when Harper was eleven years old he paired up with another young pickaninny named Dave Shaffer and together they formed a group called Two Clever Pics. Audiences laughed at their buffoonery and jokes, but the songs that, they sang were so sentimental the crowds were reduced to tears and gladly gave the young boys handsome cash tips out of approval and pity. The Two Clever Pics performed their debut at the Pantopia Theatre in Birmingham, Alabama and acted so fabulously that they were instantly picked up as the top lined featured act.

Harper and Shaffer traveled the Southern circuit and performed to sold-out houses nightly. At first when the Two Clever Pics toured the Southern circuit of theatres, they did a lot of hard country road walking. The stage manager for their show was a Mr. George Freeman who doubled as a struggling comedian as well as a producer. George Freeman was also a man out of his bloody mind although he did have a keen eye for recognizing talent and he immediately scooped up young Harper because he saw that the kid had a magical style of his own. Freedman was not big time, but with a kid who bore natural born theatrical skills like Harper, he assumed that one day they both could become famous and wealthy.

George Freeman started a group called George Freeman and his Two Clever Pics. After a four month road engagement at the Globe Theatre in Jacksonville, Florida, Harper and Shaffer demanded a name change, a business move well beyond their years. Shaffer took things a few steps further, telling a very cautious Harper, that if the billing changes didn't come into effect soon he might have to cause harm to Freeman. Harper and Shaffer were well aware of who the real box office draws were, and forced the old man's hand. They became the Freeman-Harper-Shaffer Trio. Lucille Hegamin, the fifteen year old "Georgia Peach" blues singing teenager, linked up with the traveling tent show stock company.

The Freeman-Harper-Shaffer production team traveled with two male piano players who also carried their "first class" wardrobe for them. They also had one scenery artist who functioned as the carpenter and character man. One big treat for the trio was when they mingled with the affluent, white theatre patrons of Arkansas. They enjoyed eating continental French sandwiches for the first time with Mr. J. W. Howell Jr., the well-known and moneyed President of the Hot Springs Mountain Observatory Company high atop the 180 foot mountain towers looking at the city below. The bread looked peculiar but tasted "ok, alright and good".

Even though the Freeman-Harper-Shaffer trio, were considered a "Screaming Success," there were times when the act made little or no money and had nothing to eat. Harper went for three days without eating and had to troupe 43 miles on foot from Cordele, Georgia all the way to Fitzgerald, Georgia. During this time Harper became as thin as a dime and was laughed at by all those who saw him. To add further insult to his hardship, when Harper and the rest of the company arrived in Fitzgerald exhausted as all get out; they came to find that the show and their payday had been cancelled.

George Freeman fired the less talented rough and unruly Dave Shaffer as he concentrated on capitalizing off of the many stage gifts belonging to Harper by forming the Freeman and Harper Team. This new duo signed on to do a hit comedy show at the Central Theatre and the Duval Theatre in Atlanta, Georgia. Their show was called, *Mr. And Mrs. Brown.* It was now 1911 and Harper was a mere twelve years old but he took up the female impersonation role quite convincingly. As a matter of fact, Harper played Mrs. Brown so realistically that while donning make-up and dress it could not be figured out if he was of the male sex at all. The success of *Mr. And Mrs. Brown* came with a very high and displeasing price for young Leonard who was often teased, humiliated and rumored on. Some hecklers in the audience called him Freeman's wife, or Madame Leonard Harper and his sexuality was derided off stage. Deep down inside Harper knew that it was only an act and as a professional actor the work was much better than cleaning toilets or plowing and picking cotton fields so he grinned and bearded it. Harper had to endure his *Mrs. Brown* mocking.

Clarence Muse, a stiff little dramatic church reader, who was a few years younger than Harper, saw one of the Freeman-Harper traveling shows and was so awestruck that he immediately wanted to break out of his shell and go into show business. Little Clarence did so well during his on-the-spot audition with his strong tear inducing, dramatic church readings that Freeman had no choice but to hire him. In the book *Every Step a Struggle: Interviews with Seven Who Shaped the African-American Images in Movies-Scarred By History* by Frank Manchel, Muse called to mind his first meeting with Harper, "Muse: And there were a couple fellows who put me in a stock company…One was named Freeman, and the young chap in shorts who was named [Leonard] Harper… And before I knew it, they had wiggled me around to the point where I bought third interest in the stock company." Muse summoned up the difficulties his new partners underwent "[Muse's new partners] owed people in every county they had ever been in, and every sheriff in the South was looking for them. I got a kick out of the fact that on the marquee my name went out "Freeman, Harper, and Muse." So that was big enough for me."

Thus the Freeman-Harper-Muse Trio Stock Company was formed and was comprised of fourteen people, which included support staff. Muse did a base solo that was to die for and married his child bride, Miss. Ophelia Belle Moore of Jacksonville, Florida. Muse also received a promotion from Freeman and was elevated to business manager of the troupe after a few performances and an accurate recounting of ticket slips.

In 1912 the Freeman-Harper-Muse Stock Company played Frank Crowd's Globe Theatre in Jacksonville, Florida. The play was called *Stranded in Africa* and Harper enacted both the straight and female impersonation roles as Muse portrayed the grotesquely clad and hilariously ugly King Gazu. The cast wore lots of freakish makeup for dramatic effect in their roles as African Zulus. Backstage gambling quickly became a favorite pastime for the troupe. Crowds of people wanting to see the show were turned away nightly.

It was now George Freeman's turn to take a wife not for love or romance but out of convenience. He needed an additional worker. Mrs. Gussie Freeman was the new costumer for the stock company and spent most of her time sewing. Her husband promised that one day soon she would be able to join his stock company as a lady character actress. But first she must continue laboring on as the costumer.

George Freeman was known to be eccentric, and when his brother Silas M. Freeman died he went off the deep end. Silas was in the theatre world just like his eccentric brother. He was a member of the Golden Gate Quartet in a show called *Down in Dixie* when he passed away in Atlantic City, N. J. on January 13, 1913. Brother Silas Freeman was buried in Birmingham, Alabama and George Freeman took a three week break to be with his family. Harper took advantage of this long overdue break and was able to spend some quality time with his mother and brother. He was happy to be home again with his loved ones, who he now supported. When it was time to go back on the road Freeman could only get Harper and his wife Gussie to rejoin him and come back to work. Muse and the other company members were tired of Freeman's wild and bizarre outbursts and abandoned the company due to his ever-increasing odd and erratic behavioral patterns. Although Harper was put off by Freeman's strange behavior he also had a sense of loyalty to George, the man who helped him get work early on, so Harper reluctantly returned and joined back up with the company.

Gussie Freeman got her big chance and became a full-fledged member of the Freeman, Harper and Freeman Trio. The troupe toured the South with Harper playing the role of a comical burglar. The new troupe opened up as headliners on stage and did, quite well financially. They even took side gigs becoming the first colored motion picture posers in the film industry as actors who danced in silent moving pictures for the Educational Film Company. Harper, at only fourteen, defiantly refused to wear the formulaic "Nigger's", battered pug hat, white gloves, baggy pants and gunboat shoes.

The Freeman-Harper-Freeman Trio extended their stay in Birmingham for a while longer. George Freeman said, "And as my family wished me to stay at home for a while I was asked by my many friends to introduce vaudeville there. As I, was the first man to introduce vaudeville in the city of Birmingham, Alabama, which I, did." The Freeman-Harper-Freeman Trio opened up in the Lincoln Theatre and sold out every night before they moved on to the Bon Ton Theatre in North Birmingham for standing room only shows.

To make extra income George Freeman went into a little side talent booking for the Thornton Trio who, were out of work for so long they were left stranded and hungry without clothes or money. Freeman said, "Some of them (The Thornton Trio) carry salt and pepper shakers in their pockets and sprinkle it on each other and eat themselves raw". The Thornton Trio needed any type of work that they could get so Mr. Freeman arranged for them to play shows at the Lincoln Theatre which he also double booked for the very luscious and eye-catching Whitman Sisters.

The Whitman Sisters were not just stunning, sexy and gorgeously high kicking, yellow toned black women with long "Legomania" legs, but they were also the type of girls most full blooded males would always desire in their company. In other words they were big male audience box office draws. The Whitman Sister's with their ravishing looks were also trouble for Freeman's wandering and degenerate eyes.

Trouble for Freeman came in the form of Mattie Whitman, who accused Freeman of owing her nine dollars and cutting short her payment for one night's worth of work. Freeman explained that he could not find Mattie to pay her because she and a female friend were arrested and thrown in jail. Freeman went on to say that Mattie was guilty of a very disrespectful act. He said that Mattie had committed a crime against nature by taking the place of a man with another woman who acted as the wife in a "most shameful act". Freeman made these malicious statements even though he had repeatedly propositioned and begged Mattie for her sexual affections. Freeman was also jealous that he was not invited along for the loving with Mattie and her girlfriend and this was his way of getting back at them for not including him in and making it an erotic threesome.

The sexually obsessed Freeman was so unraveled and agitated that he lost track of all his show business ambitions. When he finally came to his "senses" young Harper was gone for good. Harper had grown weary of Freeman's foolish backstage sideshow shenanigans, which had temporarily taken him away from his trade, his art, his pure devotion of performing, and all that he had grasped at such a young age.

Harper got a remarkable offer to join the Venable and Owens vaudeville team formerly called the Owens Sisters who were bound for New York City with promises of making heaps of money. Miss. Sarah Venable did what was called a male impersonation on stage, and her stage maleness was the real life 'butch' persona that was her character twenty four hours a day and seven days a week. Partner, Miss. Beatrice Owens, on the other hand was the ultra, feminine, womanly element of the act. Both women were a little on the chunky side but their plus sizes didn't hamper their refined stage moves one bit. Harper's enthusiasm and blazing skills allowed him to fit right in. It was a refreshing change for the young lad to get the opportunity to work with these two remarkably talented, free-spirited and open minded, stable women.

The Venable-Owens and Harper Trio traveled the South and Mid-Western states with a strategy to eventually wind up in New York City. At the Crown Garden Theatre in Indianapolis their music was said to have an operatic effect. The trio sang a butter-milked version of *Way Down Yonder in the Cornfield* costumed as rustics. Harper voraciously read dance books and copied the diagrams and then implemented a lot of flying foreign leaps and buck danced around the rest of the trio. They finished the show by tapping with rhythmical dance steps and singing with blended harmonious voices a song titled *Following the Crowds*, something none of this dramatic threesome, to their credit, ever did off stage.

Unfortunately, once the Venable-Owens-Harper Trio arrived in New York City, they were unable to get booked in theatres. Because of their race and the color of their skin they were rebuffed over and over again. The trio faced strong resistance from the biased white Broadway booking agents who refused to consider hiring "race" or African-American women for theatre work. Harper became their impromptu spokesman and repeatedly attempted to crack open the locked doors which blocked the players. Many theatre owners wouldn't even talk to Harper and the few that did only spoke to him because he was a male. Harper's backstage political efforts proved fruitless as the regressive minded theatre bookers continuously slammed the doors in his face while restating their discriminatory rules "No Race or Colored females, period".

It was very upsetting for the Venable-Owens-Harper act to have to stomach being locked out of the theatre world in New York. Broadway was to be the big break for Harper and the ladies, a safe haven where they could rise up in show business ranks, but instead it turned out to be just another one of their personal American nightmares. In place of flowers backstage they were repeatedly hit with racially closed doors shut hard.

Harper tried futilely to cheer up the shattered and defeated Sarah Venable and Beatrice Owens, as they traveled west to Chicago for work. While Harper felt the displeasure of having to tolerate the racial obstacles and setbacks that were positioned before the trio, and was unhappy by the recent ordeals of being locked out of the New York City theatre world, he didn't view it as a career ending catastrophe and didn't share in any feelings of defeat or immobilization.

Harper was instead more determined than ever to become a success, and had a big dream of returning to New York to open up the doors of the Great White Way for himself and the entire contingent of fellow locked out African-American theatre people. Harper exited the company with the prayers, blessings and good will of his former trio of Venable-Owens, leaving them to become a duo once again.

Harper temporarily joined a stock company with the celebrated showman Bob Russell called the Russell-Harper-Smith Stock Company with up-to-date whirlwind singers and dancers. They had mediocre success and Harper realized, for the first time, that he had a marketable solo box office name that could sell theatre seats in Chicago. Within his short existence, and for all of Harper's brief years as a childhood performer, he had created quite an upbeat buzz about himself. People rushed to purchase tickets to see him, so the rapidly ripening Harper decided to go solo at the mature old veteran's age of sixteen.

HARPER & BLANKS WITH LOVE

Part of Harper's immediate solution for success in his quest to make a bigger name for himself was that he had to start performing as a solo act on larger stage bills comprising of up to at least twenty five other selected acts or artists. One of the other acts that performed on some of the same bills with him was the delightful female duo called the Blank Sisters. The Blank Sisters were comprised of two favorite young ladies from the Chicago theatrical community who originally hailed from Saint Louis, Missouri. Osceola and Berliana Blanks were both known for singing popular blues and rag songs like *Memphis Blues* and *Baseball Rag* and for adding frisky skits that matched and dramatized the lyrics. The Blank Sisters used an innate comicality and pathos and they also dressed and costumed attractively.

Osceola Blanks, the prettiest of the two Blank Sisters and the one with the cute baby like dimples was also considered to be as pleasing as a picture. Osceola was more distinguished and elder looking in appearance, even more than Harper, but it was her grand elegance and captivating aura that caught Harper's backstage notice. Harper couldn't keep his eyes off of Osceola and one day while rehearsing, he attempted to show off in front of her with some of his quick dance moves. She laughed while shyly looking away, but at the same time Osceola was thoroughly amused by Harper's boyish flirtations. Harper was transfixed, by her graceful appearance and by her bright seal skinned complexion.

Harper was on the bill as a solo act with the Blanks Sisters when they played the Grand Theatre in Chicago in the *Grand All-Star Minstrels of 1918* presentation and they appeared together in a comedy musical farce in the tabloid form called *The Wedding Day*. This production had an additional twenty five variety acts featured. *The Wedding Day* was about a guy who mistakenly bought a dog license instead of a marriage license on his wedding day. Harper sang *Dixie* with the Beluah Blues Quartet comprised of four sweet looking young gals who stood in the background. The Blank Sisters sang the song *Asleep in the Deep* and the more shows they all performed together with Harper the closer he and Osceola got. Harper and Osceola romanced, and at, lighting speed they became an instant couple. Once they started dancing, singing, and spending quality time together, they became inseparable. Love was new for Osceola and Harper, with feelings that they had never felt before, a close, warm tingling sensation that within a thespian/dancer's heart spun into explosively strong pulse palpitations. Osceola took up sewing fine new suits by hand for her man and even put shiny new taps on his shoes whenever he needed them.

Forgotten sister Berliana Blanks was diminished into standing alone and taking a back seat to her partner and sister's romance to Harper and she didn't like it one bit. Berliana contemplated the notion of leaving the theatre profession and going back to the St. Louis school teaching field where she previously labored before the show business bug bit her. Rage and jealously factored in for Berliana who always had to do a little more work in the beautification department than her sister Osceola anyway. Berliana's anxiety was compounded by her real fear that Harper might break up the sister duo for good and damage the sibling closeness that she and Osceola worked so hard to develop and enjoy.

Osceola went back and forth from the new duo of Harper and Blanks to the old Blank Sisters duo. From 1917 to 1918 Osceola tried to appease both her boyfriend and her sister at the same time. It was a tug of war between Harper and Berliana for Osceola's time and talents. This waffling by Osceola between her professional and familial faithfulness to her sister, and her romantic/star-imagined future with Harper exhausted her emotionally and began to strain and damage her performances. Even though Osceola was in the power position, with Berliana and Harper vying for her exclusivity, she was perturbed and just as eager as they were for a resolution in this matter. Time and situation eventually made for a conclusive outcome for all parties involved. But before there was to be any conclusion, Osceola repeatedly became dizzily tugged apart while going back and forth from one duo to the other.

One of the tabloid shows' that featured Harper as a solo artist along with the Blanks Sisters traveled to Nashville, Tennessee. The producer of this outing was the jocular Sidney Perrin, an African-American performer known for donning hilarious Chinese outfits which enhanced the allure of the Orient as he sang songs with titles like *Chop Suey for One,* as the very animated and effeminate Afro-American-Chinaman in the comedy farce called *Virginia Days*. Perrin quit the tour Midway, without leaving professional notice, and as a consequence Harper was left in charge as the producer. It was Harper's big break and he used this opportunity to establish the new song and dance team of Harper and Blanks as a permanent fixture in show business. The Blanks Sister act dissolved so to smooth things over with sister Berliana, Harper promised to assist her with her new solo career. There was still too much pain and anger however within Berliana's heart to let Harper manage her, so she left the new Harper production altogether to join up with the traveling Billy King Company.

Eventually, after a period of years, Berliana Blanks received top billing singing *You Can't Shake Your Shimmy Here,* with the Billy King Company, which rapidly elevated her as one of Chicago's favorite vocalist in the production of *Hawaiian Rhapsody*. She toured with them all over the mid-west, east coast and southern states and made somewhat of a name for herself. Time healed her wounds and allowed forgiveness to enter her heart. Berliana later worked for Harper in many of his future productions with a trio of female performers called the Three Dixie Songbirds.

At 22 Harper married Osceola Blanks while they toured in Indianapolis, Indiana. The newly established song and dance team of Harper and Blanks toured the African-American circuit of theatres in America warbling songs like *Old Green River* and *Dreamy Panama*. They concluded their shows with some bewitching Spanish dancing and a particular version of their new dance creation *Walking the Dog* based on the 1916 Shelton Brooks instrumental.

The Harper and Blanks dance hit version of *Walking the Dog* helped to inspire and make popular the close partnered cheek-to-cheek couples style of dancing together. They received screams and raves from their audiences. After Harper and Blanks first presented their *Walking the Dog* dance moves to Chicago audiences it became a craze that took over the windy city like a cyclone. The fresh duo crafted superb and celebrated reputations for their act wherever and whenever they played. Right from the start Harper and Blanks headlined and closed out the big shows along with opening acts such as Blaine and Brown, Dade and Dade, the corking Snow Fisher, Butter Beans and Miss. Lester and White & Bradford known as the black faced singing comedians in a dark town flirtation. Sometimes Harper and Blanks opened up for silent photoplay movies.

Harper and Blanks were billed as "Whirlwind Singers and Dancers, Late of the Russell-Harper-Smith Stock Company, Quality Vaudeville Actors", or "A Wonderfully Costumed Act", who danced themselves into popularity and into the hearts of audiences everywhere they played. Direct from a successful run on Loews New England Time, a sampling of some of their general reviews stated, "Harper wears cork but is better without it. Harper reminds one of those classic Russian dances which have been all the rage in this country. They are considered the best dressed duo and in addition they carry their own scenery. Their style is pleasing with nothing grotesque. Osceola in her own right is complimented for having a very nice figure and carriage and for being one of the best specimens of a colored beauty, wherever she appeared." The team was noted for their performances although their pay did not increase, reflect, or parallel, the boost in their box office ticket sales at the time.

Harper and Blanks toured on what was commonly known as T.O.B.A. time, or, 'Theatrical Owners and Bookers Association', which black people called "Tough on Black Actors." The contracts were damaging for the artist's as they agreed to owe the managers a "liquidation damages" fee of $1,500 if they failed to perform for any reason. The African-American talents also had to agree to make payments of damages of $1,500 to the theatre or place of amusement contracted if they were caught in any venue other than the one on the circuit tour that they were on at, anytime in the same city. The thespians must also agree not to appear in any other theatre in the same city ninety days before their show or sixty days after their engagement, and if caught in violation of these directives, they would be impaired by any number of other stiff financial reparations.

The actors who worked the T.O.B.A. tours took to sleeping in the far back barren southern fields of unkempt farms for protection, hidden totally away from the whites who wished them harm. One amusing exception to the rule, as legend had it, was when big Bessie Smith chased away the Ku Klux Klan, threatening to beat their asses with a sizable stick, after the Klan attempted to take down and remove her performance tent.

The Harper and Blanks duo were contracted by the McCormick Amusement company to co-star in the production of *Put and Take* at Town Hall in New York City. This 1921 show was written and staged by Irvin C. Miller with music by Spencer Williams both African-American men and this all black production would never have been funded unless *Shuffle Along,* another black Broadway musical, hadn't made a profit during that same year. *Shuffle Along* was more of a comedy than *Put and Take*. *Put and Take* was tagged as "a spin from Georgia to Broadway," and was far richer in action, as it displayed lots of fast dancing, which was right up Harper's alley. Ex-boxing champion Jack Johnson was the marquee name star of the spectacle and he was guaranteed a weekly box office salary of $2,000. An enormous number of gifted Afro-American vaudevillians were featured in the musical that was also complemented by a large chorus of thirty African-American players.

The City of New York which ran the Town Hall theatre at the time, closed *Put and Take* even though it generated whopping box office ticket sales. The production sold through the roof but the Town Hall was controlled by a woman named Mary Cleveland who complained that the Town Hall was built for civic purposes and town meetings, meaning, not for African-American actors. Cleveland had, in the past, approved the showing of movies, and allowed for the Hall to be used for other commercial purposes, but she had manufactured a foul hindrance with the featuring of an all, African-American theatre troupe in *Put and Take*. African-American actors dressed in fine garb just didn't fit into Mary Cleveland's racist stereotypical concept of what black people should look like and it caused her under-bloomers to bunch up into a knot. There were reports in the press that the stage crew and the cast members of the show were not paid all of their salaries even though the producers rendered massive proceeds.

Jack Goldberg, Harlem's Shuffle Inn owner and *Put and Takes'* producer was driven to look for other Broadway area theatres to house the production. The only theatre that would have them was the Century Promenade on Sixty-third, Street. The financial backers considered the Century Promenade offer but wound, up eventually nixing the idea altogether because they would have been restricted to only playing midnight shows. Nothing became of *Put and Take* and eventually it just faded away into the annals of forgotten theatre history.

There was a silver lining in regards to *Put and Take* for Harper and Blanks. It was such a breathtaking show that the white audiences dug it in spite of the racial resistance. The white directors and producers were also astounded by the stage abilities of the African-American performers and were educated in the art of a brand new style of Southern rooted stage tricks ferociously performed by the darker skinned talents. The *New York Times* reported in *Put And Take Is Lively,* on August 24, 1921 that of *Put and Take* "there is its ceaseless activity—the best word to describe the proceedings is simple pep. There is about twice as much energy expended as is needed to run the average Broadway revue, but most of it is to excellent purpose." What the Town Hall audiences experienced was a show that didn't lag or have any sags or long pauses, and the encores were only delivered when necessary.

In an un-sourced September 1921 newspaper clipping theatre critic Patterson James wrote a very curious review about *Put and Take*, "The show moves. The opening act chorus starts like a whirlwind and never stops. The smiles of the chorus girls are real, not 'prop' attempts, and the chorus men are performers, not back row fillers. Everybody works as if it was a pleasure, not a labor. Also there is no dirt, no three-quarter stripped women, no filthy dialogue, and no profanity. In this particular show the Negro writers and comedians put their white brothers to the blush. What is responsible for this spirit of cleanliness, I do not know. It may be because Negro actors as a class are poor talkers and their lack of fluency serves as a dam to the expression of unpleasant ideas. Or again it may be that the Negroes as a race are not inclined to unclean speech. But whatever the reason and however different things may be off stage, the colored actor never descends into the sewer for his comedy material. There is not even a borderline joke in "Put and Take". — The finale of the show is an exhibition of dancing, singing madness, which approaches, a frenzy. A climax like that to any other musical show on Broadway would be a cyclonic triumph. It is all of that at Town Hall."

Theatre owners the Shubert Brothers, Lee and J. J. were in the audience of *Put and Take* and adored the show. The Shubert Brothers swiftly scooped up and contracted the Harper and Blanks team. They signed the Harper's to be the first black act to work and tour the Shubert circuit of all white theatres. The Shubert's had Fred and Adele Astaire, Eddie Foy and his Family, Sophie Tucker, the Gish Family and now Harper and Blanks.

The exceptional team of Harper and Blanks obtained a major publicity workup with pictures along with background stories for the large budgeted advertisements that were placed in all of the trade papers. The announcements read *"Opening Bill of Shubert's Select Vaudeville HARPER and BLANKS the Smart Set Couple".* It was at this point that Leonard and Osceola were deemed two of the most "dapper" and stylish of African-American performers to ever set foot on stage. Audiences ogled at Harper's superbly tailored suits that Osceola stitched for him to wear along with his spit shined reflective tap shoes, and they were overcome with admiration as Osceola hoofed her groove thing while in her fashionable home-made dancing gowns. The team acquired the managerial services of A. E. Johnson of the, Blumenfeld and Company, Inc., office and were on their way as the new fashion conscious African-American performance twosome.

Harper and Blanks opened at the Forty-Forth Street Theatre then moved to The Winter Garden Theatre with the top star on the bill being Miss. Nora Bayes who had just returned from Europe with new material. Ticket prices went up from 25 cents to a $1 and were promoted as three dollar's, worth of entertainment just for the price of $1. The Shubert production featured Eleven Wonder Acts. Harper and Blanks shared the second spot on the show and burst full of swinging pep and jazz. Harper and Blanks did so well at the Forty-Forth Street Theatre that the jealous white co-acts on the bill made up baseless and false complaints about them. When the full cast moved on to play at The Winter Garden the Harper and Blanks performances were cut short. Critics unaware of the backstage resentments grumbled that the entire Harper and Blanks routine could stand another duet. Because their time on stage was unfairly cut short, Osceola was not given a chance to show off her lovely voice and it was sorely missed by eager audiences and critics.

Within these Shubert Vaudeville shows were *Bud Fischer Cartoons,* comedies and the Shubert News Pictorials with the theatrical finale featuring the entire cast closing the show by exiting off stage in a grand high kicking, march. The Vaudeville acts left New York City and went on the road traveling to Brooklyn, Baltimore, Boston, Chicago, Cleveland, Detroit, Philadelphia, Pittsburgh, Washington, Detroit, Dayton and

Newark, New Jersey. Because of race, Harper and Blanks were forced to take separate and unequal lodging, traveling, dining and all other accommodations while on tour.

Harper quietly planned to turn his lifelong theatrical showcase desires into reality and produced his *HARPER and BLANKS Revue*, which opened at the Lafayette Theatre in Harlem under the personal direction of the Coleman Brothers during their Grand Spring Carnival Week of May 15, 1922. Harper featured and starred himself and Osceola along with acts such as Love and Shenk, the Clifford Trio, the McLarens, Caseman and Sanders, Ed Green, Dave and Tressie and the Big Folly Beauty Chorus along with budding jazz great James P. Johnson as his musical director.

The *HARPER and BLANKS Revue* had a triumphant run for a few weeks and two big moneyed theatrical backers named Maurice L. Greenwald and Jimmy O'Neal scheduled a meeting with Harper to discuss his future after viewing one of their performances. O'Neal and Greenwald told Harper how impressed they were of his work at the meeting and made an on the spot deal with him to come up with another newly created show of his own, similar to the *"HARPER and BLANKS Revue"*. Leonard titled the new show, *"Plantation Days,"* and the revue musical opened in Chicago's fashionable Green Mills Gardens. Green Mills Gardens was one of the most famous and exclusive dancing and entertainment pavilions in all of the United States. Harper was informed by O'Neal and Greenwald that his production budget had no limits as long as it was all spent for the betterment of the show.

Plantation Days was billed as the all-Southern Musical Revue and was compared to *Shuffle Along,* another popular African-American musical show. Harper made a few minor cast changes and tweaks but retained most of the old cast members from the Harlem mounted *Harper and Blanks Revue* production. The show had twelve principals acts comprising of Harper and Blanks with their eccentric jazz stepping, Dave and Tressie who did acrobatic and Russian dancing, Blondi Robinson a dance and comedy act, Marjorie Sipp soprano singer with the Plantation Four who harmonized old jubilee songs with tones that hatched goose bumps inside the listener's ears and musical director James Price "P." Johnson who was five years older than, Harper.

James J. P. Johnson was the *Charleston* songwriter and inventor of the "Stride," whose piano style was responsible for unmasking to the world the innovative brand of music called Rag Time Jazz and he was Harper's official *Plantation Days* bandleader. J. P. Johnson was so damn skillful when he jammed his hit song the *Charleston* on his piano that he had people dancing into such a frenzied state of excitement that quite a few shoddy old dance hall walls and ceilings came tumbling down. Osceola Harper was in charge of the wardrobe and costume creations. The chorus line of eight, were responsible for dancing specialized numbers like *International Vampire Babes, Ukulele Blues* and a thing called the *Broadway Glide*.

A shifty guy named Lawrence A. Deas, an African-American, was hired as the stage manager by an all too trusting Harper because Deas, the masquerader, claimed to have staged the musical *Shuffle Along*. To further secure his position on the production, Deas also announced that he had the right to give permission to the *Plantation Days* company the use of some of the songs from *Shuffle Along* free of charge. Deas, the half-baked opportunist, passed himself off as the producer of *Plantation Days* whenever Harper wasn't present. The very cunning and dastardly Deas was able to finagle his cute little five year old daughter, Theda Deas, into the show. Baby Theda was featured in one of the big Harper dance numbers. Baby Theda was quite a decent little entertainer.

The settings and the wardrobe for *Plantation Days* were very luxurious and the revue was staged outdoors with the big cash and high class socialites who patronized the Green Mills Gardens, while making being seen there a must for anybody who was somebody or anyone who wanted to be considered in vogue. Ada Brown, known as the Queen of the Blues, was one of the featured stars of the show, and she tore up each song adding rhythm on top of rhythm with each lyric.

Harper's *Plantation Days* was originally booked for just ten days and sold out to standing room only every night as onlookers loved the never before seen African-American dancers move with such radically inventive agility, speed, class and grace. South Side Chicagoans' made so many repeat visits to catch the *Plantation Days* performances that the producers had to reschedule special midnight extensions of the show and were obliged to hold it over by popular demand.

Harper was able to use his dancing girls in *Plantation Days* just the way he wanted to, and he choreographed all the steps and movements totally within his own artistic revelations. Harper took those former café girls from Green Mills Gardens and converted them into top class $2 entertainment, training them to play in all the upmarket theatres in Middle West, Southern and East coast cities. It was a carnival of jazz. The *Plantation Days* Company went on the road with the first stop at the Avenue Theatre in Chicago, before heading out across the country to capture the hearts, minds and attentions of every attendee who was lucky or blessed enough to see the show.

Plantation Days was forced to close at the Avenue Theatre because the house was bound by a contractual agreement to feature another new show at the same time. If it weren't for the legal obligations of the Avenue Theatre *Plantation Days* could have played there forever. The *Plantation Days* production continued to tour cities as well as smaller townships in the mid-Atlantic and Eastern parts of the country. While on the road the sharing terms for the gross business was seventy percent going to the company and thirty percent to the theatre with an audience that usually cleared upwards of 1500 people. This was the first African-American hit show where the audience was eighty percent white that played to standing room only crowds with at least six hundred theatre aficionados turned away at every opening night. *Plantation Days* broke box office records at every venue and Harper's *Plantation Days* was the longest running Black show of the time.

COLORED DARLINGS OF LONDON?

With the United States tour of *Plantation Days* about to wind up the company arrived in New York City for its presumed final performances as the public clamored for a piece of Harper and company. Sir Alfred Butt, the British producer and member, of Parliament with extensive connections in London, showed up at a performance of *Plantation Days* and fell in love with it. Straightaway producer/managers Greenwald and O'Neal signed a deal booking *Plantation Days* with Sir Alfred and director Albert De Courville with plans for it to play at the Empire Palace Theater in Leicester Square, London. The Empire Theatre was a house with a royal history of being on the site of Saville House, the former home to King George the Second. Producer Maurice Greenwald made attempts to sign Ethel Waters to be featured in *Plantation Days* just before they were bound for England but she turned down the offer because she believed that Negroes couldn't make any money on Piccadilly Circus, and besides, she didn't trust white people all that much, having been harmed racially in the past. Ethel was also hesitant to travel so far while under a white producer's economic control.

Before Harper and company left for London they had to appear at the Lafayette Theatre in Harlem. All up and down the streets of Harlem full sized posters and advertisements were put up as well as paid promotional placements in all the local African-American newspapers. The glitch in all of these wonderful developments came when Harper and Blanks refused to honor their contracts at the Lafayette Theatre. They did this because an African-American detective named Sheridan A. Bruseaux, owner of the Keystone National Detective Agency, had been hired by the songwriters from the 1921 musical *Shuffle Along*. The *Shuffle Along* songwriters were, Eubie Blake and Noble Sissle and they charged the *Plantation Days* revue with piracy for the unauthorized use of their legally copyrighted material without permission. This added a big monkey wrench to the grand plans of showcasing the final leg of *Plantation Days* tour in America at the Lafayette Theatre. The Harlem performances were to be a kicking off point just before the company sailed off to Europe. It was a fact that Eubie Blake and Noble Sissle's production of *Shuffle Along* sometimes followed *Plantation Days* while touring America and when audiences paid to see *Shuffle Along,* they complained that they wanted their money back because they had already heard some of the same songs previously in *Plantation Days*.

The man liable for the illegal usage of the lifted songs was the artistically feeble scoundrel Lawrence Deas who got his job as stage manager of *Plantation Days* by falsely claiming that he had full rights and all the legal permissions to use the said Sissle and Blake tunes. The songs exploited without legal permission were *Gypsy Blues, I'm Craving for That Kind Of Love*, and *Bandanna Days* which were all written by Eubie Blake and Noble Sissle and they were the hit numbers that Harper staged for his show. Harper, for his part, was at fault for being too trusting and lacking in contractual sophistication.

Detective Bruseaux had his investigative agency contact Scotland Yard and his Keystone National Detective Agency also filed motions before a United States federal judge. An injunction against *Plantation Days* was issued preventing the cast and crew from sailing off to England. Harper was livid and refused to go onto the Lafayette stage to perform until all of the legal glitches were resolved. To add insult to injury, the new and questionably illicit *Plantation Days* Lafayette theatre credits read, "Production Staged by Lawrence Deas, the Producer of '*Shuffle Along,*' with Music by James P. Johnson "America's Greatest Jazz Pianist" with Harper and Blanks mentioned as only a secondary part of the cast.

Harper did some quick on the job learning with very little time to take care of these snags. Although it was only partly his fault Harper didn't feel it was necessary to have others sharing in the blame or assisting him in the resolution. Harper, more than anyone, knew how important this trip to Europe was in regards to his and the company's future occupational advances. Osceola meanwhile watched proudly as her dear, husband took up the reins as a full-fledged producer and worked it to the max.

With everything resolved, by Harper eradicating the *Shuffle Along* songs and numbers from the *Plantation Days,* he made some very crucial and necessary casting and crew adjustments. Harper clarified and refuted his own culpability for the predicament of the appropriated songs to many in the press "All this was done against my wishes by the former stage manager. I greatly regret the circumstances but nobody can hold me responsible for this breach of ethics. The blame is not properly mine."

Plantation Days finally opened at the Lafayette Theatre with an entirely new cast, some original songs, and numbers selling out the house as soon as tickets went on sale. O'Neal and Greenwald did not punish or fire Deas for any of his wrong doings due to their own cunning future financial plans. Their disciplinary immobility towards Deas was purely a production business decision. With Harper taking his real *Plantation Days* to Europe they wanted Deas to produce a similar yet artificial copy of *Plantation Days* and have it travel within the United States so they could double their profits.

Another problem arouse for Harper and company in the form of one racially predisposed Caucasian theatre producer named Lew Leslie who had his own production titled *The Plantation Revue* starring the great African-American stage star, Florence Mills with many of the former cast members from *Shuffle Along*. Leslie wanted his production to go to England first, and now that *Plantation Days,* headed by Harper would beat him to the punch, Leslie freaked out big time while trying to block *Plantation Days* from going on stage in England. Leslie, who thought all blacks were second rate to whites, had accepted the idea that Afro-Americans couldn't be objective in terms of producing their own African-American shows because only white males were able to form the proper creative perspective to stage, and interpret African-American life in theatre.

What infuriated Lew Leslie was that a colored man like Harper was even thinking about going to London with a hit *Plantation* show at all. Leslie got all of his London contacts in place through British producer

Charles B. Cochran and used Sam Salvin, owner of the Plantation Club in New York City, and glamorous movie star Tallulah Bankhead, to bear witness on his side in the British courts. Leslie made a pathetic bid to try to block Harper's *Plantation Days* from using the *Plantation* name and it didn't work. According to a March 22, 1923 article in *Variety* titled "Plantation Title Not Prevented in London-Court Decides Against, Cochran in Butt Injunction Matter". Sir Alfred Butt and his counsel promised the British courts, with their fingers crossed behind their backs, that in order to avoid any confusion they would change the title of their show to *Plantation Land* and that they would only use *Plantation Days* for a small scene in the show. With no intention of changing the title, as soon as Sir Alfred legally thwarted the injunction in court, he went back to using the original *Plantation Days* title.

Leslie and Cochran also claimed in court that they had a copyright for their version of *Plantation Revue* and that it was dated well before Harper's *Plantation Days* production. The British courts motioned to have Leslie's claims thrown out instantaneously. Being a member, of Parliament, *Plantation Days* producer Sir Alfred Butt, did have a considerable amount of clout in his homeland courts. Sir Alfred also proved in court that he had earlier rejected a proposition to bring Lew Leslie's *Plantation Revue* to travel London. Sir Alfred had indeed formerly passed on Leslie's offer because he demanded that Butt pay him a fee of 1,300 pounds weekly and Sir Alfred thought the price was much too exorbitant. Sir Alfred's London competitor Charles B. Cochran was Leslie's second choice and they secured *The Plantation Revue* starring Florence Mills for London's Pavilion Theatre. When Sir Butt found out that *The Plantation Revue* with Mills was bound for London he quickly moved and out maneuvered Cochran by hastily turning up in America and securing the rights to Harper's *Plantation Days* under his Palace Theatre Productions, leaving Leslie in New York and Cochran in London scrambling and doing damage control while trying their best to halt Harper and company from bringing his smash hit jazz revue to Britain.

On March 3, 1923, after having the *Plantation Days* Company departure delayed for one week, twenty four year old Leonard Harper and the troupe finally headed for England aboard the Red Star Line Steamer, named "The Finland". They departed from New York's Pier Fifty-Eight at North River. Harper, along with his wife Osceola and his most trusted and talented composer/musical director James P. Johnson and his Syncopated Orchestra, Harper's Pepper Chorus, the Four Cracker Jacks, the Silver Tone Four, George Stamper, Josephine Stevens and lastly the super fine-looking and nimble Miss. Wilhemena Steptoe the New Orleans soul food cook with a celebrated culinary history all cheerfully left America. The rest of the *Plantation Days* ten member crew made it a total of forty people on the voyage to England. Young white composer George Gershwin was aboard and was offered $ 1,500 dollars and a round trip ticket to write additional music for *The Rainbow,* the British production which sandwiched *Plantation Days.* All shows were credited as being produced by Albert De Courville including *Plantation Days.* Gershwin was a year older than Harper and was a Harlemite as well, who resided on 110th Street at Central Park North. Once, the American players both black and white stepped foot on British soil a whole new set of complications were there to greet them.

The British press got into the act right away and the concoction of European racism and anti-Americanism turned matters into a foreign style of ugly. Author Bill Egan wrote in his book *Florence Mills; Harlem Jazz Queen* that "The leading complainant, stirring up mischief with spiteful glee, was prominent journalist Hannen Swaffer. Swaffer used his columns in the *Sunday Times* and the *Daily Graphic-London, England March 6, 1923,* to promote his populist prejudices. In an article headlined "The Scandal of Negro Revues," Swaffer took swipes at both Cochran and Butt, asserting that "while the actors and actresses of England are concerned about their bread and butter... Sir Alfred Butt and C. B. Cochran are quarrelling apparently about which niggers they have got." Egan moreover wrote about how Swaffer repeatedly scrawled more racially odious commentaries with headlines such as "Nigger Problem Brought to London."

The *Baltimore Afro-American* printed an article titled "Negro Artists Not Wanted In London", on April 6, 1923 in which London scenic artist Robert Law, who painted the plantation scenes for *Plantation Days* demeaned the current nature of his work. Law rationalized why he painted the stage sets "so that niggers can act it front of it." Law was further quoted referring to Harper's cook Miss. Wilhemena Steptoe by saying "That they are even bringing over a black cook. So 'Aunt Jemima' of Virginia, the Coal—Black Mammy of all time will make waffles which you could eat forever, and still, want more."

The same Hannen Swaffer, London press piece stated how white film producers felt about casting Afro-American people while entitling the African-American imports as ignorant "White actors would not act with them for one reason and for another. There are no Negro actors of ability. They haven't enough intelligence. No white woman film actress would act in a scene where a Negro had to touch her, or to make love to her, and if she did, the film would be too revolting to show." Swaffer pronounced that "The Negroes produced one good actor. Bert Williams. But he's dead now." An American, staying at the Savoy Hotel was quoted saying of Bert Williams that, "He was liked because he knew his place and did not make himself aggressive. I like Negroes—as servants and as workers—but not as actors. Why have Negro actors when so many white people can act so much better?"

Harper stepped into what was akin to a British whirlpool submerged with positive and negative elements but at its onset the situation was primarily negative. With almost 2,000 white British musician union members out of work many local subjects had already started to blame their lack of labor on the influx of the hot African-American jazz bands which were all the rage. They also held the nationalist belief that home grown English musicians could get down and play jazz music just as expertly as Classical Negro American Jazz instrumentalists.

Not only did Harper and Osceola have to put on a wonderful show with the rest of the team but he alone had to keep the spirits up of his fellow *Plantation Days* cast and crew members, some of whom wanted to go back home to the United States immediately. At least the racism in America was on familiar soil as opposed to England where they didn't know what they might encounter or be hit up with. The British even had the gumption to protest musical artist, non-Brit, white man, George Gershwin, because he was an American Yankee taking up British jobs. The protesters said all the Americans should return to the United States.

Below are a few of the many initial obstacles placed before the *Plantation Days* company while they were in London.

1. The Empire theatre ushers positioned ropes in front of the stage to keep the African-American *Plantation Days* cast from touching the all-white audience patrons as theatre union members protested their arrival outside of the theatre.
2. The Empire theatre attempted to pay all, of the African-American cast less money than promised contractually for their acting and performance services.
3. The *Plantation Days* cast member's dressing rooms were transferred down into the basement from upstairs and they were driven to dress by dank and leaking water pipes.
4. The show times and *Plantation Day's* length were shortened from twenty nine minutes to fourteen minutes to accommodate the envious white cast members of *The Rainbow* which, triple-decked Harper's production.
5. The *Rainbow's* producer's attempted imposing drastic salary reductions which were as a direct result of finely printed obscure and vague clauses in the *Plantation Days* contracts and the interpretative finagling of minor details.

The British Actor's Association registered a Foreign Invasion Protest against the African-American theatre workers with the inane anticipation of farming out their *Plantation Days* roles to the out of work white English vaudevillian actors and they also proposed an additional new rule that stated that all alien American productions and or bands must leave the country first before any new alien performers could enter England for work. The British Actors Association also attempted to get the London County Council to deny the *Plantation Days* troupe a permit to perform.

Producer Sir Alfred Butt originally had much more elaborate plans for the *Plantation Days* production but had to scale things down in light of all of the racial and anti-American resistance. Sir Alfred wanted Harper and company to perform at least two additional shows per night in a cabaret/supper club within the Empire Theatre and he also desired that the interior design of the supper club look like authentic Southern cotton fields with wood cabins, trees and picket fences. Along with this concept Sir Alfred fancied a change of look for the Empire Theatre's entrance way. He wanted it to model a "real" Southern Plantation with Harper's dancers intermingling and dancing with the curious British public. Sir Butt also intended to have a Soul food take out sampling of some of Miss. Wilhemena Steptoe's dishes, all of Sir Alfred's ideas were ways to drum up more business and entice theatre patrons into buying tickets to the show.

The quandary for Butt was that the front entranceway of the Empire Theatre, specifically the sidewalk, had a history of being a major hang out and pick up spot for hookers. In the recent past the Empire Theatre had to be shut down on a few occasions because of health concerns in a struggle to stop the prostitutes from spreading sexually transmitted diseases. The British authorities nixed Sir Alfred's ambitious ideas fearing that the local prostitutes might flock back to the area to sell their wares. It was widely assumed that a downtown London thoroughfare with African-Americans dancing and singing on the sidewalks along with Southern soul food dishes being sold and served from an outside sidewalk café just might once again attract the unwanted crowd of local street walking ladies and their sex starved customers.

The Empire Theatre was billed as the Cosmopolitan Club and the Rendezvous of the World and *The Rainbow* played two shows nightly with the *Plantation Days Revue* inserted in the middle of the show. The billing was "PLANTATION DAYS" 32 COLOURED SINGERS, DANCERS AND MUSICANS FROM THE SOUTHERN STATES OF AMERICA". Harpers' show started off with an opening chorus number performed by James P. Johnson and his Syncopated Orchestra, with the entire company joining in. Harper and Blanks and the Pepper Chorus hit the stage with a number called *Simply Full Of Jazz,* the Four Cracker Jacks did a Ragtime Jubilee number then the Silver Tone Four broke out with some harmonizing and were followed by a *Plantation Days* number. Singers George Stamper and Josephine Stevens were the last acts in the show before the Entire Company returned for the finale staged by Harper with original music by James P. Johnson. These *Plantation Days* numbers were flanked by the first and second acts of *The Rainbow,* which by comparison, was a rather lackluster monotonous and unemotional undertaking.

James P. Johnson displayed a few piano tickler tricks of the trade during rehearsal down times to the very willing and eager to learn George Gershwin. Contrary to popular revised and historically inaccurate reports it was not J. P. Johnson who took lessons from George Gershwin but the other way around, even though many historians instilled with automatic racial supremacy seemed keen to propagate the false myth. The Johnson and Gershwin impromptu jams had the down home rag and soul from James P. with Gershwin adding his very own unique fascinating rhythms into the musical mix.

The *Plantation Days* cast and crew, got to merry-make together with their "rival" African-American show people from Lew Leslie's *Plantation Revue* once they disembarked in London. The cast members of both companies had many things in common being African-Americans in a foreign land and thespians unlawfully discriminated against on both sides of the ocean. None of the animosity that had been exhibited by the show's producers existed between the two company's fellow acting members. Harper was not only enthralled and enticed by Florence Mills but cultivated quite a close bond with the dainty and fragile stage idol and star of the *Plantation Revue*. Florence Mills possessed a distinct bewitching power of attraction about herself which made people want to protect, hold, worship, and make love to her, all at the same time and Harper though happily married was not immune to her star power.

Both *Plantation* companies and the West Indian Cricket Team were honored guests of a Black British social club called "The Coterie of Friends", a small and self-described well educated isolated group of socially and serious mined people of African descent from the West Indies, native Africans and native British born blacks who were either living or just traveling through England. The Coterie had been founded four years ago by Edmund T. Jenkins, a black classical composer, who had a closeted affection for jazz music. Jenkins, a scholar, built a substantial library of books and clippings all pertaining to the history of African people and their ancestors.

Harper was persuaded into being the proceeding's Master of Ceremonies. His evening callings included the showcasing of the talented performers who were the "Guests of Honor" like Florence Mills, Will Vodery, Shelton Brooks and J. P. Johnson. The British press ridiculed the black get together, and the awfully stuffy British theatrical circles snickered at them but that didn't stop some of curious wealthy and prominent English whites from showing up at the gathering. Nora Bayes, the Broadway vaudeville star who headed the bill at the Winter Garden Theatre in 1921 when Harper and Blanks became the first African-American act for Shubert Vaudeville, went to the party as well as Paul Whiteman the famous American jazz composer/conductor along with many other Americans working and visiting England. Nora Bayes had also worked with Florence Mills and her husband U. S. "Slow Kid" Thompson some six years back so for both Mills and Bayes it was a wonderfully joyful surprise reunion. Nora felt a sense of pride for what she had done to further the careers of some of these talented African-American people and reveled as she was showered with their immense gratitude.

Another white actress with a completely different set of motivations was at the gathering that, night. Her name was Daphne Pollard, originally from Australia. Daphne had joined the cast of *The Rainbow* as the lead star attraction. She was not officially invited to the mostly black affair but because she had some semblance of fame in British theatre and because she was currently featured in *The Rainbow* she was allowed to crash and muscle her way in. Daphne came to the event with a deep-seated hidden detestation for Florence Mills and she seethed with envy as she stood alone in her corner while the cute African-American star tantalized all the guests. Mills had the look, style and talent that Pollard wished God had bestowed upon her. Pollard's eyes burned at every charming Mills gesture, laugh and inflection. Pollard was further outraged because Mills was a dark girl and because nobody was paying any attention to her at the party. Pollard's rage and jealously boiled up inside of her at the Coterie of Friends event and it wasn't until later on that year in New York City that she acted upon and revealed her true maniacal stripes.

At the Coterie of Friends dinner-bash all, of those in attendance mingled and later jammed it up Harlem style. Harper and Osceola were on such good terms with Florence Mills and her husband, U. S. Thompson, that they were later able to borrow cash from the Mills' to help pay for some disconcerting unforeseen future occupational expenditures.

Something unpredictably upbeat happened to the *Plantation Days* Company by way of the Royal family. Queen Mary's godchild, Miss. Elaine Lettor, was the premiere danseuse in *The Rainbow*. Her father was the superintendent of his Majesty King George the Fifth's wardrobe and one of the oldest inhabitants of Ambassadors Court. All of the Royals went to witness *The Rainbow's* opening night. The theatre party included Queen Alexandra, Lady Patricia Ramsay, the Grand Duchess Marie, the Princess Royal, the Duke of Connaught, Prince George, Prince Henry and the Duke and Duchess of York with many of their upper crust servants in tow.

The British Royal family immediately fell in love with the delightful *Plantation Days* piece as some of the Royals were known to be jazz devotees. Buckingham Palace, under the direct supervision of King George, had already staged a hot jazz performance. This approval from the Royals helped gain the favorable reception for *Plantation Days* as many of their fellow open-minded British subjects followed suit and relished in a electrifyingly pungent show.

The trendy London pleasure seeking upper crust ladies' man and unemployed gossip dandy of leisure Mr. Fynes Harte-Harrington wrote in *After Dark the Nocturnal Adventures of Fynes Harte-Harrington* No. 17, London, April 1923 of *Plantations Days;* "Within the show (*The Rainbow*) is a segment called The Plantation, comprising a coloured entertainment set on a mythical Southern plantation on the Mississippi which has caused a little furor." *"I particularly liked Lola Raine and Alec Kellaway's pretty singing duet' Sweethearts."* Says Pricilla (one of Mama's latest matches) afterward as we walk through Soho. "*The 16 Empire Girls were superb in this number too. But, I also rather enjoyed the Plantation.* "Well I must admit I rather liked that bit too. It is good to see something completely different. The dancing was amazing especially Leonard Harper and his wife Osceola Blanks and the acrobatic Archie Ware in the Crackerjacks troupe."

The adverse confrontations encircling *Plantation Days* just wouldn't go away and on opening night George Gershwin was booed off stage during the finale of *The Rainbow*. Gershwin was blasted by boos and hisses for being an American and taking work away from unemployed British songwriters. Gershwin was embarrassed and wounded and made plans to go back home to America and leave London within three days. Gershwin was in fear of his safety. Also, one of the British supporting cast members of *The Rainbow,* a character actor named Jack Edge who played the tragically outrageous red headed comic transvestite and female impressionist, for laughs went into an impromptu unrehearsed reckless speech at curtain call. Edge anxiously protested the entire production of *The Rainbow* and questioned the inclusion of *Plantation Days*, claiming "I can't find De Courville the producer of *The Rainbow*, but I want to say I was engaged as a low comedian and have been given only one scene with no sufficient scope in the, piece". After being jeered and taunted by everyone in the audience, Jack Edge was grabbed by his neck from two hands that appeared from behind the curtain and physically pulled off stage and fired. Edge was replaced by Ernest Thesiger in the role of *The Rainbow's* Miss. Violet Vanbrugh the catastrophically humorous grand dame who sang *The Price of Love*.

At the same exact time that Sir Alfred Butt brought Leonard Harper and his *Plantation Days* Company along with George Gershwin for *The Rainbow* his American producing partner Alex Aarons brought Fred and his sister Adele Astaire to London to star in the musical *For Goodness Sake*. According to Bob Thomas' book *Astaire, The Man, The Dancer* Fred and sister Adele Astaire attended the opening of *Plantation Days* and were regaled by Sir Alfred Butt and his business associate Alex Aarons. Thomas stated that "During their early period in London, the Astaire's had an alarming experience at the Empire Theatre. They attended the opening night of a revue that failed to find favor with the audience. Patrons in the galley talked back to the actors, boos and whistles punctuated the performance. The curtain brought a chorus of disdain. Fred and Adele stared at each other with trepidation…" In Bill Egan's book titled *Florence Mills; Harlem Jazz Queen* Egan wrote that comic transvestite actor Jack Edge's "outburst triggered some cries from the audience of 'Send the niggers back.'"

Within all of the stagy excitement of the *Plantation* Days opening night being attended by the Royal family and with the boisterous and at times deafening booing of George Gershwin by many of the unruly spectators along with the offensive unpremeditated eruption by the disgruntled transvestite actor Edge, Fred Astaire sat in the audience and watched Harper with piercing intensity as only another great dancer could.

Fred tried to get his sister Adele to concentrate on Harper and the entire *Plantation Day's* company's work ethic and tap dance arrangements. Fred badly wanted Adele to take her dancing more seriously like the performers up on the Empire Theatre stage. As Fred examined every precisely measured step coming from Harper and company he repeatedly nudged and pleaded with his unfocused sister Adele to stay fixated on the acts in the show and to pay less attention to all the upsetting off stage sideshow shenanigans and to stop making flirtatious goo-goo eyes at all the available wealthy and potential European suitors in the audience.

The review in *The Illustrated London News* stated that *The Plantation Days* "scene, rendered by colored artists, is not at once amusing and bizarre, or that there is not a certain gorgeousness in the scenic effects". Another paper clipping read "*Plantation Days* and it is just a usual darkey song and dance entertainment with a very discordant 'syncopated' orchestra and some lively acrobatics at the finish in the style of Arab tumbling acts. It would seem to have been a waste of time to bring these performers all the way 'from the Southern States of America.' There should surely have been enough resident colored folk in London able to do the same thing with the same lack of distinction."

An excerpt from *The Sunday Times of London* dated April 8, 1923 subtitled "The Negro Turn" stated "The Negro "plantation" turn to which there has been so much unreasonable opposition has now been greatly subordinated. Personally, I do not think much loss would ensue were it to go altogether, for the character of dances and the noises made is the reverse of pleasing."

But it was the April 8, 1923 *London Observer* that was the most offending review. It stated that the Negro performers should "come under the Performing Animals Act" and the "chorus of black maidens, with black knees and pink-and-white make up daubed over Negriod features is a "decadent" spectacle for the London audience". H. G. the author of the review ended his piece by stating "I will merely say that it (*Plantation Days*) seemed to me stupid, vulgar, and dreadfully ugly".

Harper was very much mindful that *Plantation Days* was being written about in the major African-American American Press as well as widely distributed theatrical publications like *Variety* distributed from its London's cable office at Trafalgar Square. To set the record straight

Harper came off with his own bit of profile-raising press in the way of a very personal letter.

In a letter printed in the *Baltimore Afro-American* newspaper titled "Colored Actors Write of Prejudice in London" on May 11, 1923 Harper and Blanks wrote to newspaper man J. A. Jackson from the Empire Theatre in London. Harper penned the following "In spite of adverse propaganda in the "dailies" which began about three weeks before we arrived and the nastiness of the critics of said papers, "Plantation Days" was the outstanding hit of the show. We are doing only fifteen minutes in the show which is just long enough to hold up proceedings in each performance. We had a great deal to overcome from the antagonism caused by the jealousy of the English Variety Artists Federation and the Actor's Association and English Musicians who adhere to their slogan, "British Theatres for the British". The public however proved that they care for American entertainment and especially colored performers."

Next Harper went into negotiations with some well-connected French businessmen for the *Plantation Days* company revue to tour the entire European continent. Harper's new proposal never got out of the starting gate because the other *Plantation Days* artists wanted to go back home to America. His chorus girls wanted to get on the steamer back to Harlem as soon as the run of the show was over. The cast mate's skins were show business thick but simply not thick enough to bear any more foreign racial denunciation and humiliation.

All of the cast members of *Plantation Days* prepared to head back to New York City posthaste. They boarded the White Star Line steamer dubbed "The Cedric" and Sir Alfred Butt cunningly swapped their tickets from second class and substituted them for the cheapest steerage third class packages. Sir Alfred impishly pocketed the discount as the shaken *Plantation Days* troupe members were escorted to the shoddy bottom of the ship. The gorgeous showgirls grumbled to Harper and mostly everyone elected to pay the difference of the ticket prices on their own so they could sail back second class, just as they arrived. Harper borrowed extra money from Florence Mills and her husband

U.S. Thompson so he could upgrade some of the travel arrangements for the less frugal of the *Plantation Days* cast members.

The London press got hold of the ticket transferring episode and disclosed the fact that Sir Alfred had also illegally withheld for himself 300 pounds of the *Plantation Days* cast and crews profits from the following week. The press also uncovered that another British producer named Charles Gulliver made an offer to Jimmy O'Neal for the company to stay in London to perform matinees at London's Palladium for a fifty percent sharing of the earnings, but that Harper and company, much the wiser this time around, necessitated up-front financial sureties of which they weren't granted and the proposition was nixed.

Sir Alfred Butt, having made a significant financial yield from *Plantation Days* and legally ripping off the cast and crew of the production with his innovative bookkeeping, further exploited the incidents in the press in an effort to redeem his reputation in terms of importing employment as a pro-British, anti-American and anti-Afro-American producer newly aligned with his fellow Englishmen. Sir Alfred then spun his decision to bring the black acts to England as a hedge against forthcoming opposition, just in case he wished to import more African-American, talents to London in the future. Sir Alfred also used the fact that the Royal Family very much enjoyed the *Plantation Days Revue* on his angle as a potential hawking point.

HARPER MOVED TO HARLEM & DID THE LINCOLN THEATRE

Back from England and new resident New Yorkers, Harper and Blanks moved into a spacious new Harlem apartment at 2067 Seventh Avenue, between 124 and 123rd. Streets one block away from the famous Hotel Teresa. The Harper's had filled their new digs with romantic soft lights, gorgeous pillows, handsome rugs, and a battery operated radio, along with a wind-up Victrola record player that played jazzed-up marching band recordings and an elegant baby grand piano.

This calm atmosphere didn't last all that long for the Harper's because they took in two budding jazz musicians and their families as boarders. One of these lodgers turned out to be a young dynamic musical genius named Edward "Duke" Ellington and terrific things were about to materialize for both him and Harper.

Upon their return from England Harper produced the *Plantation Revue Junior* featuring Harper and Blanks at the Lincoln Theatre on Lenox Avenue at 135th. Street in the heart of Harlem. The Lincoln Theatre was owned by a Puerto Rican woman named Marie Downs who sold it to businessman Frank Schiffman. The Harper presentations at the Lincoln consisted of variety acts and big bands and as the acts changed so too did the titles of the productions; *Harper's Famous Bronzed Revue with the Ginger Chorus, The Sheiks of Harlem, Creole Follies, Magnolia Revue, The Jazz Time Revue* and *Harper's Crossword Puzzle Revue*.

Thomas "Fats" Waller, who labored as a Harlem deliveryman for a neighborhood delicatessen owned by the Immerman family, methodically used to sneak into the side door of the Lincoln Theatre to see Harper's shows. Later on, a very young and shy unassuming current New Jerseyite named William "Count" Basie parked in the back row of the Lincoln Theatre mesmerized in unreserved fascination by the rapid deployment of the floor pulsating Harper stage shows. Both Waller and Basie imagined of one day being allowed the chance to play the big Lincoln Theatre organ and pluck the keyboards with the same quick and tuneful rhythm patterns as the Harper Chorus line did when they shifted their feet. What Harper, Waller and Basie had in common was that their spirits were filled to the brim with the language of rhythm. The huge Lincoln Theatre organ was primarily used to accompany the incidental-filler music and effects for the silent motion pictures that starred the likes of tall dark handsome and rumored to be "colored" Rudolph Valentino and silent movie actress Pola Negri. These soundless films played as a separate feature to Harper's live productions. Fats

Waller eventually did get a gig as the house grand organ player and the instrument swung.

The Lincoln Theatre turned out to be a primary main stay for Harper from the early 1920s until the late 1920s. It was a theatre space where he always either produced a local showcase or mounted a touring show to be dispatched out and exhibited around other parts of the country to generate extra revenue.

Harper sent out his shortened touring versions of his Lincoln Theatre revues, what they termed as "tabbed-out" or "tabloid" to other theatres with acts like Morat and Warren from Argentina, current boarder Duke Ellington and his Washingtonians, Princess Yvonne and her Marvelous Revelations from Harper's *Ciro's 2 AM Revue, the Kentucky Club Revue, Brown Skin Models of 1929, Midnight Steppers of 1929,* Champion boxer Jack Johnson with movie star Fredi Washington who starred in *Harper's Crazy Rhythm Capers* in 1929 and even the young piano mastermind Thomas "Fats" Waller got into the act as Harper billed him as "Senior Fats Waller" in his 1926 *Creole Follies.*

Fire Marshals repeatedly shut and locked up the doors to the Lincoln Theatre because the admission tickets were over sold by the grabby owners as Harper's shows were always sold out. To Harper's credit and knack as a stager there was never enough seating for many of the eager fans.

In the late summer of 1923, after Harper was well settled and ensconced in Harlem, his former manager/producer Jimmy O'Neal along with producer Irving Tishman and Lew Herman traveled to Paris a short time after the London, closing of yet another imitation of *Plantation Days* for British audiences. These theatrical backers had high hopes of opening up new opportunities and markets for themselves in France. They attempted to open up a Parisian version of an American cabaret and dance hall featuring some of New York's finest African-American artists utilizing Leonard's directorial skills but they were unable to procure a deal. Forced to return back to the States, lacking any solid agreements, Jimmy O'Neal and Tishman decided to hook up with Harper once again to produce a condensed version of *Plantation Days*. Harper employed a company of twelve talents for the vaudeville Pantages Theater and its circuit of many playhouses. Word spread quickly around the inner circles of the theatre district that Leonard Harper was back in New York producing and directing. It was just a matter of time before he became a major theatrical force to be reckoned with during the Golden Years of the Great Roaring 20s and the sweet era of the Harlem Renaissance.

CHAPTER TWO
(1923 to the Early 1930's)

HARPER DID CONNIE'S INN

Throughout the concluding part of 1923 Harlem was like a two-sided coin for the dapper twenty four year old Harper and his proud wife Osceola Blanks. On one side of this Harlem coin you had the Harper's smack dab in the middle of the "Harlem Renaissance," a burgeoning movement where African-Americans with proficiencies in arts and culture were able to use their creative gifts to humanize their race as full people to a white America. The world listened to the songs of the African-Americans and saw their performances, read their books and viewed their paintings then curiously inquired about the lives of the artists behind the works. This cross racial inquisitiveness in turn forced the white people to look at blacks with a more three dimensional perspective and some of them couldn't help but start seeing black people as full-fledged, if not equal, human beings.

The other side to Harper's Harlem coin was tainted with the hostility of bigotry. To stroll just one block away from the Harper apartment onto the busy through-fare of 125th Street one found that he and his fellow folks of the darker hue were not allowed to shop in most of the white stores. The few shops that they could enter into would not permit African-Americans to touch or inspect the merchandise unless they bought it first. Harper watched and bumped into the black veteran soldiers of the 369th Army Infantry Regiment who had recently returned to

Harlem from their stints in World War One. These soldiers were filled with pride and dignity but had very little money in their pockets and few options for employment or income. The black patriots who came back from fighting and spilling their blood for their country wrongfully believed that after they put their lives on the line for America they would see better days. These thoughts turned out to be unpleasant nightmares as the gruesome reality for these veterans of color set in. Instead these loyalists were driven to stand on food lines in soup kitchens for their meals and if more than four of them were congregated on a corner they were shoved harassed and mistreated by the all, white law enforcement officers.

For Harper specific aspects of Harlem life reminded him of his adolescence as a juvenile pickaninny when he was dancing in Medicine shows because his new neighborhood was filled with some of the world's most prodigious African-American entertainers. Just seven blocks away from the new Harper apartment on Seventh Avenue rested the magical "Tree of Hope," a fading old elm tree stump said to possess unearthly powers. All of the black show business people rubbed and touched the "Tree of Hope" for good luck.

Nightclubs and tented cabarets were everywhere and they were jam-packed with swinging piano players jamming all over the place and anyone who heard them were either put into a musical trance or moved into a rhythmic submission. Waiters, waitress' and service workers all stepped with a distinct beat and looked as if they should be up on stage while they serviced their patrons. Some club interiors had sunk in and had weakened with bouncing walls, not because of poor construction but because just like the drinks on the table they repeatedly shook and shifted to the riveting musical tempo.

On Sundays in Harlem just about every block had a church filled with the soulful singing of their Gospel Chorus men and women whose intonations were so sweet and wholesome that even the Lord was obliged to snivel. Harper had no idea that he was about to become the centerpiece of the one and only genuine Harlem Renaissance.

On Thanksgiving in 1923 while producing a monster dance concert featuring himself, his wife Osceola, and friend Dewey Weinglass, with the famed Russian Dancing Demons and a host of others, Harper got a proposition to produce, direct and star in a nightclub show at a new club called "Connie's Inn." The new swanky Black and Tan nightclub spot where both white and black customers were to be allowed was located at the former Shuffle Inn. Connie's Inn was situated on Seventh Avenue right below the Lafayette Theatre down in its basement area where Harper had just finished staging *Plantation Days Junior*. The Shuffle Inn had a reputation for being a very hot place for the past two years largely due to the dreamy virtuoso of ragtime "bandleader to the millionaires" Lucketh "Lucky" Roberts who ran the Shuffle's rhythm shaking house band.

The Immerman Brothers, George and Connie were German immigrants and were the proud owners of the new nightclub property. At the outset the Immerman's experienced racial difficulties with fuming local African-American Harlemites who rallied at the all-white construction crews who installed their big red exterior canopy. The Immerman brothers were able to get a reprieve from the local demonstrators because they were able to persuade the Harlem community that they already had employed seventy one African Americans including the entertainment talent pool and the brothers announced that they were planning on hiring even more African-American neighborhood residents.

Inside Connie's Inn nightclub one got the sensation that they were in an enormous cave with an interior space exquisitely particularized with elaborate decorations that encased the tables and chairs for 500 people. The chairs and tables were cramped together bungalow style, not for intimacy, but to provide for as many paying customers as possible.

The Immerman brothers had controlled a very prosperous delicatessen and illegal bootlegging delivery operation in Harlem with their mother. Mother Immerman was staunchly opposed to the idea of her two son's taking their share of the family sandwich sale profits to fulfill their pipe dreams of owning a Harlem nightclub. Mother Immerman was right to be uncomfortable because of the danger factor as her two boys might have to transact with the murderous racketeers of the nightlife world. Part of Connie Immerman's big plan was to serve exotic Chinese and regular American dishes with their prohibited "Hooch" liquor and he purchased a huge imposing white organ to overwhelm the club with jazz reverberations.

Harper appeared at times like an army drilling sergeant occasionally having to demonstrate the dance movements himself to his chorus girls. He physically took the hands of one of his girls while he whirled a South American shawl about her derriere. Harper let the dancers know first-hand how it really should be done. Connie's Inn chorus girl Ruby Dallas Young, who later went on to work at the Cotton Club, recollected "Leonard Harper built a wall around himself. He was hard to get to know and very strict." Some of the more disobedient young lovelies who misbehaved by taking brakes when they were not supposed too or reported back to the staging area late forced Mr. Harper to either fine them or dock their pay or yell at them with as a last resort having to fire them. The one undetectable and very sensitive cautious male transvestite in Harper's all-girl chorus line cried a lot at first till Harper had the rehearsal band play a hard driving butt jerking musical number that built up his/her confidence. At the end of every hard day's rehearsal the final result for Harper and his girls and the rest of the production company brought about some remarkably proficient revue spots that were weaved within the overall texture of the show.

If the girls showed the spectators something special or brought out some otherwise hidden star potential they might be upgraded to feature talent status with a pay raise. Harper picked each of the girls out of a first-rate pool of hundreds of would be dancers because of their artistic talents. He firmly believed in each and every one of their showgirl abilities. But Harper pungently cautioned them that if he should ever find any of them being lazy or awkward or showing up to work late or using too much dirty language or eating too much food, causing their figures to get out of shape and if he ever caught anyone misbehaving by upstaging any of his principal performers they would find themselves out of work. Some of the more unruly girls laughed at him and rolled their eyes while popping chewing gum behind him. Harper was informed about the slights from one of his assistants but let it roll off his back because those few untamed girls just happened to be the most vigorous and sexually charged tempting dancers of his lot.

Osceola Blanks was content and delighted to be Harper's self-respecting wife. She co-starred with him on stage and on the domestic home front she took great joy in sewing her man's clothes, setting his taps, and always having a warm dinner basket full of fried fish, chicken and fixings on top of the oven. Her sister Berliana had patched up her stormy relationship with Harper and he promised to feature his sister-in law and her group the Three Dixie Songbirds in some of his forthcoming productions.

Osceola did get mildly disheartened from time to time because she had failed in her frequent bids to get pregnant and start a family. She also all too often found herself unhappily waiting up nights for Harper to come home from work. Harper, when home was cheerful but coming back to the apartment became an increasingly infrequent circumstance due to his work overload. Harper did miss his mother Sarah and his brother Gene so he tried to convince them both into moving from Chicago to Harlem even offering to pay for the move. It upset and saddened him that his younger brother Gene was so jealous of the theatrical success that he had worked so hard to achieve. Leonard wished that Gene would instead be congratulatory toward him and celebrate all the good things that had come his way.

While eating a late night dinner Leonard told Osceola that some of his musician friends had asked him if he would admit another border in their sizeable apartment. At this time in Harlem history African-Americans were limited as to which street blocks they could live on. The Harper's already had all around jazz musician and sax specialist Otto Hardwick and his wife Gladys staying in one of their smaller rooms. Otto Hardwick was a childhood friend of the up and coming pianist

Edward "Duke" Ellington and gave Harper his highest recommendations on his pal Ellington. Harper asked Osceola if it would be all right to rent out another one of their six bedrooms and he explained to her that this Ellington fellow and he were the same age and he was a brilliant pianist from Washington D.C. Besides the rent money from the new lodger once he got on his feet he could help them financially by bringing more money into the household. Most importantly the Harper's knew just how hard it was for African-Americans to find good available living quarters in the current racially segregated Harlem and were empathetic. Osceola approved of the idea saying yes to opening up another one of her apartment bedrooms for the new boarder.

When Ellington moved into the Harper Harlem apartment, he was at first unassuming and reserved as he played beautiful tunes on Harper's baby grand piano. Fascinated by his wizardry on the piano Harper wrote several letters of introduction on behalf of Ellington to all in the African-American entertainment community. In his dispatches Harper testified about just how gifted his new roomer was and asked all of his professional associates to meet with Ellington so that they could hear his music and consider hiring him.

An enthusiastic bug-eyed and clearly awestruck Ellington was familiarized with Harlem's fast and uninhibited nightlife by Harper. Ellington was flabbergasted by all the unrestricted and bouncy soulful activity. These two young men hung out with people like the hot tempered hoofer and gambler William "Bojangles" Robinson, who always reminded everybody that he had a big silver handled pistol in his pocket and would use it just in case they had any thoughts of ripping him off. Ellington gravitated towards what he likened to an Arabian Nights fantasy Harlem style which was fertile with jazzy jamming musical tapestries and audio atmospheres beyond one's wildest imagination. The greatest pianists in the world populated Harlem during this time, guys that took broken beat up old pianos with missing keys and were still able to make music come out of them that sounded like paradise delivered jazz orchestra concertos. Little did the green and unripe Ellington know that one day very soon he would be the Sinbad genius with his skillful fingers while his piano turned into an uptown Magical Lantern as all of his Harlem based Arabian Nights fantasies would come true.

Ellington strived to establish himself but it was to no avail. Harper encouraged his temporarily down in the dumps boarder by convincing him that there would be more prosperous days ahead for the both of them. Harper listened endlessly to the incredible Ellington sounds that floated around in his apartment from his concert carved piano. Harper would often dance and rehearse in one of his back rooms as Ellington jammed in the living room. The walls to the Harper crib pulsated with amazing rhythms and beat sounds so astonishing that they were without equal. To get Ellington out of his funk Harper momentarily hired him to work at Connie's Inn playing piano during his mid-day rehearsals. Ellington was enamored by the Connie's Inn nightclub operation as he rehearsed the show tunes with some of Harper's former *Plantation Days* production cast members. While at Connie's Inn, Ellington went to African-American Musical Comedy school uptown style where he listened attentively as many eye popping backstage tales were told.

Edna Ellington, Duke's wife joined up with her husband in swinging Harlem and relocated into the Harper apartment once her wishes were known. Harper, ever the producer, keenly observed Edna Ellington as she gracefully ambled about in his apartment from the bedroom to the kitchen. Harper presented Edna with a chance to be one of his Harper Connie's Inn chorus girls and she accepted. The revenue from the work that Harper provided for the Ellington's helped the couple establish themselves in Harlem.

Three weeks into rehearsals at Connie's Inn and it was like an exciting circus of kaleidoscopic energy with rhythms from tapping feet and rapid fire music which commanded and lorded over anyone and everyone within hearing range. Anyone within earshot of the beat was compelled to drop whatever task or pleasure they were doing and tap their feet on the floor. The audio and the visuals of the chorus lines at many of these performances rose above and beyond the level of the anticipated senses and created a temporary numbness in the listener's and observer's spinal cord because of an exhilaration overload.

Harper's chorus girls carried on interviews and deliciously postured for photographers looking racy, spicy, naughty, and near naked, in exotic see thru robes with jeweled and feathered multi-colored headdress gear. Harper proudly viewed his new posters that read *LEONARD HARPER'S REVUE FROM CONNIE'S INN.*

Leonard held a swift run thru with some of the principal acts like Leroy Smith and the Jazz Kings, the Green Dragon Orchestra with Wilbur Sweatman "The King of Jazzdom" who played three clarinets all at the same time and would swing patrons into obedience and the Acme Syncopators who were accused by some of originating jazz. Song titles ranged from, *The Rosary* to *Cross the Way* and *Down in the Deep*. Harper also watched the rehearsals of the vaudeville category of acts that he set on the program like the comic dancer named Earl "Snakehips" Tucker a former circus snake charmer who previously danced poisonous cobras and rattlesnakes into near death trances. "Snakehips" dazzled with his rubberized hips and slithering legs and lips that were at times painted bright devil red. "Snakehips" juggled his body while wearing a loose shaking colorful satin outfit with ruffled sleeves and a shiny belt buckle that casted off blinding rays of light whenever he bounced or gyrated, his hips or plunged his pelvic and gigantic endowments at audiences. Only the most daring of the wealthy upper crust downtown women would hang out and allow themselves to be hypnotized by this super virile jet black specimen of a man. As rumor had it even dancing close up with a fully clothed Mr. "Snakehips" might lead a lady to get an unexpected pregnancy.

Standing in the wings at the Connie's Inn rehearsal was a short thin dapper butch lesbian woman in men's clothes and blue lipstick. She's the new Master/Mistress of Ceremonies and she couldn't wait to belt out a racy song. Meanwhile Harper scrutinized his romantic couple act that, were costumed handsomely in Mediterranean garb. Mr. Harper then had his chorus line of very long legged tall dancing girls pace themselves while going through the motions. These Mademoiselles knew how to recoil their erupting breasts with phenomenal cleavage in a delightful rhythm sequence like waves in a milky and sudsy ocean all in a congenial syncopated unison a movement that titillated all audience members no matter what their sexual predilections. Even the fully married Harper perspired after one of their robust and fleshy charged routines. When Osceola entered the room the Harper and Blanks duo teamed up to show everybody how it's really done, jazzy style.

Gangster Dutch Schultz disrupted one of Harper's rehearsals at Connie's. The "Dutchman" communicated in pugnacious timbers and bullied the Immerman brothers with the threat of bodily harm if they didn't give into his money shakedown demands. Dutch Schultz soon became a Connie's Inn regular as he and his gangster associates never had to pay a dime for anything while receiving the very best special treatment.

Harper had a tight-lipped summit with the often volatile and the easy to offend "Bojangles" and the rail thin diva Ethel Waters who were both at the top of their games entertainment wise. Together they planned a few special surprises' for the Harper floorshows at Connie's. Bojangles and Waters were both guests of the nightclub and appeared to be in the audience just like every other patron but Harper gave the Master of Ceremonies a cue for the bombshell revelations of visiting guest celebrities in the audience and when the lights turned to either Bojangles or Waters they sprang from their seats and did special solo performances. These exclusive talent ambushes were broken up with Bojangles during the first act and Waters at the second act and if they wished to be part of the finale it was an unbelievable icing on the cake. Both stars had an open invitation to perform at any of Harper's shows and at any time in the future.

An often smashed and pudgy Fats Waller was another one of a handful of top line regular entertainers who frequented Connie's Inn and jammed till the break of day. Waller tickled the piano keys with magical dexterity while at the same time exhibiting his famously clownish jocular facial expressions as he emitted smoking first-rate jazz music.

Well-heeled whites from downtown jaunted uptown by car or cab and like bees to honey entered the nightclub to get their fix of uptown soul during opening night at Connie's Inn. A few of the local African-American Harlemites who arrived on foot tried to gain entrance but only a handful of the most noticeable and smartly attired looking black people were permitted inside. Once the African-Americans had penetrated Connie's Inn they were instructed that they could only take the shoddiest seats in the house by either the steaming hot kitchen or next to the smelly back toilet area. The African-American locals who were left hanging outside struggled to maneuver past the considerable rows of Cadillac, Roll Royce and Dusenberg limousines that dropped off the affluent patrons on a continual basis. In most cases the barred Harlemites wound up hitting a dead end and were shooed off or shoved away from the entrance way and were consigned into gazing at the festivities from across the street behind the big red velvet ropes as the privileged customers opportunely entered and enjoyed the floorshows. The majority of the local African-Americans who remained on the pavement heard the blasting jazz music only at the brief intervals when the doors to Connie's Inn open and closed.

Harper operated out of Connie's Inn for more than a decade and the nightclub became his central headquarters and the nucleus for many of his floorshow productions. Harper's work at the famous club thrived well into the early 1930s. Connie's Inn served as a catalyst for Harper and was at the core of some of his most highflying amusement operations as he marked, stamped out and catapulted his very specific brand of African-American Musical Comedy DNA on the world of theatrical attractions.

Singer Bricktop was utterly elated when Harper outfitted her in a rose flower costume for her debut as a pretty and flirtatious soubrette. Leonard staged Bricktop in a floral floorshow production number along with the chorus girls who he bedecked in dissimilar flower costumes fabricated from her prototype.

Harper knew that to get remunerated he would have to at times re-establish the white audience's fictitious sense of racial supremacy over the African-American actors who performed on his stage. If Harper hadn't incorporated some of the old thrown back insulting stereotypical racial rudiments, many of his white audiences would be alarmed and question "What happened to the good will and colored's need to appease us?"

Harper's use of exotic romantic love scenes on stage contradicted the idea of African-Americans as animals because it showed and paraded passionate black romance in front of both white and black audiences in America for the first time. The soft expression of an African-American sentimental courtship with a duo act crooning about their fondness for one another further humanized a black race that had been stripped of its humanity for decades.

Most of the regular struggling coffee-colored New Yorkers were never permitted in to see the floorshows at Connie's so as to not offend many of the white patrons even though the club was promoted as "Black and Tan" establishment. The few non-famous African-Americans that were sanctioned entry could not enter the club on its most popular Thursday, Friday, Saturday or Sunday evenings and if your casing was either sable black or seal skin even the off week nights were iffy.

Some of the Connie's Inn patrons were absolutely blown away with an over, abundance of liquor consumption. These rowdy nightclub customers often grabbed at the body parts of some of the theatrical and non-theatrical African-American staff. The disruptive displays of unrestrained and perilous lust blended right in with a dose of suppressed guilt. The curious touching and hugging of the taboo race by some of the uptown visitors were viewed within the obscure corners and silhouettes of Connie's Inn.

African-American Broadway theatre great and grand highbrow thespian Charles Gilpin, the Drama League Honoree who was famous for reading Eugene O'Neill's *The Emperor Jones,* invited some of his white friends to come uptown with him to Connie's Inn. Gilpin's friends were hurriedly escorted inside the club along with thirty other white customers but Gilpin was not recognized to set foot near the club this night.

The bouncers claimed to have no more seats available and no more room even though it was Gilpin who made the reservations in the first place. As the snubbed but proud Gilpin objected he was manhandled by the Connie's Inn bouncers and shoved away from the front door then flung onto the sidewalk. No matter what Gilpin's theatrical credentials were while he laid slammed down on the dirty city pavement and as his friends reveled inside Connie's Inn he was reminded that he was no more than just a common "Nigger" with a Drama League award in this America.

Harper's shows brought in throngs of glitterati regulars like Mae West, Jack Pickford, Joan Crawford, George Abbott, Hilda Ferguson the blonde beauty of "Follies," Mayor Jimmie Walker, Beatrice Lillie, Gertrude Vanderbilt, intercontinental banker Otto Kahn, Tallulah Bankhead, Hoagy Carmichael, Max Schuster of Simon and Schuster, Jack Dempsey, Eddie Condon, Mark Hellinger, Benny Goodman, Rudy Vallee, producer Florenz Ziegfeld, the Marx Brothers and a young columnist named Ed Sullivan along with damn near every luminary with a pulse beat all looking to pump up their plasma systems with some perky uptown fervor.

The high society customers enjoyed trying to guess which of Harper's Chorus girls, was truly a male or female. Harper kept everybody speculating with at least one passable and eye-catching transvestite in the bunch. Bonus audience participation came with the bewilderment as to whether some of girls were of the Caucasian race or if they were blacks who just lacked darker pigment as some of the girls were high buttery mulatto or so light toned in complexion that they passed for the white race if they so desired.

Harper himself was not immune to certain racial episodes within Connie's. It perturbed Harper immeasurably when a few white guests cited to the Immerman brothers that the nightclub was much too swanky for all of the, Black and Tan race mixing stuff and that some patrons were scared that they might get beat up. The Immermans were counseled by a few other customers that some of the whites in the audience were terrified at the thought of rubbing up with some of the common blacks who sat by the kitchen and the brothers were advised that they must keep the racial lines divided so as to advert any loss of their well, heeled yet at times ill at ease clientele. The Immermans were also petitioned to get rid of the browner skinned chorus girls because the fairer skinned girls, who looked more, white and appeared less threatening and menacing were more in synch with the well-off Park Avenue type patrons. The feelings of the racist yet more well to do customers was that the high-yellow African-American gals intermingled much better with the audiences and were more able to dance up close without petrifying anyone.

In an effort to enact a less racially offensive policy the Immerman's pressed Harper against his wishes to dismiss his darker skinned dancers and keep only the high-yellowed skinned chorus line dancers so as to put some of the white customers at ease. Harper had always casted his chorus line dancers based on stage talent alone irrespective of their skin shades. Dark and light skinned blacks hoofed side by side with the occasional white girl or male transvestite performer. The Immerman brothers emphasized to Harper that the new skin tone club policy would not affect the featured or principal star acts. Many of the star acts were of browner skin and the Immerman brothers had no choice but to engage them or cut back on their star talent pool significantly.

Once the new Connie's Inn chorus line complexion sterilization policy went into effect many reporters fell, victim to the racial identity confusion. The press reported that some of Harper's girls were white or dead ringers for white until the dancers started to throw "their business around" which unmasked the Caucasian camouflaging "with moves like that, they must be colored". Connie's Inn called itself a "Black and Tan" club yet the more popular the nightclub became the more the Immerman's forbade the number of African-American patrons, admission.

After famous gossip columnist Walter Winchell's first visit to Connie's to view one of Harper's floorshows he predicted that Harlem would be the new nightlife entertainment center. Winchell called it the New Broadway—north of 125th Street and said "Harlem came alive tonight." Romeo L. Dougherty editor of *The New York Amsterdam News'* Theatre page on April 20, 1923 wrote "Among the younger generation of colored theatrical producers during the era that brought the revue form of entertainment into its own, Leonard Harper has been one of the most prominent and successful. With becoming modesty he has done his work, never seeking the puerile publicity that means so little to the intelligent members of the profession."

Another validation of Harper's knack and aptitude as a stager/producer was the way in which he incorporated current newsworthy events into his floorshows. In 1926 he featured the African-American female champion swimmer of the world in his revue. The swimmer's name was Izzy Ringold and Harper conceived a new dance number for her called the Channel Crawl. The Channel Crawl dance was tailor made for the popular swimming diva. Harper also catered to corporate company sponsorships like the time when he produced a specialty number titled *Candyland* and had the chorus girls decked out in *Love Nest* candy bar costumes blatantly financed by the Love Nest Company for advertising and pure financial purposes.

British royalty from London would pop into Connie's Inn from time to time like when Princess Alexandra Victoria of Scheleswig-Holstein the daughter of King Edward the III and granddaughter to Queen Victoria traveled uptown under wraps to attend Harper's floorshows. Jazz appreciation ran stoutly through the British monarchy bloodlines. The well-mannered Princess Alexandra Victoria was one of Harper's foremost European fans having attended *Plantation Days* in London. As the favorite godchild of the late Queen Alexandra the privileged and irresistible Princess Alexandra Victoria loved to party uptown at Connie's as she would always leave her crown at the imperial flat, let her hair down and have her noble booty shaking north of Central Park. The eye-catching Princess was always accompanied by her platonic friend Magistrate Charles A. Oberwager and the debonair Mr. Bernard Weller, the wealthy manufacturer, who was Alexandra's secret casual boyfriend and swiving partner who her mother discouraged from ever marrying. Bernard Weller never identified himself or let on that it was he who was the recipient of the bonny Princess Victoria's amorous and bodily cravings at least in most public places but in the bounds of Connie's Inn they had a tendency to let it all hang out.

It was rumored that on one obscure night a reedy and agile gracious white gentleman with a pleasurably well-matched grin entered Connie's Inn and gently stood within the dark unlit walls. During a fast song and dance number the rhythm took command of this gent and obligated him to blast from the back floor area to the stage. He started to dance and wound up stunning the crowd. When finished the unassuming fellow received an enthusiastic round of applause from the patrons. As he softly withdrew from Connie's some of the African-American dancers patted him on the back and told him that he was so good that he should be a professional showman. As he ambled out the man elegantly acknowledged the dancers and it was said that he was none other than Fred Astaire himself.

Some of Harper's other Connie's Inn floorshow titles were *Harper and Blanks Musical Revue, Home Again* where Julia Moody sang *Everybody Loves My Baby* as Bessie Alison lead, the routine of *Harlem Mammas In Pink Pajamas* and some of his other creations were titled *Court Of Harmony, Hot Harlem, Connie's Inn Revue, Spades Are Trumps* and *Ace In The Hole*.

Harper's conceptions at Connie's Inn proved to be exceedingly fruitful and advantageous for him and his Connie's Inn Chorus Line received the well-deserved reputation of being some of the best dancers not only in Harlem but in the world. In 1935, Connie's Inn relocated downtown to Broadway and Forty-Seventh Street, and then closed in the fall of 1936 with the downtown version of the Cotton Club taking over its prior Broadway location and shutting its doors four years later. Neither downtown variations of the once famous Harlem nightclubs lived up to their past reputations while being stationed in the predominantly white Times Square area.

HARPER DID THE LAFAYETTE THEATRE

In the late fall of 1923 Harper was under a great deal of pressure to continually churn out fresh new productions at Connie's Inn. He had the added predicament of having to figure out what he was going to do with the out-going current acts, talents and show themes that were so well received at Connie's from the preceding weeks. Harper's solution came in 1925 by the way of Frank Schiffman, the new owner of the Lafayette Theatre.

The Lafayette Theatre had a 2000 seat capacity with nonstop performances six days a week and had been conveniently located right above Connie's Inn nightclub. The gap between the two buildings was called Lafayette Square and it was often used by Harper. Once Frank Schiffman secured the Lafayette from the Coleman Brothers and bought the Lincoln Theatre and the Harlem Opera House, Harper's conundrum with what to do with his numerous one-week-old weekly Connie's Inn floorshows were solved.

Harper "tabbed" his nightclub floorshows out into theatre settings and the only thing that was missing was the liquor. As in most theatres of that day, African-Americans were obliged to sit in the balcony area and that was only if they were permitted to enter the theatre in the first place. Many theatres held a strict white's only policy as the African-Americans were impeded from entering except on special black's only show nights. The white audiences had entirely separate performances. The first show might be just for the white people and the second show was restricted to African-American audiences. Years later a lawsuit would legally modify the prejudiced seating and entrance policies in some theatres.

Schiffman proposed to Harper that he transfer all of his nightclub floorshows from Connie's Inn right upstairs into his Lafayette theatre. With a smidgen of tweaking and in a modicum amount of rehearsal time Leonard revamped his nightclub shows into African-American Musical Comedy theatrical pieces quite effortlessly. Harper subscribed to Schiffman's business arrangements and launched his practice runs for the Lafayette Theatre at the Elk's Lodge auditorium. Schiffman also made a deal to "tab" out Harpers shows on the Afro-American "wheel" on the multi-state touring circuit. Schiffman accepted offers and committed to farm out Harper's productions to venues such as the Royal Theatre in Baltimore, the Howard Theatre in Washington and the Earle Theatre in Philadelphia…. These theatres were all lined up in a mini-monopoly pact to guarantee that everybody involved got steady employment, wages and returns. Years later Harper would disclose to a reporter that "in three years-time I had earned over $20,000 but lost most of it to bad investments."

The traveling talent consortium was paid a fixed rate during performances while another one of Harper's brand new weekly shows were in rehearsal at the Elk's auditorium for the subsequent week. As Harper's other current productions were on stage at either, Connie's Inn, the Lafayette or the Lincoln Theatre, his previous week's productions were "tabbed-out" on road tours. When one show concluded its weekly run Harper recycled and transported the new show that he had just finished showcasing at either Connie's or another New York theatre.

Schiffman, a very clever and pioneering businessman, concocted a little ruse in which he compensated the talent with very low wages but submitted two totally different contracts to them. One of the contracts had a completely bogus higher rate of pay. The low paid performers were encouraged to use the phony contracts with a greater rate of pay at other venues to negotiate better deals for themselves, while gratefully accepting the decreased salary from Schiffman.

Harper had several assistants like Charlie Davis, Clarence Robinson, Addison Carey and Teddy Blackmon who traveled with the troupes on the "tab" tours and he also interchanged them as stagers in the Lafayette Theatre. His aides were useful and capable but they didn't yet possess the knowhow or faculty of how to operate big productions at this time. Some of Harper's directors weren't able to dance or demonstrate their stage commands like their boss did. Harper was adept at physically demonstrating to his talent the steps and what movements he wanted his line to execute because of his background as a dancer. Harper said it with his feet and body movements, then articulated it vocally, while many of his subordinates were restricted by their performance limitations and were consigned to merely verbalizing the directions or by drawing sketches.

Harper also found the time to drop in on some of his "tabbed" shows while they were on the road and when he was in a rhythmic frame of mind he would participate himself by performing in a mixed-bag of roles with the players. These productions were mini-vaudeville styled African-American Musical Comedy presentations comparable to the touring Medicine shows that germinated from Harper's recollections as a youth and were manifested before his live audiences. Most of the talent in these productions had to holler out loud into the balconies just to be heard because in those days the theatres didn't have microphones. Wallace Thurman wrote about the Lafayette Theatre in his book *The Blacker The Berry* where he described what it was like being in the audience "There was much noise… much passing to and fro, much stumbling down dark aisles…Then people were always looking for someone or for something, always peering into the darkness, emitting code whistles, and calling Jane or Jim or Pete or Bill. At the head of each aisle…people were packed in a solid mass, a grumbling, garrulous mass, elbowing their neighbors, cursing the management, and standing on tiptoe trying to find an empty intact seat—intact because every other seat…seemed to be broken."

Traveling "tabbed" shows like Harper's were labeled by the independent theatre circuits as *Round the World* tours although they, for the most part, only journeyed in the eastern and southern parts of the United States. Harper to his imaginative repute deviated from the orthodox everyday nightclub floorshow blueprint by adjoining different scenes and boosting the design detail and splendor of the sets.

A few of Harper's sample Lafayette theatre revue titles were as follows: Bill "Bojangles" Robinson in the *Pepper Pot Revue, Ballyhoo* Revue, *A Night in Harlem,* Leonard Harper's *Frolicker's, Adam & Eve in*

Harlem, Chocolate Music Box Revue, *Fireworks of 1928, Bandannaland, Parisian Nights, Monkey Shines of 1928, Red Cap Follies, Slippery Elm* Revue, *Double Check* with Duke Ellington, *Easter Parade, Whoop It Up, Rhapsody in Rhythm* Revue, *Rhumbaland,* Harper's *Oriental* Revue with Jap Salmon, *Merry Whirl*…"From America's leading Colored Theatre nowhere in this city could you find better entertainment under the direction of Frank Schiffman. The Fastest, Merriest, Peppiest revues of them all."

In Harper's *A Night In Harlem* the team of White and Sherman were telepathists and in his *Midnight Steppers* Mabel Nichols warbled a *Steamboat Sally* number and it showcased "Peg Leg" Bates the dancer with a peg leg who also had his collection of wooden legs painted different colors so that they matched his many colorful suits. "Peg Leg" glided across the stage while shrouding his physical discomfort from the audiences. Harper also managed Bates under the Leonard Harper Management Company from 1927 to 1935.

The pubescent Wilhelmina "Tondaleyo" Gray became a background dancer for Harper but when the truant police officers found out that she was playing hooky from Junior High School she was driven from the Lafayette theatre stage in the middle of her piece and commanded to go back to school. Back in class Tondaleyo was not interested in the least in book study but instead she researched dance movement on her own while fantasizing of the day when she could once again jiggle and shake it in another Harper show as an adult. Harper figured out that Tondaleyo and some of her talented adolescent chums could perform in the state of New Jersey without getting into trouble with New York school officials. So it's across the Hudson River and off to the stages of New Jersey and goodbye to the New York City truant officers for Tondaleyo and some of the other super gifted Harper chorus teenaged hoofers.

Wilhelmina Tondaleyo Gray procured her stage name of Tondaleyo from a South-Seas character who, awakened dead Englishmen and turned the seedy British sailors into natives after they watched her shake her impassioned hips while gesticulating her energized buttocks at them. This particular South-Sea scene came from *Tan Town Topics* one of Harper's voluminous Times Square area theatrical productions.

In Harper's *Brown Ginger* at the Lafayette he featured the specialty act of Morton Downey Sr. the white singing drummer who opened up the program for the handsome Paul Meeres who executed a dexterous dance rendition of a "Frankenstein monster" routine. In Harper's *Ballyhoo Revue* Paul Meeres the immaculate looking specimen of a man heartthrob glided his honey glazed winding body with the muscles of a Greek God and performed a *Voodoo Tabu* dance number with Miss. Bessie Dudley who never left a wriggle go un-writhe. The theme of Harper's *Cocktails of 1932* was about people who drank too much wine, just another example of Harper giving his audiences what they wanted to see.

The teenaged Edward Sisters dance act came to Harper by way of legendary theatrical producer Flo Ziegfeld's confidante and adviser Mr. Jay Eddie Edwards who happened to be the girl's father. Jay Edwards informed Harper that Flo Ziegfeld thought that Harper was a genius. Ziegfeld was so enthralled with Harper's spectacles that he would sit in his revues take notes, jot down stage tips, appropriate revue concepts and even use partial production numbers without the thought of any compensation for Harper. The uptown chitchat propagated that Harper had the ability to train wild animals to dance and that he had the chops to instruct farm and circus beasts in the art of syncopation.

Jay Eddie Edwards took the casting people from the original 1930's stage version of *The Green Pastures* uptown to the Lafayette to meet with Harper. Many of the African-American show people such as "Jazzlips" Richardson Junior and Edna Mae Harris who were cast in the original *The Green Pastures* were hired under Harper's advisement. Harper casted Mr. Edward's dancing daughter's the Edwards Sisters in his *Candyland* revue about a candy factory and introduced them as the "Female Nicholas Brothers". In *Candyland* Harper also casted Maude Russell who was costumed in male evening garments for a lesbian love themed number. Maude sashayed her stuff while singing to a coquettishly sassy

Mary Perval who chirped a song of love right back to her female object of affection while the Harper chorus line of dancing damsels wobbled their titillating fiery peppers behind them.

The Nicholas Kids were interchangeably presented as the Nicholas Brothers and they performed in an oversized number with Harper's Chorus line in his *Wet and Dry Revue* at the Lafayette. Harper's production of *Fireworks of 1928* jumped off with real live fireworks, drums and guns on stage along with soaring kicking female and male dancers that went on and on non-stop. Miss. Rookie an eccentric dancer in full get-up dressed as "Topsy" from the book *Uncle Tom's Cabin* enacted lively convulsions that, exploded.

Harper's barber, Moses Weinglass's son Dewey Weinglass along with his Four Dancing Demons Company, were identified as the best African-American Russian Dancers this side of the Mississippi. Dewey and his Four Dancing Demons appeared on stage with arms folded and broke out into some stupendous Cossack twirls and Ukrainian spins that had the Harlem audiences believing that they were in the middle of Moscow. Harper even had Chick Webb the celebrated big band leader with a growth disfigurement pop out of a paper-mache flower bulb on stage in his *Roseland Revels*. In Harper's production of *Paris and Harlem*, he transformed the Harlem stage into Paris, France for the week's engagement at the Lafayette where he utilized the arena for three big scenes one in a hotel lobby another on a dance floor and he closed the floorshow with a glimpse inside an erotic Parisian dressing room.

Harper did undergo a few complications like the time when he borrowed "Sunshine" Sammy aka Ernest Morrison the Afro-American *Our Gang* child slapstick movie star from Hal Roach. "Sunshine" Sammy was always marketed as this darling infant because he looked so babyish, but the smiling sugar-child possessed the sexual libido of a fully grown macho man in other words, nobody should ever let their daughter alone in the playpen with him. Pintsized Sunshine Sammy was constantly on the run from the fuming mother of his underage chorus line girlfriend at the Lafayette Theatre. During one of Harper's shows Sammy's sweetheart's momma hounded, captured and pounded Sammy with an umbrella backstage before a performance. After another show the diminutive "Sunshine" Sammy was taken to court for getting his chorus line darling pregnant. As a consequence Sunshine Sammy Morrison was indicted with the crime of seduction and had to watch his back for fear that his girlfriend's mother might revisit the backstage area and bash him out with her bulky umbrella again.

Sammy did enjoy some degree of success years later when he shaped an eleven piece nightclub band. Induced back into the film acting field for monetary reasons "Sunshine" portrayed, the always spooked, panicked and affable African-American member of the *Dead End Kids* and the *Bowery Boys* series of comedy films. The charismatic and contagiously irresistible Sammy was always the first one to dash from the haunted house when the lights went out or away from the police if someone stole an apple.

On one evening a handful of audience members stormed out of the Lafayette theatre to protest an offensive "hot dog" song in Harper's *Rhumbaland* which was sung by Mamie Smith. Harper also staged two Cuban men who sang a tune titled *Peanut Vendor* in *Rhumbaland*. After the Cuban actors fandango themselves out of bondage while wearing chains and singing a slave song they then flung actual bags of peanuts out into the audience. An eye-catching seemingly Spanish woman enlisted the men in a bouncy merengue tailored tango and calypso movement then they were joined by the Harperettes for a conga finale.

Acts like the twenty five Rose Midgets, Princess Zulieka the mystic who could answer all of your questions, the Six Strutting Dandies, the Three Yorkers, and the Five Racketeers, Baby Fisher, the hilarious raspy voiced and tooth challenged comedian Jackie "Moms" Mabley along with fellow jester "Pigmeat" Markham all were semi-regulars who supplied much enjoyment at countless Harper Lafayette theatre shows.

A small sized insurrection set off outside of the Lafayette Theatre by dance aficionados who were unable to procure tickets for the Harper produced Bojangles *Pepper Pot* revue. Connie Immerman praised

Harper's showgirls who out danced Bojangles in those specialty numbers swaggering their feet up and down the stairs and in time tit for tat on the theatre's stage. Connie bid Leonard to do a similar production of the Bojangles-Harper chorus line dance-off challenge for the patrons at his Connie's Inn nightclub.

During this time period "Bojangles" Robinson who was branded to keep a not so nice temper while laying bets also went after anyone who endeavored to pilfer his signature dance steps or sought to imitate his rhythm routines. Bojangles' fixation with being ripped off was evidenced in an "over the top" and exaggeratedly threating full page advertisement that he took out in *Variety*. Since Bojangles and Harper initially worked together on the stair dance steps Robinson had no problem if Harper or his chorus girls used or shared his steps. Sharing the great Lafayette Theatre stage with, the searing Harper chorus girls in a dance competition compelled Bojangles to tighten up his steps while perfecting his already cooking with rhythm dance act.

A quote from a newspaper extraction about Harper's *Swanee Revue* declaimed the following "Swanee Revue, from the moment Leonard Harper's show opened at the Monday matinee and the band paraded across the stage to take their places in the pit, the audiences went 'wild.' From the opening chords of the stirring overture through all the fun in the circus, the action in the Spanish bullring through Willie Jackson's ride in the airplane 'Spirit of Africa' and the languorous dances in Mexico, there was a succession of laughter and applause. Never before had so many performers stopped the show, with almost every one of the principals getting a tumultuous reception as they finished their work. Harper has created a wonderful machine."

In Harper's *Bare Facts Revue* he showcased himself as an unaccompanied dancer and singer with fine-looking girls singing and dancing in a beach scene as he lead the chorus in his interpretation of *Adeline*. Harper's enactments on stage reminded everyone in the audience of how much of a seasoned stage player he was and just how highly he still ranked as a well, rounded talent. One journalist who sat in the audience penned of Harper, "He knows his vegetables when it comes to crowd pleasing and his feet can be turned every which way but loose." At that particular *Bare Facts* performance, Harper and cast had to take a total of six encores after each exhibition.

Another reporter elucidated "There comes a time in every reviewer's life when the English language fails him in his efforts to do justice to a particularly inspiring show. This is the case now when attempting to describe Leonard Harper's new Revue Hit show *Jazz Fantasy*." In Harper's *Brown and Pink Revue* he casted the show with fifty black and white entertainers who deviously battled against each other in a turbulent race against race dance-off on stage. It was the black dancers, verses, the white dancers and the entire audience found it irresistible when two of the white boys tore up the stage in a high speed moving foot ricochet tap number titled *Painted Doll*.

Harper's *Red Cap Follies* was a production that was originated by the executives of the New York Central Railroad as a publicity gesture. The New York Central Railroad organized and formed a jazz band from its hundreds of musically gifted African-American Red Cap workers. Red Caps were the African-American baggage handlers that toiled for railroad trains. These Red Cap positions were very high-status jobs for black men who for the most part were locked out of America's mainstream labor force. The jazz band delegation of Red Cap railroad train employees performed in Harper's show under the headship of band conductor Russell Wooding and they legitimized their musical credentials at the Lafayette Theatre with a bombardment of jazz sounds that cracked full of passion.

Harper's early teen year's collaborator Clarence Muse, the former dramatic church reader, with the golden voice was now a big time screen star in Hollywood and he came to Harlem to star in a Harper staged show. Harper had specially assembled the Lafayette theatre production to suit Muse's renowned large screen persona. A March 1933 *N.Y. Amsterdam Newspaper* theatrical press piece read as follows *Hollywood Sends Screen Star Home to Harlem, Muse Heads Harper Revue.* Muse, having just concluded an advisory position at the Fox Film Corporation in conjunction with his leading role in the feature film *Hearts of Dixie,* was now ready for some good old uptown Harlem action. Clarence Muse sampled dramatic bits from *Trilby* as Svengali. Contained within the same *Home to Harlem* showcase were the Nicholas Kids who performed impressions of Louis Armstrong with Harper's breakneck nimble chorus-line all dancing up a storm in a giddy *Reefer Smoking* number. The jazz band did a rare swinging version of the *William Tell Overture* as Harper was able to bring out the live and dramatic stage flair of his one-time childhood pickaninny partner and buddy.

Harper and the artists who worked at the Lafayette Theatre had to endure a few payment glitches from time to time. Frank Schiffman made nice profits for himself but as for Harper, regrettably, there were times when he wound up owing the Lafayette Theatre money even after many of his sold out capacity revues played. It was rumored that Frank Schiffman the owner/manager necessitated that Harper procure the uppermost salaried stars from downtown then Frank would make Harper forfeit his proceeds with a salary deduction to compensate for the orchestra and for half of the movie leasing fee to offset the production going over budget.

Leonard Harper productions at the Lafayette would regularly gross between $10,000 and $15,000 and he would earn additional monies from his other interests in connection with the theatre such as his many "tabbed" touring road shows. For instance a Harper show might be guaranteed $3,000 a week with anything over $5,000 as a possible yield for him. But if you factored in all of Schiffman's creative hidden and additional production costs and fees Harper could very easily wind up indebted to Schiffman at the end of a sold out hit show depending upon how imaginative Schiffman's bookkeeping pencil was during any given week. Schiffman's ability at bookkeeping assured that the numbers and takings didn't usually total up for anybody but himself.

The tradition of seductive and erotic components on stage, were absorbed and picked up by young Harper very early on as he examined his actor dad William Harper duet with female thespians. The remainder of his sexual instruction had been harvested from his own personal theatrical experiences as an adolescent pickanniny during his post-minstrel days of traveling medicine and circus shows. The completely seasoned Harper ascertained immediately that when it came down to it, audiences always hungered for a little titillation when they came to see a show. Vaudeville was known for displaying women fan dancers who also sometimes held some otherwise dubious talents. These sex pots uncovered themselves by eliminating portions of the fan, feathers or balloons as they romped or adagio danced about on stage, then these lasses would craftily strip naked and unmask their comely shadowed unembellished zones.

It was only a natural progression of events for Harper to have incorporated many of these sexual elements in his acts especially given the dark and magnetically powerful enticements that went part and parcel with the risqué nightclub floorshow world. Some observers attributed the sexually charged naked and stripping phenomenon in theatre beyond normal everyday human curiosity and voyeurism and ascribed it to the anxious pent-up tensions of post, World War One angst. Musical comedies during this time provided all the fantasy, escapism and anxiety respite that craved to be released by war weary and fun starved American audiences.

Harper was no different than any other stager/director so he liberally fused lots of flesh, nylons and lace for the fetish challenged. Young misses with locks of gorgeous hair and sporting nothing but an unrestricted string of pearls performed sphinx like movements that held audiences under a spell. This was a typical and stimulating vibrational occurrence in the course a regular Harper staged show. No sexual rating systems existed at the time but because of prohibition against illegal liquor sales and the rampant consumption that went along with it certain righteous anti-freedom of expression groups popped up from time to time making unreasonable pleas for raids from the rare few law enforcement officials that were not on the take. These clean cut law enforcement assignments were to bust up nightclubs and speakeasies by imposing the immoral and indecent act edicts that, for the most part were just on the books. Harper was not untouchable from these extremist civic bluecoats and he got tangled up in the middle of a great big police raid at one of his *Kentucky Club Revue* productions at the Lafayette Theatre.

The *Kentucky Club Revue* obscenity sex case was dismissed by authorities on the grounds that police, were incapable of securing any statements from the devoted Lafayette Theatre audience members or establish any eyewitnesses to come forward and testify against the show. The general public and theatre going spectators believed that the *Kentucky Club Revue* cast and production staff had undergone enough by being arrested with the $500 bond being imposed upon each of them. As a consequence lots of public commiseration was engendered towards all of those implicated with the much maligned *Kentucky Club Revue* production.

Harper and Schiffman were able to capitalize and escalate their earnings for *Kentucky Club Revue* during the police bust hullabaloo and this was not the first time or the last time that a Harper production would have to encounter this type of legal scrutiny. Frank Schiffman hired Nathan Burkman who was Charlie Chaplin's attorney to represent the Lafayette theatre and its personnel. Harper uniformed his chorus women as zesty diminutive tramps for a future production. The girls drew tons of cheers as Harper's Charlie Chaplin Maidens captivating all as they "Tramp" walked with canes then bopped into a fueled high kicking dance routine.

The *Kentucky Club Revue* received extra publicity with photographs of the semi-nude female dancers ornamented in bikini like undergarments and formless fabrics over their flesh divulging shoulders with headlines reading *How Could Anybody Arrest This Group?* While calling the cops who locked them up, "a mighty heartless lot to haul these pretty chorines before a jury in their stage cleanup drive last week". Another print item read *Take Your Pick* with photos of the girls, who caused so much questionable trouble for Harper and Schiffman. Some of the girls were clad in tiny Dixie maid sarongs as others were geared in see-through undraped bikinis as they coquettishly solicited the public to rule on whether stockings improved their legs and if they ought to go with or without nylon hose.

Adverse reports asserting that the *Kentucky Club Revue* was "The most indecent show ever" only increased the ticket sales with curious male audiences keen on getting their jollies off. The Lafayette Theatre was a stage showplace and not a cabaret nightclub so Harper was pressured into cleaning up his shows and modifying segments of the risqué moments in future productions at the venue or encounter persistent police monitoring.

The *Kentucky Club Revue* didn't only consist of tempting sensual titillation because Leonard Harper was savvy enough to embrace wholesome entertainment in the form of an adorable young lad who went by the stage name of "Jazzlips Junior". Jazzlips Jr. at only eight years old was unusually undersized which made him appear much younger than he actually was. His father "Jazzlips Sr." was one of Harper's fully-grown entertainers who generously shared and spread his theatrical gifts right on down to his son little "Jazzlips Jr." Harper had "Jazzlips Jr." team up with his single and divorced mom Anna Mae Fritz who did a *Mammy* number with her son "Baby Jazzlips Jr." who sang hopped and paraded his stuff to capacity crowds while on the *Kentucky Club* road tour. Any lingering dishonor of an excessively fleshy *Kentucky Club Revue* was put to rest once clusters of fans came to check out the appealing fresh-faced talents of little "Jazzlips Junior." and his mommy.

Harper carried on producing his distinctive trademarks of swift multi-treated African-American Musical Comedy Theatre at the Lafayette well into the early 1930s while he concurrently conceived more of his brilliant and racy nightclub floorshows downstairs at Connie's.

HARPER DID THE NEST CLUB

The Nest Club was an authentic Harlem quasi-public/private after hour establishment in every sense of the word and was owned by Johnny Carey and Mal Fraizer who both were very pale skinned African-American men. The Nest Club was relatively close to both Connie's Inn and the Lafayette Theatre and addressed at 169 West 133rd. Street. It was, in point of fact, stationed down in the basement of the Monarch building over a vacant lot. This exclusive uptown hangout site was done up rather attractively with aged rose and gold interior designs. Harper was snapped up and appointed to produce the floorshow revues at the Nest Club because of his reputation as a distinguished producer and because he could generate the stars. Harper got going hooking the Nest Club up in late August 1923 for a mid-October opening and word spread rapidly from 133rd Street to Palm Beach and all the way over to the French Riviera. Two early gangster shootings in the Nest Club gave it a street creed reputation as a hazardous yet jumping joint and it drew hordes of club goers who deemed it exhilarating to rub elbows with real live racketeers.

The Nest Club was a "Black and Tan" joint purporting that both black and "slumming-uptown" white people could hang out together and nobody would mess with either assemblage. Mae West the famed movie and stage star was a regular at the Nest because the African-American co-owner Johnny Carey was her beau. Mr. Carey could be spotted squeezing his hands between Mae's big hour-glass thighs in the back of the bar regularly. Certain incensed downtown and west coast show business executives were furious at Mae West because she was expected to be "the ideal All-American beauty" and with her not sticking with her own race betrayed the myth. Malicious rumors were concocted around the downtown Times Square area and people began to whisper that Mae was really a male impersonating a woman. As a longtime devotee of African-American entertainment Mae was known to use bawdy music and lyrics written by African-American songwriters in her repertoire. Mae was later able to talk Harper into producing one of her stage shows using many of his African-American acts for a small Brooklyn theatrical showcase.

Some of the steady celebrated visitors at the Nest Club beholding Harper's floorshows were Franchot Tone, Otto Kahn, Burgess Meredith along with his mother and famous bandleader Paul Whiteman. The top New York political officials and police brass were paid-off to look the other way no matter what went down at the Nest and they abided by the terms. Clients often would *"B.Y.O.B.B."* meaning "Bring Your Own Brown Bags" of liquor. But if you had the right contacts you could secure a bootleg bottle of "Chicken Cock" from under the table in a tin covered flask or canister.

Harper had a jamming Nest Club floorshow with music delivered by the Sam Wooding Creole Band using singers with names like Bee-Bee Bachelor and "Shaky" Beasley all enriched by Harper's signature Nest Club chorus girls who were always underdressed in eye-catching bird feathered costumes. The Harper Nest chorus line danced up and flared-up the stage floor and chirped about birds going to the Nest while they juddered, their voluptuous tail feathers off. The girls jiggled, joggled and detonated with rhythm every night as their boss Leonard Harper commanded substantial sums of cash for his production services. The Nest had no actual stage so the acts were all exhibited on the grand dance floor. These shows started at 9:00 pm with just music. Harper's revues started at 11:00 pm with the second revue beginning at 3:00 am until the 5:00 am closing breakfast show.

HARPER DID THE COTTON CLUB

The Café De-Luxe Club was located on Lenox Avenue and 142nd Street and was owned by former prizefighter Jack Johnson. Johnson assumed that his renowned name and his latest cracks at acting in Colored Musical theatre world would be a magnet for Broadway nightclub patrons to voyage up to Harlem and into his showplace but he was wrong and his moniker alone was not enough to bring in big money business. Johnson, who was exhausting his funds rapidly at the Café De-Luxe, was coerced to sell his Café De-Luxe Club in 1923 to gangster Owney Madden by hook or crook. The liquor bootlegging Owney Madden was freshly out of prison and ascended by the blood of his rivals to control illegal cigarette, laundry and taxicab concessions and became part owner of the downtown high end Stork Club. Madden with his squeaky Irish accented peculiar voice lorded over the Irish mob with a blood stained iron fist. With images of African-American slaves picking cotton under white supremacy in his head for the interior of the Harlem nightspot Madden changed the name of the Café De-Luxe to the Cotton Club once he obtained the club.

Former East Harlem inhabitant and Chicago mob boss young Al "Scarface" Capone was the silent financial co-investor behind Harlem's latest nightclub extravaganza the Cotton Club. During this time period Al Capone familiarized himself with Harper's production abilities. A decade later Harper was to be commissioned to stage and produce at intervals for Capone at his various nightclubs in Chicago before completely moving into the hoodlum kingpin's hotel and becoming his principal floorshow producer.

Owney Madden's new nightclub's policy only permitted white customers who after entering would become fully regaled by a tremendous African-American jazz band and a swinging Harper produced floorshow. Co-manager and fellow thug George "Big Frenchie" DeMange was employed to make sure things went according to Owney's designs. Black talent and servers were not authorized to use the white restrooms as Madden felt it was not his responsibility to comfort his African-American employees especially when it came to their relieving themselves. The Afro-American staff was on their own as far as restroom services were concerned so they were driven to use their own ingenuities like scurrying out into the back street area or carrying their own brown paper bags for their eliminations. Harper was signed to stage and produce the first two of three Cotton Club premiere show openings and Harper's breathtaking skillfulness facilitated the Cotton Club and helped garner the celebrated hotspot its initial worldwide recognition.

William "Sonny" Greer, the famous singing drummer from New Jersey who worked with Harper and became Duke Ellington's drummer from the early 1920s on, talked to writer Stanley Crouch in an interview for the *Jazz Oral History Project* which is on file at the Institute of Jazz Studies, Rutgers University, New Jersey and the Smithsonian Institute:

Sonny said "No, the first show at the Cotton Club? Oh yeah. It was heavy. The, guy that staged the show was Leonard Harper. He had all them, girls and different acts, of course, the first time we had a regular Broadway production up there and it was all right, you know, it wasn't, nothing difficult about it, but we had exact timing. We had the Nicholas Brothers, the Berry Brothers, Peg Leg Bates, Ethel Waters, they were the head, a dance team and oh, 16 prettiest girls you ever saw, in the chorus… but opening night, everybody in New York was there. Sensation. That's the first time we really played what you call a stage production; we had a natural Broadway show like these shows on Broadway nowadays, ain't nothing. They ain't nothing. Them, girls stopped the show. Oh just the girls, the chorus. Stopped them cold. You had to be somebody and know what you were doing to follow them, girls! Sixteen of them, they were hand-picked, like you pick a beauty contest. That's how he picked them girls. He screened them. The prettiest colored, girls in the world. They looked pretty on stage and when they are on the street, down on Broadway shopping, people would turn and look at them. They never, seen nobody, like that. That was the Cotton Club girl's, famous. "

Sonny continued "Productions, because the producer, he had a guy called Clarence Robinson, was assistant to Leonard and every year he would go to Europe and see the different shows, they would come back and give ideas to our show. We had special writers, Harold Arlen, Jimmy McHugh and Dorothy Fields. They were writers they were on the staff, that's right. It was a production, man, just like Ziegfeld put on a production. That's what we put on there. We had that."

Some of the world's most recognized V.I.P. visitant patrons that let loose at the Cotton Club were J. Edgar Hoover and partner Clyde Tolson, Ethel Merman, Mark Hellinger, Marlene Dietrich, George Raft, Emily Vanderbilt, Cole Porter, Charles Chaplin, Franklin D. Roosevelt Jr., Lady and Lord Mountbatten who were special fans of Harper's *Plantation Days*. Lady Mountbatten came to dub the Cotton Club "the Aristocrat of Harlem". Sadly the exalted king of the blues W.C. Handy was forbidden to step foot inside the Cotton Club because of the discriminatory "no coloreds admitted" door policies. W. C. Handy was pointed away from the entrance doorway and snubbed by the Cotton Club.

Leonard Harper later directed a revue which yielded its foundations from the Cotton Club. The show which maintained a very lengthy run at the ritzy Harlem hotspot was titled *Cottonland* and was billed as the fastest floorshow in town. Harper's *Cottonland* was eventually relocated to a new Chicago based pleasure resort named the Plantation Café nightclub in November 1924. The Chicago form of the new Plantation Café was managed by Jimmy O'Neal, Harper's former manager/producer and business associate from *Plantation Days*. Power hungry and very dangerous Mafioso Alfonse Capone was reported to have had financial interests in the Chicago Plantation Cafe after having invested in the Cotton Club. Harper was able to cast his formerly alienated sister in-law Berliana Blanks who at the time warbled with a trio of women who called themselves the Three Dixie Songbirds.

When *Cottonland* launched in Chicago it ran for two weeks before going on the road in other parts of the country. Three years later in 1927 Harper returned to Chicago's Plantation Café, with another groundbreaking new African-American Colored Musical Revue that was so well received that it ran past the four weeks that it had been committed for with further annexations into its booking options.

Harper had at the very least nine concurrent productions on various stages at this time along with a few specialty tap shows as well as a few limited one night only recitals. Harper was not able to devote all of this time to the new Cotton Club because of his demanding work load. With his main floorshow attractions arising from Connie's Inn Harper had no choice but to consign the Cotton Club position of floorshow stager and its responsibilities to his assistant Clarence Robinson. Robinson made up for his dancing ability deficiencies by making use of his keen eye for artistic detail and his noteworthy interpretations of the choreography by doodling sketches of his impressive directorial concepts. Clarence Robinson did some unbelievable work at the Cotton Club and would go down in the annals of nightclub history as one of its most important creators.

Harper's choice not to remain at The Cotton Club and stay at Connie's Inn as its main in-house producer demonstrated to be one of the most prudent professional decisions he was ever to have made. Harper's sixth sense, theatrically speaking, helped him take the correct critical occupational route because in time more "above the line" prospects were presented to African-American people at Connie's Inn as opposed to the totally bigoted enclave of the Cotton Club. The Cotton Club was operated by ruthless blatant racists who frequently stole outright the original stage creations of their African-American workforce. Little credit and measly payment was allotted for the hard working behind the scenes African-American Cotton Club artistic sources and occasionally the creative burglary would go well beyond small bits with the outright thief of entire theatrical productions.

The picturesque and enduringly soulful Lena Horne was one of the Cotton Club's paramount stars and even she underwent the indignity of not being able to have her family come into the club to see her perform as they were lead away from the doors. All time song and dance comedian Honi Coles reminisced about the Cotton Club's past when he chatted to AFP reporter Mel Watkins in 1979 for a commentary titled *That Vaudeville Style: A Conversation with Honi Coles, How Hope Started.* Honi said of the Cotton Club: "It was an all-black show, and had all black help, except for the Chinaman in the kitchen. But there, were no blacks in the audience-none. And we had no resentment at that time; it was normal.

That was the way of life. If you were brought up in that period, there was no reason to even think about changing things. Comics thought the same way, they reflected the times."

The throaty voiced Connie Immerman with his curly blondish red hair was not the same type of man that Madden and the rest of the ruffians who operated the Cotton Club, were. Connie's Inn did more business by a hair than the Cotton Club did and Connie was canny enough to understand that Harper was one of the main reasons responsible for the enormous profits. Plus the Immerman brothers collectively were quite aware that they owed much of their early achievements to the African-Americans who patronized their uptown family delicatessen in the years before they had the cash to acquire their popular nightspot.

Harper reappeared later on from time to time at the Cotton Club to stage the dance numbers for Dan Healy and Elida Webb like the *Stormy Weather Revue* with the Nicholas Brothers, Cab Calloway and a team of Fan dancers. This nightclub version of the *Stormy Weather Revue* was mounted years before the motion picture of the identical name was ever envisioned, filmed or contemplated. The *Stormy Weather Revue* had a nice three months run at the Cotton Club then traveled out on a road tour under the directorial supervision of Irving C. Mills.

In 1935 Harper staged the dances and supervised the rhythm numbers for the *Cotton Club Parade 26th, Edition.* Ted Koeher penned the *Cotton Club Parade 26th Edition* book and lyrics with Rube Bloome as the musical source and the orchestration was handled by Will Vodery. The cast had Lena Horne and she was promoted as the Bronze Looker, comedian Mantan Moreland, Flournoy E. Miller, Butter Beans and Susie, the Rhythm Rascals and Nina Mae McKinney. Nina Mae McKinney also shared the starring credits and was the chorus girl who danced for both Leonard Harper and his white rival Lew Leslie before she became Metro Goldwyn Mayer's first light skinned black motion picture star in 1929. McKinney rose to national fame by portraying a sexy African-American prostitute in King Vidor's colossal sound film about African-American life titled

Hallelujah. Nina Mae was lucky enough to have secured a multi-picture deal with M.G.M. studios before becoming aware that her big screen cinematic career had come to a surprisingly instantaneous halt. All of the Hollywood studio heads which included the executives at MGM changed their minds and determined that they no longer wanted black women procuring lead roles so they agreed to let McKinney's contract peter out.

This 1935 Harper co-choreographed production of the *Cotton Club Parade 26th Edition* was a short-lived and futile shot at bringing the once grand aura of the Harlem nightspot and its high caliber of sparkling entertainment back to the life of its glory days of the Harlem Renaissance after those times had long waved goodbye. Although this edition of the show was somewhat of a mini triumph the Cotton Club nightclub itself was regrettably unable to turn back the hands of time and capitalize off of what it once was. Bill Bojangles Robinson, Lee Shubert, Mark Hellinger, Walter Winchell, Ethel Moses and a host of other show business dignitaries appeared for the opening night merriments. Sam Goldwyn was in the audience checking things out after having just contracted MGM's new high gingered golden, skinned African-American actress Nina Mae McKinney under the yet to be dead-ended Metro Goldwyn Mayer studio deal.

The original uptown Cotton Club nightclub of Harlem closed right after the *Cotton Club Parade 26th Edition* opened and toured just as the new reworking of the Cotton Club nightclub opened up on Broadway and Forty-Eighth, Street on Times Square with expectations of a fresh downtown inauguration. Innumerable Editions of the *Cotton Club on Parade* toured and played in big city theatres like the Apollo. In 1938 Clarence Robinson staged yet another converted rendering/edition of the show that sailed to Buenos Aires, Argentina. Harper was present at the lively bon voyage party which saw the cast and crew off before they sailed away from the docks of New York.

HARPER DID THE HOLLYWOOD INN / KENTUCKY CLUB

During the first week of September 1923 Harper produced for the Lincoln Theatre, Connie's Inn, the Lafayette Theatre and the Cotton Club while staging a whole host of benefit productions. Additionally he also found the time in his schedule to establish an association with a downtown Times Square producer to direct an, all African-American revue in a, new nightclub right in the heart of the "Great White Way". The nightclub was called the Hollywood Inn and it was formerly known as the Palais De Dance located at Forty-Ninth Street and Broadway.

Recently back from their trip to England, Harper and Blanks were the principals of his original new Hollywood Inn show which contained a company of seventeen which included a high speed moving chorus of dancing beauties. Dabney's Ginger jazz band of six furnished the music. Harper's new production packed the nightclub in with hordes of aficionados like cans of standing room only sardines cramming the interior and filling the space with inquisitive Times Square onlookers who wanted to set their eyes on the cabaret revue that the press pronounced as "elaborately staged with several new effects brought from Europe by Mr. Harper."

Promoter Joe Ward teamed up with Harper and both fellas had major designs to mount similar original spectacles in a number of other nightclub cafés across the country. The proposals for a traveling circuit of African-American cabaret nightclub revues and all the other new projects under the management of Harper with Joe Ward never materialized and their plans were blocked from ever getting off the ground. Nightclub owners and management people with more cash on hand, street muscle, and knowledge, became aware of Harper's talents and gobbled him up while driving Joe Ward away.

Harper's show at the Hollywood Inn initially did only fairly well and the proprietors believed that business could be a bit healthier so they agreed to let Harper's production be farmed out as a form of marketing to the Cinderella Dance Hall as a profile-raising trick to drum up additional nightclub customers. The general public paid to get into the Cinderella Dance Hall and Harper's newest floorshow got such good word of mouth it enabled the Hollywood Inn to draw in a totally new assembly of patrons once the revue returned to the new nightspot. The Immerman Brothers, from Connie's Inn, got-wind of this stunt and made a comparable deal with the Cinderella Dance Hall for Harper's Connie's Inn *Black and Tan Revue*. The Cinderella Dance Hall patrons went crazy with encores for the Leroy Smith's Band in the Harper revue and screamed out pleading for more red hot tunes. Leroy Smith, the temperamental musician, ignored the outcries and pigheadedly refused to answer the audience's appeals for more and curtly concluded the Connie's Inn promotional stunt.

Harper's downtown undertakings at the Hollywood Inn unsealed many previously unexpected opportunities for the in-demand producer with a reputation for furnishing audiences much more enjoyment than they had expected. Historically, many of the all-white theatrical institutions had opposed "White and Tan" mixed race shows on Broadway until Harper and his *Hollywood Follies* came along and spawned enormous profits. Money halted the complaints and condemnation of "mixed race" productions from most of the downtown theatre executives. In mid-1923 Broadway Burlesque stood trite and uninspired with diminishing audiences until Harper came on the scene and used fast jazz dancing chorus lines a phenomenon that the white theatre going crowds had never beheld before. Harper's stage masterpieces were a much craved shot in the arm for everyone in the theatre world.

The African-American Musical Comedy format that Harper bestowed upon to yawing and somnambulant Burlesque theatre buffs was about to give a wider range of audiences reasons to wake up and recharge their systems while sitting on the edges of their seats. Broadway producer Joe Hurtig was so awestruck with Harper's Hollywood Inn revues that he signed him to direct *The Hollywood Follies* with an unprecedented all white and black talent cast line-up for the Columbia Burlesque Theatre on Times Square and Forty-Seventh, Street. Hurtig got down to it with an indeterminate booking engagement for the show and had Harper working with the largest cast ever on duty numerically in a burlesque show. Young Harper had sixty-five people from the top pick of the white burlesque litter and a one of a kind libretto with a musical score that production notes described as lively, fun and snappy. The daily matinee prices ranged from 25 cents to 75 cents and the night tickets were 50 cents to a $1.50.

Harper ushered in his own expressive style of the Charlestown Buzz and Black Bottom dance routines within *The Hollywood Follies*. Making good use of his earnings he opened up a Times Square dance studio luring in many of the white fans of his recent hit productions who wanted to be taught how to "dance dirty, just like the coloreds." Harper was on his way up and set in motion the progression of integrating the Great White Way as he accepted more offers to "pep" up white shows from behind the scenes with his inimitable panache of chorus line dance arrangements and with his assimilations and infusions of his spicy African-American variety acts.

Mixed "White and Tan" musical comedies or floorshows continued to get angry protests from racist theatrical organizations and Broadway was bound by its discriminatory creed to enact and enforce its strict separate and unequal black and white split performances and segregated seating schedules. The enormous box office ticket sales from Harper's voluminous Broadway productions forced obstinate theatre proprietors to rethink their bottom lines and they examined their antiquated regressive racial guidelines.

The name of the Hollywood Inn was changed to the Club Kentucky and club goers started referring to it as the Kentucky Club. The Club Kentucky had become the main, downtown hangout for big time gangsters with influence and authority like Charles "Lucky" Luciano and Legs Diamond who were annoyed at competing mobsters for burglarizing their alcohol and ice trucks.

Luciano often snickered to himself while at the Hollywood Inn because he had Harper working for him downtown at his hoodlum ruled nightclub which pissed off his uptown crime rival Dutch Schultz who wanted to claim Harper's theatrical services exclusively for himself in Harlem.

    Revenue police were always in and out of the Club Kentucky because of its high profile locality. The cops were either trying to bust the joint or better yet they came to pick up their sizeable under the table graft payments. When the clean stage law enforcement officers attempted to raid the Club Kentucky, Harper had his semi-unclothed dancing Misses pose as motionless and lawful artistic naked model/statues dressed in flowing see through robes or have the ladies appear as sexy cigarette sales girls. Harper always hoodwinked the purity police at the Club Kentucky who always ambled away with a wink, a nod, and a chunky pocket.

    Luciano booked Harper out of the club one night to set up a hush-hush show for some of his ruffian associates at a neighboring hotel. When Harper's chorus girls arrived to work they were instantaneously hounded by some of Luciano's sloshed and bad-mannered crime partners. These gangsters took to grabbing and feeling up some of the chorus girl's figures before the girls could change into their performance apparel. Most of the girls freaked out but a slight few of Harper's more hardened and street wise dancers were more than willing to do anything for a price and requested generous up front gratuities for the implementation of any supplemental services. Luciano expressed his regret to Harper for the discourteous behavior exhibited towards his chorus girls and reimbursed him and his panicky dancers for their time before discharging them. Luciano telephoned Madame Polly Adler also known as the "Queen of Tarts" to dispatch some of her most beautiful lily complexioned professional hookers without delay to do all those particular things for his guests at his hotel party that nearly all of Harper's chorus line dancers were reluctant to do.

    The Club Kentucky's oddly low-slung ceiling was always damp and for some strange reason the club was cursed with several periodic fires and equipment burnings. Many declared that the repeated fires were set with the intention of either acquiring insurance money for free renovations or to enable the management to weasel out of substantial contractual payouts. The Club Kentucky's stage area was quite tiny and was always overcrowded with some of the greatest musicians this planet had ever known.

Huge tips for performers were the additional perks especially for musicians like Fats Waller. When Waller played at the Club Kentucky he always attached two bulky tin cans on each side of a mini-portable piano and fastened it over his big shoulders then lugged it throughout the club while amassing tips. Waller literally became a hustling gratuity machine as he walked, goofed, played, sang, and cried out loud for more dough within the thickly patronized corners of this downtown jumping joint.

Jazz musicians Jimmy and Tommy Dorsey were regulars at the Club Kentucky as was big time bandleader Paul Whiteman. Whiteman was known to have written down the jazz improvisations of African-American musical artists during jam sessions at the club and he later turned the appropriated materials into his so-called "symphonic-jazz." Symphonic Jazz was Whiteman's method of surrendering the essentially native and rhythm based Afro-American musical art form into a more harmoniously tamed, sterilized and watered down germ-free arrangement of sounds. Actor Al Jolson and multiple Charleston dance tournament champion and all around carousing chorus girl Lucille Le Seur, who later changed her name to Joan Crawford, could also be seen on a regular basis at the Club Kentucky. Joan Crawford was known in her early days for shaking her delectable nether regions in amateur dance contests. Large factions of loaded and famed downtown luminaries entered the Club Kentucky at 11:00 pm and stayed until way after the 7:00 am breakfast performances were over.

Harper encountered all, of this good occupational kismet while his gifted piano playing boarder Ellington strained to establish himself as a musical bandleader. Ellington's proficiencies were vastly superb but with so many other well acknowledged and remarkable musicians who had been on the Harlem scene much longer, meant it took him an extended amount of time to get truly recognized.

Ellington and his wife Edna had their young son Mercer come up and sojourn in Harper's huge flat. Mercer lived with his grandparents in Washington D.C. during the week and came up to spend his weekends at the Harper's in Harlem. Harper's apartment was enormous but because many people occupied it, young Mercer was asked to sleep on the couch in the living room while his parents shared one of the extra bedrooms. Mercer Ellington recounted when he stayed at the Harper's apartment and his floorshows in his book co-written with Stanley Dance titled *Duke Ellington In Person: An Intimate Memoir*. Mercer said "I was familiar with that kind of show routines they had at the Cotton Club, because when pop was living at Leonard Harper's place; Leonard was the producer for Connie's Inn. I went down there, once when they were rehearsing a big time jungle thing that had been worked out for the chorus girls. They had feathers around their hips and feathers around their ankles and they were supposed to look like Zulus."

Duke Ellington was employed by Harper to play during the preproduction rehearsal phases at Connie's Inn and at the Lafayette Theatre from time to time. It was piece meal work and Ellington didn't make any real cash until he was signed to work at Barron Wilkins nightclub. Barron Wilkins was a black businessman who loved to use light mushroom toned and almost white looking black chorus girls in his floorshows. A handful of patrons alleged that Barron Wilkins developed the concept of using near white African-American chorus girls for uptown nightclubs. Barron Wilkins club was robbed at gunpoint one evening and Wilkins was murdered while Ellington was performing on stage. The white Wilkins club goers swiftly dove to the floor for protection as Ellington and the rest of his band members ran out for dear life and away from the flying bullets. Ellington had to find another good paying gig to support his family after Wilkins death. When Ellington returned to the Harper apartment that evening he told Harper about the incident at Barron Wilkins nightclub and notified him that next month's rent might be late. Harper reassured Ellington, telling him not to worry about it because he was about to produce a brand new big musical revue at the downtown Club Kentucky and that he planned on hiring him and his band to perform the music. Ellington supposedly jumped for joy at the opportunity to work with Harper on stage and on a regular basis. Ellington was also mindful that the tips were more plentiful at the big time Kentucky Club Times Square area spot.

Ellington was interviewed by author Don George for the book titled *Sweet Man: The Real Duke Ellington*. Ellington scanned back into his bygone days and told George: "A man named Leonard Harper, who produced the shows at the Cotton Club and Connie's Inn had heard our band and liked it; in fact I had a room at his house. He said 'I got a job for you guys. A new club opened, the Kentucky Club at Forty-Ninth, Street and Broadway. Would you be interested?" Harper's new floor-show was called *Harper's Dixie Revue* and Harper's blueprints called for him to utilize lots of exotic calypso and Hawaiian numbers along with a white master of ceremonies named Burt Lewis entitled as the singer of a thousand songs and an assortment of comedians with a white female opera singer to satisfy the hunger and exotic tastes of the "cultured" Club Kentucky regulars.

Harper awkwardly explained to Ellington that the Club Kentucky proprietors required him to use a different band headed by Everard Dabney and his six piece Ginger Band and that Everard had already signed a contract of a six month agreement for his services. The good news for Ellington was that Harper said that his own agreement was based on the precondition that the Elmer Snowden Washington Black Sox Orchestra perform the music instead of Everard Dabney's band and that Elmer Snowden take on Ellington as the pianist. The inclusion of Ellington was one of Harper's main stipulations. Elmer Snowden was the leader and banjoist of his band and they doggedly rehearsed at the Strand Building. Ellington's musical gifts were so mighty that it was just a matter of time before he took over the band by his essentially innate artistic ascription. The name of the band was changed from the six-piece Washington Black Sox Orchestra Band to the "Washingtonians". The seven piece band was featured in *Harper's Dixie Revue*.

Duke Ellington was now able to disburse the rent money owed to Harper and have some spare cash on hand. Ellington wasn't the only talent to claim his coming out party during Harper's floorshow revues at the Hollywood Inn/Kentucky Club. Singer/performer Aida Ward and blackface comedian Johnny Hudgins were members of the same league that acquired their downtown commencements there as well.

Harper injected an East Asian dancer to the mix of his *Harper's Dixie Revue* and highlighted the Seven Strutters then incorporated himself as a crème de la crème solo dancer for exclusive performances. Bert Lewis jested up a cluster of socialites then teased a table full of treacherous criminals before breaking out in song with a ragtime number backed up by a trio of harmony songsters. The show also featured a female ragtime vocalist and a "Charleston" dance specialist. The performances were tight while the club still maintained a free-for-all informality. Harper and Ellington were to work on many hypnotizing floorshows at the Club Kentucky like for instance Harper's famous and widely discussed *Kentucky Club Revue*.

The Club Kentucky's horn players growled like horny alley cats that had inhaled much too much catnip and the party went on all morning long as Ellington played. Harper and Ellington worked and collaborated together at the Club Kentucky for almost five years, till Ellington received one of the biggest breaks in his early career, to gig and become the Cotton Club's main bandleader under Harper's former assistant producer Clarence Robinson. Irving Mills drew up the contract for Ellington, and his band started working at The Cotton Club in 1927. The Harper-Ellington collaborations were extraordinary. Ellington said of one Harper's Revues, "It was a hot show."

HARPER DID SMALL'S PARADISE

Harper's production services and various achievements at other nightclubs were not lost to Edwin A. Smalls the tough African-American Harlem nightclub impresario and titleholder of Smalls Paradise. Mr. Smalls had previously owned outright the colored hangout spot called the Sugar Cane Club. But on October 22, 1925, he determined that the Sugar Cane wasn't grand enough so he started up a brand new nightspot called Small's Paradise Club which was deemed the biggest colored owned joint in Harlem located on Seventh Avenue and 135th. Street.

Ed Smalls approached Harper and told him that Small's Paradise was to be a "Black and Tan" nightclub where all of the diverse races could dance, party and hang out with one another and it would be a showplace where nothing would be off limits or taboo. Harper moved promptly and had the Small's Paradise animated and ambidextrous wait staff bouncing and grooving as they served the patrons their orders in a fashion similar to his shuffling chorus lines. Some of the more able waiters and waitress spun their service trays above their heads and beneath their legs as they shook what God gave them while rotating towards the tables. Harper's new job at Small's wasn't regulated to just the choreography of his dancers in his nightclub floorshow because he had to also coach the wait staff on how to wobble their groove things like hot pepper shakers, while nimbly transporting large trays loaded down with food and drink. Customers came from far and wide and as nearby as around the block to see these outstandingly talented uptown service workers dance. They would pirouette and Charleston while circling up to the tables singing and whirling the food trays without dropping the pieces of bread, fried pork chops or dishes of butter.

Small's Paradise was slightly more second-rate in atmosphere and ornamentation than Connie's Inn but visitors got to see an original Harper show for a lot less coinage and if you had an appetite for race mingling on the dance floor then you better get your butt over to Small's because all categories of party folks were tolerated to dance as well as partake in the pleasure of observing a sizzling fast stepping Harper floorshow.

The production budgets were lesser for Harper's Small's Paradise nightclub floorshows and sometimes the Small's revues were just more scaled down adaptations of previous theatrical Harper marvels without the star power lineup. Now and again his Small's cabaret shows were preexisting Harper touring performances that had already showcased in other theatres with some marginal modifications and embellishments. For instance Harper's *Versatile Revue* opened up with the Three Midnight Steppers highlighting the music and lyrics of Andy Razaf and Spencer Williams with ditties like *Mammyland* and *Banta Baby* or tunes with compositions written by Razaf and J. P. Johnson like *Sambo's Syncopated Russian Dance* (1930) all slugged in and infused together within a regurgitated spinal cord that allowed for the redeployment of the revues at a musically calculated rhythmical velocity.

Harper's 1931 edition of his *Pepper Pot Revue* was featured at Small's but in contrast to the Lafayette theatre this time the show was installed without the irreplaceable dreamlike dancing skills of the world's chief versatile tap dancer Bill Bojangles Robinson. All of the fundamentals of a stirring Harper show endured but many of the auxiliary acts were up and coming talents pursing their big breaks. Lyricist Andy Razaf worked at Small's Paradise with Harper during their early years and their joint works of art at the club yielded what was to become a truck load full of forthcoming imaginatively fertile projects.

Leonard Harper generated floorshows during his initial period at Small's Paradise well into the late 1920s. He went missing from the club as a creator for approximately five years before resuming his express-line and perky floorshows from the mid-1930s into the early 1940s.

Harper had ripened into more than just a singer, dancer, and showman turned stager-choreographer, creative producer. He had metamorphosed into an instrumentalist-composer to a certain degree just like Ellington, Waller, Gershwin and J. P. Johnson but as a substitute for piano keys or a musical instrument he mastered the art of building pleasing reverberations by working his chorus line, their feet and the rest of their body motions.

CHAPTER THREE
(1924 to 1928)

TAKE ME UP TO *THE ONLY HARLEM RENAISSANCE*

The life-force behind the original Harlem Renaissance mainstream was bursting with black suppressed art, culture, rage, sexuality and everything else that made up the human subsistence and it was all dying to breakout and gush with self-expression.

An article was featured in the *Baltimore Afro-American* newspaper dated October 26, 1929 which was titled *Variety-Thinks Harlem Nite Clubs Have Broadway Skinned* and the publication defined and recorded some of the more interesting facts about the village of Harlem and its illustrious nightlife during the duration of the Harlem Renaissance:

1. Harlem has attained preeminence as an amusement center.
2. Its nite life has surpassed Broadway.
3. Celebrities of all walks of life "make" the Harlem joints every night.
4. Harlem has 11 white trade nightclubs. With a population of 250,000, the actual number of colored cabarets exceeds 500. This number is topped by statistics on the apartment speakeasies, called "buffet flats," there is an average of two such joints for every apartment building. Admission is two bits and the same for a drink.
5. More chop suey joints are in Harlem than any other district of similar size in the country.

6. Harlem has 300 girl dancers working in the joints. About 800 are always ready for an audition.
7. Harlem has 150 boys, perhaps the best aggregation of tap and buck dancers extant.
8. There are 15 major bands, more than a hundred others in action every night.
9. Only 1,000 white families live in the colored belt.
10. Gold eyeglasses are the rage having replaced gold teeth for class. More than $30,000,000 is spent a year in Harlem playing the "Numbers".
11. The folks up there, who live all for today and know no tomorrow, are drawing the whites closer to them.

When tap dancers Bojangles and Harper showed up at rent parties they would join in the "cutting" competition using just their feet and the wood floor as an alternative to fingers on piano keys. Their feet talked releasing brilliant tempo resonances and all of the instrumental musicians would discontinue whatever they were playing to let the rhythmical part of their brain muscles oscillate without interruption. As stated in the book *The Jazz Cadence Of American Culture* edited by Robert G. O'Meally; "The role of the chorus line dancers in the development has been consistently overlooked by jazz and dance historians. According to Dicky Wells, many jazz musicians felt a kinship with chorus line dancers: "They used to be the biggest lift to musicians, because we thought alike. They were more important than people realized. You might say we composed while they danced—a whole lot of swinging rhythm." Harper understood that rhythm, tappers were categorically jazz percussionists. Your great drummers sat down and drummed and, your great hoofers pulsated, standing upright.

Inside the veiled shelter of their brownstone apartments the African-American literati and polished elites intellectualized and contemplated the Afro-American circumstance and its outlook with pen and paper.

At the time of the Harlem Renaissance transvestitism was a novelty with men who dressed as screen actresses like Gloria Swanson and Mae

West who they worshipped. The audacious and noticeable spectacle of black men acting like famous white women was a statement not only of sexual unconventionality but it additionally took on anti-societal manifestations of defiance and an insubordination which provoked the matter to its uppermost of racially satirical depths.

Harlem was saturated with lots of Southern Fried Soul food restaurants and the affluent tourists from downtown adored munching on the ribs, chicken and fish with waffles, yams, hog maw and sweet potato pies while navigating the grease so that they didn't stain their formal suits or expensive mink coats. The rotund and burly Gladys Bentley, who was to become Harper's Master of Ceremonies at the Ubangi Club, worked in the trendy Harlem Clam House.

Harper's marriage and rapport with his wife Osceola deteriorated because of his time-consuming work schedule and all of the extra-curricular goings-on that went along with being at the epicenter of the Harlem Renaissance. With all of the perks and, complementary offerings that were showered onto successful theatre directors Harper was certainly only human and succumbed to indulgence from time to time, but never to the point that he neglected his production works. Harper's nightclub revues and theatrical shows gradually began to take the place of his better half. His stunning chorus lines became known as "his girls" and they took the place of his wife.

In spite of Harper's thoughtlessness towards her, Osceola recurrently performed upon special request, and as time went by she resolved herself to being Harper's stay at home housewife. As a case in point the Harper's traveled jointly as Harper and Blanks to do what was termed as a "clever aggregation" at Toronto's Gayety Theatre in 1926 and in 1927. Harper & Blanks also traveled as a unit with Sliding Billy Watson to Detroit's Gayety Theatre for an impressive run. These theatrical excursions took place even though Osceola's spirit was temperamentally no longer in show business.

Lodger "Duke" Ellington had an analogous set of spousal complications with his wife Edna while boarding with the Harpers. Duke

Ellington remained out late at night working just like Leonard and was setting in motion his reputation for having an eye for the ladies. Edna Ellington reacted differently than Osceola and refused to put up with her husband's wandering eyes. The Ellington's quarreled regularly while inhabiting at the Harper apartment and in due course Edna took her son, little Mercer, and left.

Leonard's brother Gene-Eugene Harper resided with their mother Sarah Harper in Chicago and for an infinitesimal interval Eugene tried to exploit his brother's fame. Eugene came by some piecemeal behind the scenes labor on a few of the stage road shows but these temporary positions faded out right along with his theatrical objectives. Gene returned home to Chicago and mother Sarah, with no choice but to stare from a backseat at his older brother's escalation into theatrical stardom.

Harper partook in an assortment of fundraisers and benefits primarily for the welfare of theatrical organizations and children's country camps. Harper treasured his involvement when the Cotton Club and Connie's Inn donated free turkeys for Harlem's poverty-stricken denizens during the Thanksgiving and Christmas holidays.

Some of the fundraisers Harper participated in were *Harper's Creole Revue* for *A Monster Carnival of Novelties* with Florence Mills and her husband's duo for The Dressing Room Club's charity event, The Negro Folk Music and Drama Society exhibited *Harper's Revues from Connie's Inn* and his *The Nest Club* with Paul Robeson who performed a solo accompanied by his group the Four Harmony Kings, Alberta Hunter, Ada Ward and Edith Wilson who performed in what was defined as a series of Negro nuances for *Negro Musical Night* at the Forty-Fourth Street Theatre. Harper and Blanks also played at a testimonial for Sam Langford in 1925 with Charles Gilpin and Alberta Hunter as well as *A Benefit for Salem Tutt Whitney* that highlighted Harper's *Lucky Sambo* cast members and his floorshow chorus lines from Connie's Inn and Cotton Club. Harper additionally tooled a fundraiser for the Theatre Boys of the Keith-Albee Circuit of Theatres and another one for their Colored Employee's Organization in a benefit at the Grace Congregational

Church with musician "Lucky" Roberts along with an aggregation of delightful complementary acts on the bill. Harper, Bojangles and Frank Schiffman were all on the entertainment committee for the Harlem Children's Center Boys Club Camp Benefit at the midnight show in the Lafayette Theatre with Harper and Bojangles mutually appearing and executing some stupefying dance sequences.

The *Billboard* show-business journal's "Black Page Columnist," J. A. Jackson inscribed that "Harper it was said always made Christmas very happy for the show folk, because he had just about everybody idle in town on "the job" in one of his productions."

Harper staged a great big show at the New Star Casino on 107th Street and Lexington Avenue in a neighborhood that would later become known as Spanish Harlem with a singular appearance by none other than his resuscitated Harper and Blanks team along with his *Hollywood Club Revue, Cotton Club* and *Connie's Inn Revues*. Harper also commandeered some scaled down one night only performance productions for the Elk's Lodge and the Capitol Palace Club from time to time. Harper presented a racy Bathing Beauty Contest for cash prizes at the Manhattan Casino for the Elk's Lodge and also furnished to the Harlem Renaissance Ballroom his *Hot-Cha Revue* in a fundraiser for the Ziegfeld Sporting Club.

Harper transferred his *Kentucky Club Revue* from the Club Kentucky nightclub with Ellington and crew to Broadway's New Amsterdam Theatre's fabulous rooftop nightclub on Times Square on off nights when the theatre became dark. The New Amsterdam theatres' rooftop was known as an entirely white bread setup famous for featuring the glamorous *Ziegfeld Follies* with the exception being when Harper brought his powerfully brisk booted chorus line and jazz jamming Afro-American floorshow revues to their stage.

With his lucrative business interests swelling up Harper secured the veteran vaudevillian Bob Slater from out of retirement in year 1927 because he required someone with backstage promotional expertise to manage the profile-raising branches of his many roadshow "tabloid" productions. The next year Leonard appointed former stage manager/dancer Emory "Hutch" Hutchinson who performed with the Three Dukes from Baltimore. "Hutch" was elevated to the position of Harper's senior manager running all of Leonard's theatrical undertakings which incorporated the road shows, revues and downtown nightclub floorshows. Under Harper's company they facilitated the management of talents like Peg Leg Bates "The Fastest Wooden Legged Tap Dancer on Earth". Nearly all, of Harper's 1928 productions grossed sum totals of from $10,000 to $20,000 nightly.

THE GREAT (WHITE) LEONARD HARPER WAY

After Harper landed back in New York from his London *Plantation Days* performances during the fall of 1923 his ensuing labors in the Times Square district of Broadway turned out to be like a magical key which would open up several doors to him as it was a commencement for the theatrical integration of African-Americans. Even though he was known on Broadway as being part of the "put out" Town Hall *Put and Take* fiasco and as the male half of Harper and Blanks the first African-American pair to perform on Shubert Vaudeville time those latest achievements showcased only his skills as a performance talent as opposed to the adept producer/stager he was about to mature into.

Theater reviewer J. A. Jackson wrote for *Billboard* in an article titled *The Floor Show a Growing Feature* that "Leonard Harper of Harper and Blanks have no less than three such shows in New York, one in an exclusively white patronized Broadway place, the Hollywood; one in a mixed rendezvous, an Inn in the upper section of the city and still another, 'The Nest' a place that is filled with colored patrons nightly." For the duration of this time Broadway theatre was drying up from its lack of inventiveness. It wasn't until Harper was unobtrusively employed to implant an African-American portion into the opening half of the all-white *Fast Steppers* revue that any unquestionable revolutions ensued.

Harper's modest trial concoction of African-American talent in a predominantly white show coupled with his staging instructions shot the box office receipts through the roof reaching $2,500 weekly according to *Variety* and his contributions didn't go undetected by Broadway's key players.

Various authors penned on about how in 1923 Harper inserted vivacity into *The Greenwich Village Follies* and George White's *The Passing Show* of 1924. Harper's work as a fragment set piece director on these productions went unattributed but a careful inspection of the talent pool comprising of Florence Mills, Daphne Pollard and Martha Graham in *The Greenwich Village Follies* and Lucille Le Sueur subsequently known as Joan Crawford in George White's *The Passing Show* implied that Harper was not only on duty but on top of things production wise.

Daphne Pollard, the actress that earlier in the spring of that year crashed the Coterie of Friends event that Harper was hosting in London, England, was in New York starring in *The Greenwich Villages Follies*. On September 20, 1923 Florence Mills was given a prime specialty role in the production of the *Greenwich Village Follies* which opened at the Winter Garden Theatre on Broadway. Leonard Harper was one of the un-credited stagers on *Greenwich Village Follies* as well as other numerous Winter Garden theatrical productions. Harper was on the payroll because Lee and J. J. Shubert were the producing partners and they were badly in need of his directorial expertise to pep up productions like these. Harper's history, along with Osceola, of being in the first African-American duo to tour on Shubert Vaudeville time and his success with *Plantation Days* in London, helped him secure these part time gigs with the Shubert Brothers doctoring up some of their more lackluster stage shows. During this time Harper was able to solidify his affectionate professional relationship with Florence Mills while he embarked on his domination of nightclubs and theatres both downtown and uptown.

While Mills got star treatment and top billing on advertisements, as she so well merited in *Greenwich Village Follies*, Miss. Pollard, the other star in the show, felt ignored and affronted. Pollard questioned out loud and often to the rest of the white cast members probing why a black girl should get the more preferential star treatment while the white cast members were handled as mere stage props? Pollard's gripes went on and on and she never shut her insolent mouth. Finally she threated the producers with an all-white talent walk-out and strike just before opening night. The producers gave in to Pollard's imbalanced demands because they feared her walkout might hurt their bottom line. Daphne Pollard's program and poster credit for the *Greenwich Village Follies* were enlarged to a comparable size as actress Florence Mills'. The contents of Pollard's twisted and sour nature was never to change even though she did go on to play the tiny wife of big Oliver Hardy in Hal Roach's Laurel and Hardy comedies providing much joy and laughter to many on the silver screen.

From Broadway's Palais de Dance publicity stunt to the Hollywood Inn/Club Kentucky floorshows big deal theatre landlord and producer Joseph Hurtig often parked himself in Harper's audience and dug what he saw. Joseph Hurtig was the guy that owned the theatre district's Columbia Theatre and was also a partnership proprietor of a nondescript modest uptown theatre known as Hurtig and Seamon's New Theatre which would later become Billy Minsky's Little Apollo Theatre. Joe Hurtig signed Harper to create for his Columbia Theatre site at Times Sq. and Forty-Seventh Street, a burlesque edition of his nightclub floorshow revue which had already been running at the Hollywood Inn.

At this time it was unheard of to have an African-American man direct a show in an all-white theatre. The revue was titled Joe Hurtig's *Hollywood Follies* but everyone knew that it was an all Leonard Harper production. Sixty five people were in the company of *Harper's Hollywood Follies* and the show was so lucrative that Hurtig along with partner Seamon kept Harper on to direct an extra show entitled *Seven and Eleven. Seven and Eleven,* was promoted as being the "World's Greatest Colored Show" with the "Fastest Dancing Ever Staged" which also contained a staged female boxing bout. Harper's production of *Seven and Eleven* was so fruitful they "tabbed" it out from Broadway off to Harlem's Lafayette Theatre then they dispatched the production to tour the African-American theatrical circuit in other major cities.

Hurtig and Seamon also enlisted Harper to bring his legendary *Connie's Inn Revue* for the Mid-Winter Carnival Week showcase into their all white Hurtig and Seamon Theatre in Harlem. Half of the Mid-Winter Carnival showcase consisted of fifty white entertainers and the other half of the show featured fifty of Harper's all Afro-American speed steppers and high soaring entertainers. The "tab" rendering of Harper's *Connie's Inn Revue* without the other half of the fifty white entertainers was offered to the booking agents of the Keith-Albee circuit of theatres with an asking price of $2,500 weekly and the show was rapidly snatched up because of the reported big box office sales and record house escalations at the Hurtig and Seamon burlesque theatres. Joe Hurtig was severely in need of Harper's expertise and his contributions to his Broadway productions and Harlem theatre and once acquired it was comparable to an injection of unadulterated, theatrical adrenaline, colored style.

Even as Harper boasted a near monopolistic dictate in most matters of theatre he still dealt with many nonsensical racial regulations from white theatre owners. For instance African-American acts were habitually not permitted to take any bows or curtsey for the duration of the applause no matter how impressive their performances and Harper had to put up with many run of the mill white acts that refused to follow African-American entertainers onto the stage. Some of the dreadful timeworn white acts claimed race as their excuse for why they wouldn't follow African-American performers on stage but the actual explanation was that countless talents of the darker shade were truly so outstanding with their crispy showmanship services that they blew just about every other lackluster act off the stage.

Harper's new Broadway audiences were somewhat atypical because they were the kind of spectators that wouldn't automatically trek uptown to Harlem or enter a nightclub that sold liquor. They were people who prized the retrograde themes of African-Americans going back to Africa or either being swindled or hoodwinked. African-Americans drinking and gambling while attempting to win back their rent money or petrified while scampering from white police or ghosts were a few of the stereotypical subjects that were acted out in extraordinarily absorbing song and dance routines.

Harper cleverly slugged in progressive sections that crafted the representation of his folks in a more real and humanistic light while eradicating the usual negative and offensive cultural characteristics whenever he could. Harper basically grabbed white Broadway vaudeville and squeezed it then shook it up by outshining a worn out old model by the use of eye-catching exotic costumes and arty sets with huge amounts of Southern theatrical soul. Harper's productions were not automatically contingent on theme, concept or story but were often held together by an array of fast interlocking bits and scenes.

It was expected that the superstars and groupies of Harper's broad and ever expanding audience base would want to learn his style of dancing. Some termed it colored or "dirty Negro" dancing and just about everybody craved to experience the personal adventure of rhythm dance. A selected few who desired to acquire Harper's dance technique had the God given skills to work with while others did not fare so well but no matter what their race or agility level paying pupils round or thin all lined up and flowed into Harper's Times Square studio shelling out for either his beginners or master classes.

Many glamorous entertainment idols assembled at Harper's studio to be trained to dance. The Marx Brothers, a teenaged Ruby Keeler, the Fabulous Foy Family, Jack Halbert and Valeska Suratt known as the "Vampire Woman of the Silent Screen", the Dooley Family a minstrel/circus act, Adele Astaire prodded by brother, Fred, Kitty Donner the great male impersonator and Mary "Ziegfeld Star" Hay, the waltz clogging Pat Rooney and Bee Jackson the Charleston Queen and Ziegfeld girl were all pupils. Against his hostile inclination Busby Berkeley was forced by

Broadway producer Moe Green to turn over his colossal chorus line unto Harper so he could school them in everything that they didn't know and what Berkeley was incapable of imparting to them. Whenever a Berkeley stage or cinema production was mounted all of Harper's trainees and anybody who ever studied under him would go to see the film or stage piece and cackle out of their seats upon witnessing how dreadfully off rhythm some of Berkeley's choreography was in contrast.

In the book titled *Duke Ellington And his World: A Biography* writer A. H. Lawrence marked that Geraldine Lockhart who danced for Harper in his production's told him that Harper "like most producers, he preferred to hire tall women with long legs. His routines were fast-paced, stately, with just a hint of sex. He could teach an elephant to dance". Lockhart recalled about the times when she would go to Busby Berkeley movies in Harlem theatres with other Harper trained dancers. "We used to laugh out loud at what he was doing. We knew Leonard could do it a lot better. Had he been white, he'd been in Hollywood by then" concluding what was a heartbreakingly ill-fated vocational observation on the Leonard Harper that she was acquainted with.

Caucasian star of *Greenwich Village Follies,* Irene Delroy appeared at Harper's Studio unable to dance and after just a few rigid instructions she left knowing how to hoof it with the best of them. Fred Astaire was displeased with his sister Adele's miscalculations on stage because of her nonexistent attention span. Fred commandeered Adele over to Harper's studio for practice lessons with hopes that she could improve her steps. At the time the Gershwin Brothers featured both Fred and Adele Astaire in their musical *Lady Be Good* and one of the breakout songs from the show was *Fascinating Rhythm*. Fred was very aware of how crucial it was for Adele to be taught fascinating rhythm and trusted Harper's Dance Studio was the place where she could attain it. Three years later Adele revisited the studio for some instant supplementary preparation when she and her brother Fred topped the bill in *Funny Face* on Broadway.

The Harper Studio was registered in the Broadway Blue Book as soon as its doors flew open commercially. Harper had another fellow of copper skin in this enterprise, his business partner Billy Pierce was the general and office manager of Leonard Harper Incorporated and he also accepted requisitions for new nightclub floorshows of which Harper was to direct like Jack Curley's Forty-Fifth Street-Club, The De-Luxe "Cotton Club", cabaret contracts and all of the Hurtig and Seamon deals for the Columbia Circuit of theatres. Originally Harper and Pierce opened up with one big room on the top floor and the spacious escalation within just four years made Harper's conservatory the largest space for coaching and dramatizing dance in the world while the leasing fees for the space ballooned to $6,000 a year.

Harper couldn't instruct all alone so he hired a workforce of eleven people and they held twenty-seven dance sessions a week. The interior walls to the studio were covered with autographed photos of every important celebrity that came through the Harper studio for instruction. All of his dance educators were salaried at $2,800 total for the week with eight teachers to a class for one course alone. Lessons commenced at twelve noon and ended at seven pm each night. Gargantuan mirrors were installed and Harper had showers, baths and a private V.I.P. workroom and teaching space areas were set up which had been particularly decorated with dancing figures painted in brown, red and orange. Regrettably, peepholes had to be ensconced in the bounds of some of the dance workshop walls because some of the male and female trainers were spotted getting "much too" sociable with each other. If they were seen partaking in the act of sexual intercourse or in any other compromising position they were quickly dismissed and replaced.

Harper instituted reservation only lessons for a select group of celebrities in the art of the Sugar Foot Stomp, Syncopated Buck, Eccentric Buck, Devil Dance, Jungle Stomp, Dirty Dig, Flapper Stomp, Harlem Hips, Black Bottom, Stair Dance, Zulu Stomp, the Charleston, Black Bottom and a mixed bag of other knee drop kicking and soft shoe, routines.

In October of 1924 the Leonard Harper agency via manager Billy Pierce was commissioned to handpick eight African-American chorus girls for a new revue at the Moulin Rouge in Paris, France. Mr. Salibert the administrator of the French company had heard all of the glowing reports about "The Leonard Harper System" of dance and appealed for Harper's choreographic assistance. Due to previous contractual obligations Harper couldn't travel to Paris but he was able to drill and produce the dance compositions for show from his New York studios. Before sending the girls on their way to Paris, Harper designated them to be called "The Brown Skin Vamps". One of his aides, Emma Maitland, was positioned in charge of overseeing the dancers for the mixed race show while they were away in France. The Brown Skin Vamps had to grapple with some very unpleasant racial problems surfacing from their white American "sister" chorus girls almost immediately after disembarking in Paris.

A white American chorus girl named Doris Lloyd, who was part of an eight white Follies chorus girl contingent in the Moulin Rouge show, complained about the all racial fraternization that went on backstage with Harper's "Brown Skin Vamps" chorus girls and the whites. Miss. Lloyd felt she needed to be the spokeswoman for the white dancers and she was also against certain numbers where the white girls and the black girls danced together. Lloyd was not permitted to open the show and was fired after she declared that she would never be caught strutting, her stuff with "browns". After Lloyd was sent back to New York the seven other white chorus girls were notified by Salibert that the show would go on with or without them and that in France entertainers were selected by talent not by color. The Parisian producers hinted that professional jealously might have been the source of the trouble.

The indigenous Parisians were esthetically liberal and had little difficulty with white and African-American performers on the same stage. The French relished Harper's exported fresh Cake Walk routines that he altered into a more soulful and formalized French "Can-Can" with that little something extra in the hip department. It was unfortunate that the shadow of American's repulsive racial white supremacy decrees would follow the Brown Skin Vamp ladies on their Parisian visit.

The other American dance directors felt overlooked and neglected as Harper's studio gained all of the newspaper press so a hoax quarrel was concocted to question which choreographer actually created many of the fashionable African-American rooted dance steps of the time like the Black Bottom and Charleston. The wholly publicity purposed manufactured attention getter as to who should be credited for the dances instigated nightclub table chatter for a short-lived period of time.

In Mark A. Knowles book *The Wicked Waltz and Other Scandalous Dances: Outrage at Couple Dancing in the 19th. And 20th. Century* the author wrote that black composer Will Marion "Cook points out that the Charleston was first done on stage in a production called *How Come?* And was performed by an African-American man named Leonard Harper."

Under pressure Harper totally vacated his dance studio because of his massive amounts of pre-production and production duties and he allotted everything to manager Billy Pierce. Just before Harper left he appointed a former bus boy from Connie's Inn named "Buddy" Bradley to take over his instruction obligations. Harper discovered trained and selected Buddy to be a member of his Connie's Inn Revue four years prior to hiring him to take over at the studio. Bradley was a good apprentice of Harper's and a superb dancer as validated by the thoughtfulness he collected from Stella Doyle the white British actress who was so delighted with the way Buddy tutored her in the art of Black Bottom hoofing that she gifted him a French antique cigarette case inlaid with six uncut diamonds and ornamented with two rubies said to be worth $150. An unappreciative "Buddy" Bradley would later appropriate all of the credit for the Harper Dance Studio in interviews by completely editing out all of Harper's involvement in his own studio.

Leonard Harper Dance Studio affiliate and general manager Pierce did his best to keep the studio open but he was an administrator and not a dancer or teacher. Without Harper's association and his ability to instruct learners on how to jiggle, waggle, wiggle and juggle, the dance academy folded after a few years. Harper on the other hand had grander and bigger theatrical challenges to overpower on the Broadway African-American Colored Musical Theatre horizon. In 1933, eight years after the termination of the Leonard Harper Dance Studio, Billy Pierce perished in insolvency departing with an estate of only $250 to his name.

Tan Town Topics was Harper's subsequent majestic 1925 Broadway production. The premier of *Tan Town Topics* kicked off in the latest nightclub on Times Square dubbed the Plantation Café Room on Broadway and Fiftieth Street and was stationed within the Winter Garden theatre building. The Shubert Brothers, Harper's first significant break-out Broadway employers, owned a fifteen percent stake in the Plantation Café Room. The Immerman brothers, proprietors of Connie's Inn, were on board as partial financiers of the *Tan Town Topics* bankrolling team. Harper shared his director's credit with William Seabury a white man.

It was relatively customary on Tin Pan Alley for African-American songwriters and composers to not only share their profits and capitulate, their authorship copyrights, but to also divvy up their credits with the white publishers who didn't tender any artistic contribution, in order to get compensated. If the black musical artists didn't subscribe to these unfair and insulting arrangements they wouldn't be able to peddle their compositions and thus would be incapable of generating a livelihood in the show business profession. Scores of whites in show business saw Negroes as just fly by night outsiders who were all too eager to tolerate minimal fees for their creative products. Harper regularly went along with these same racially belligerent contractual understandings with his theatrical transactions although not as habitually as the composers and lyricists perhaps because his craft was schematized to primarily staging live performances and the songwriters musician/works were chronicled with sound recordings and the publishing rights of sheet music.

The billboards and the advertisements for *Tan Town Topics* had a cartoon drawing of a little African-American girl in the nude in cornrows sitting on a block of ice while wolfing down a big watermelon with cotton bolls bordering the signage. With the title of the nightclub being called the Plantation Café, Broadway patrons gleefully anticipated morsels of bigoted Dixie delineations on the Great White Way. The occasionally fouled mouthed Ethel Waters' played the central top billing star in *Tan Town Topics* and each and every time she warbled she disseminated like the cabaret deity that she was. The fledgling and slightly too trusting emerging star Josephine Baker was also casted in *Tan Town Topics.* Will Vodery the brown skinned composer who was recognized by the celebrated Broadway columnist Walter Winchell as having discovered George Gershwin "because he got Gershwin his very first job as rehearsal pianist on the musical *Miss 1917*" was in command of the orchestra and baby it cooked. *Tan Town Topics* was considered to be one of the greatest floorshows ever and one of the best staged presentations in New York. It was said by one journalist that "Josephine Baker and Ethel Waters please in their specialty number."

The go-getting Josephine Baker was not only multi-talented but she stole the show from Ethel Waters, elevating her career to the uppermost point with some managers incorrectly deciphering and attempting to take advantage of her towering objectives. Certain close women friends sensed that Baker's private irritations at not being an instant box office lure was her Achilles heel and made efforts to use this inside information to charm her sexually. These advances were futile because all Miss. Baker actually desired was to dine; ride in limousines and dialogue about her future prospects in show business.

As detailed in Jean Claude Baker and Chris Chase's book titled *Josephine: The Hungry Heart* we discover that luckily for Josephine, producer Mary Louise Howard came to see *Tan Town Topics* and the minute the Harper/Seabury show ended Howard brought Josephine to the Champs Elysee in Paris for attendances with imbursements of $150 a week. From her alluring Parisian showcases Josephine Baker converted into the idolized international megastar that the world recognized her to be.

Harper was later able to tab-out to other theatres altered forms of *Tan Town Topics* with all new dance numbers and this time without having to apportion any of his directorial credits to William Seabury. Thomas

"Fats" Waller along with Clarence Williams composed the music and Eddie Rector with Spencer Williams carved out the lyrics for one version of the revue and Andy Razaf completed another. *Tan Town Topics* delivered Thomas Fats Waller's first important hit song entitled *Senorita Mine*. The featured tune *Senorita Mine* was staged using a Spanish bullfight sequence. Additional ditties were titled *Valencia, Charleston Hound* and *I've Found a New Baby* which were all enacted live at the Lafayette Theatre.

As an extension of Harper's dance studio coaching work with pupil Ruby Keller she arranged for him to be signed to stage a few of her upcoming shows. Keller considered Harper the finest dance tutor that she ever had. While employed with the former Western-rodeo sharpshooter and El Fey speakeasy nightclub owner Texas "Hello Sucker" Guinan, Keeler was hyped as one of Texas Guinan's "Ten Little Glorious Girls, Who Don't Need Glorifying."

Harper attained significant progress as he moved further and further into the white production show world while still upholding his dominance in Harlem. Burlesque producer Morris Cain of Cain and Davenport retained Harper to produce *Harry Steepe's Own Show* and then contracted him for additional production stage directing with the Columbia Wheel attractions. Rube Bornstein also engaged Harper to produce numbers for his show *The Bathing Beauties* as he was simultaneously contracted by Alphonse Delmonico to create wholly white shows for Delmonico's Restaurant on Fifty-first, Street. Harper then staged the first totally black incarnation of *Temptations, Seven-Eleven* a mixed *4-11-44* and then mounted *Step on It* for Hurtig and Seamon. British actor Charles Laughton was said to be a regular at the Hurtig and Seamon theatres. At that time a robust Harper also found the time to guide the production numbers for the entirely white Morrissey-Harry-Bastry's spectacle titled *Watch Out*.

Harper worked at resuscitating Jimmy Cooper's (all Caucasian) graveyard bound revue from its abruptly dwindling box office receipts. Harper inserted an early version of his *Hot Feet Revue* from Connie's

Inn nightclub and it became the finale attraction on Jimmy Cooper's half white, half black line up. Harper graciously outfitted white producer Jimmy Cooper's revue with Thirty Four Real Hot Dancing Feet who danced to Julian Arthur's Ten Real Hot Jazz Hound's Band. Harper shared the bill with Cooper's stale first act of played out old vaudevillians such as the Seven Pashas an "Arabian" tumbler team and a wearied nude act called the Illuminated Curtain. The semi-racial mixing and the utilization of Harper as an African-American stager/producer and all of his talented performers was not racial altruism on Jimmy Cooper's part instead it was all about the cash and rescuing his corny production from extinction. Harper's second act of ostentatious, fervid and, unconventional dancing performers always stole the show away from Cooper and his first set.

Harper accomplished all of the aforementioned while producing a radio show which broadcasted live from the WHN Loews' State Theatre building radio station on Times Square and from the Kentucky Club every day after 2:00 am in the morning. Leroy Smith's Band from Connie's Inn was on board with a lineup which included a group of visiting pop-in musicians from Harper's several nightclub floorshows.

An offer to voyage back to London to stage the floorshows at England's new Hippodrome Club came his way with huge money propositions but because of his other occupational commitments in the States the vigorously toiling Harper was unable to accede as he multitasked like a mother. Harper found great gratification in unearthing a new young Caucasian talent named Ray King. Harper came across Ray King singing on a showboat and it was kind of like a reverse throw back for him from his own days as a pickaninny dancing on the Southern levee. Ray King was a white boy steamboat act from Louisville who fooled and snared his audiences in by speaking in the Negro dialect to perfection before singing in an amazingly soulful croaky baritone voice. Harper casted Ray King in a Blackface show wearing black cork which further deceived, puzzled patrons that questioned whether Mr. King was a black or a white man.

A music publishing company was founded by musical ragtime great James P. Johnson with his comrade and collaborator Harper. This publishing company was short lived and unproductive due to both Harper's and Johnson's lack of dedication to it and because he and Johnson could not economically compete with the established white publishing companies that paid African-American songwriters cash money, on the spot for their songs and compositions.

In 1926 Leonard Harper presided over the staging of *Lucky Sambo* the African-American Musical Comedy on Broadway with the personal direction credits going to theatre owner Joseph Hurtig. *Lucky Sambo* was the story of unrefined Negro hotel porters who get hoodwinked into buying valueless property then learn that they have new found wealth with the discovery of oil below their land. The instantaneously affluent porters and the destitute townspeople break out into a song and dance prancing about in front of Aunt Jemima's Log Cabin set with uncontrollable rhythmic movements similar to a spastic Charleston. Afterwards the cast of actors and dancers agree to rejoice in front of the town's hotel, jail house and oil wells culminating Act One with a big parade. At the conclusion of Act Two a nightclub cabaret scene is staged at Jim Nightingale's club. Jim Nightingale was also the town's resident crook who was just about to go off to jail. Some of the song titles in *Lucky Sambo* were *Anybody's Man Will Be My Man, If You Can't Bring It, You've Got To Give It* and *Charley From That Charleston Dancing School*. All of the wicked people in *Lucky Sambo* go to jail and the virtuous folks either get rich or fall in love to live happily ever after. *Lucky Sambo's* incidental plot really didn't matter for it was all about the unique floorshow style of choreography staged by Harper that had hordes herding into the Columbia Theatre to revel in the show.

Sister in-law Berliana Blanks was cast in *Lucky Sambo*. Berliana who had been performing with her trio the Three Dixie Songbirds was electrified to get the role and Clarence Robinson, Harper's Cotton Club assistant portrayed the antagonist charlatan Jim Nightingale who unloaded the "worthless" property on the gullible hotel porters. *Lucky

Sambo originally kicked off in 1924 with the title of *Aces and Queens* but the first initial materialization of the musical ran out of financial resources compelling the orchestra to refuse any further performing until they were compensated.

In 1926 Hurtig and Seamon bankrolled *Lucky Sambo* principally because of Harper's association with it. One of the posters for *Lucky Sambo* had a cartoon drawing of a black male in blackface with enormous white lips wearing a bolder hat with a bulky piece of jewelry around his neck with the words reading "The Black Diamond Speed Chorus." After leaving Broadway *Lucky Sambo* toured the Columbia Wheel circuit of theatres intact and then visited the African-American circuit of theatres for a year. *Lucky Sambo* drew in healthy profits for its principals. Unknown musical virtuoso Louis Armstrong went to see Harper's *Lucky Sambo* at the La Salle Theatre in Chicago and little did he know that two years later he would be introduced and launched into stardom by Harper to Broadway audiences in his *Hot Chocolates'* staged Colored Musical Comedy revue.

In February of 1926 Harper directed a floorshow for Ciro's downtown nightclub using a number of the entertainers that he supplied to Connie's Inn. Ciro's club was where the Park Avenue hoity-toity "creme de la crème" gathered with Harry Richmond as a fixture on the piano. The Immerman's were thrown into disarray with the notion that Harper might snatch away more of their on-stage talents for other nightspots. Connie Immerman and brother, George "dropped a dime" and snitched to law enforcement authorities that Ciro's nightclub didn't have a legal dance license nor did the club possess the proper paperwork to legally operate as a nightclub establishment. The tip-off was a very hazardous thing for the Immerman brothers to do because Ciro's was in point of fact owned by the notorious Harlem gangster with a nasty temper Ciro Terranova who also happened to be a partner in crime with "Lucky" Luciano. Harper's *Creole Follies* went on without any hindrances as Ciro's was permitted to remain open with or without the dance license or the appropriate paperwork.

Harper dispatched a touring edition of his *Creole Follies* from Ciro's and the first stop was Harlem's Lincoln Theatre and the show's title was modified to *Ciro's 2AM Revue* with press announcements declaring the show to be "Smart, Spicy, Fast."

⸻

LEONARD HARPER & FLORENCE MILLS

Imaginably it was her sweet vulnerability as a celebrity with her potent captivating theatrical magnetism not to mention the polished patent leather hair style that she sported or those flawlessly trim legs that went with her thin bright "Betty Boopish" intones when she sang *"I'm a little Blackbird lookin' for a Blackbird too!"* that attracted Harper to her. But for some reason, or for all of those reasons, ever since Harper became friends and got close with Florence Mills he was dying to work with her. In London, England when his *Plantation Days* company and her *Plantation Revue* played the two of them got along swimmingly. When both theatre companies returned back to New York, Harper was able to work out the staging with Mills during her Winter Garden stint in the 1923 version of *Greenwich Village Follies*. Florence Mills was considered the prime-most African-American female star ever during this time period of the mid-1920s. Audiences flocked to her like bees to honey and she lived up to everyone's promise and imagination. Mills was on her way to being the breakout African-American star and this time both black and white people who witnessed her stage talents concurred unanimously that she exhibited an irreplaceable acting quality while they fell in love with her huggable slight *Blackbird* persona.

While Harper was in the thick of producing his all-time ground breaking African-American Musical Comedy revues he still found time to work as an actor in a musical with Florence Mills. To perform on stage with Mills, Harper had to swallow his pride because she was presently under contract with his adversary producer Lew Leslie. The production was titled the *Brown Skin Quinan Revue* in its earliest shape and

Mrs. Mill's spouse U. S. Thompson was in the show with Will Vodery's orchestra, Edith Wilson and Johnny Nit with the remainder of a full cast. The 1925 production of *Brown Skin Quinan* was first displayed at the Plantation Club on Times Square and the very next year producer Lew Leslie converted the show's title into *Blackbirds of 1926* modeled after Florence's real life personality. The Lew Leslie *Blackbird Revue's* upheld a very long shelf life for Leslie as he made copious alterations of it on different renderings throughout the years. An early Vincent Minnelli was appointed to stitch the costumes and wardrobe for *Blackbirds* because of his fashion sensitivity.

During the musical comedy's transformation from *Brown Skin Quinan* into *Blackbirds of 1926* Harper was surreptitiously seeking to sway Ms. Mills away from Leslie to star in one of his own productions. Lew Leslie's *Blackbirds of 1926* had a Harlem premiere at the Alhambra Theatre on Seventh Ave. and 126th. St. While performing in *Blackbirds of 1926* Harper absorbed some of Lew Leslie's promotional ploys like compensating phony audience members to applaud deafeningly in front of passing theatre goers generating a fabricated pre-buzz for the show well ahead of its opening. Leslie worked it, enticing and setting up the public and the result was that large volumes of tickets were always purchased in advance.

While Harper was engrossed with his act in *Blackbirds of 1926* he also had his own uptown edition of *Tan Town Topics* playing with Fats Waller and Maude Mills who just happened to be Florence Mills' less talented sister. Harper's *Tan Town Topics* played just four blocks away from *Blackbirds of 1926* at the Lafayette Theatre and operated in direct opposition to Leslie's show at the Alhambra Theatre. Schiffman and Harper had dropped the cost of the entry fee for *Tan Town Topics* to further undercut the fierce competition coming from Leslie's *Blackbirds of 1926* production.

Being no stranger to propaganda Leslie systematically boosted the fact that the dearly beloved Florence Mills would be saying goodbye to Harlem and her home base fans to live in Europe conceivably for many years. Leslie's marketing "mantra" was "you better see her right now in her farewell show because she might not be back here again for years." The enraptured Harper was in Florence Mills paradise as he appeared with the little *Blackbird* in her showcase while directing a production with her sister Maude Mills, right down the street.

In *Blackbirds of 1926* Leslie highlighted Harper as a supporting star in his own plentiful Southern country tap dancing scene in plantation clothes with the Famous Plantation Beauty Chorus line of adorable women. All of Harper's Famous Plantation Beauty Chorus girls were clad in evocatively erogenous country duds and though they were all African-American most of them were so light skinned they seemed as if they could pass for white. Harper also acted in bit roles with the rest of the cast. One scene featured female pirates with Harper as a jail escapee. Leslie also staged a birthday cake bit with Harper as a waiter with a dancer popping out of the pastry prop ripping up the dance floor with fabulous footwork. These scenes were done underneath a big humiliating watermelon prop painted with massive seeds and in the background scenery a dark painted ship was stationed while a liquor bar set was positioned at the center of the stage. Trees edged the sides of the stage left and right.

In regards to *Blackbirds of 1926* one un-ascribed April 6, 1926 review titled *Sing a Song of Sixpence* by a D. N. wrote "The gods should send down a watchmaker from heaven to discover what makes Florence Mills tick. The rest of us might be gayer if we knew. A drool, dainty creature, like a human–sized mosquito that draws laughter instead of blood, her skin more alive than whiteness, she goes flitting about, billing our funny bones or she is a mad bewitching monkey, or a flippy–floopy, flirty blackbird." A *New York Sun* review stated "Florence Mills is prancing and singing in her well known fashion and bewailing that she is a poor little black bird, looking for a blue bird and without anybody to love her." The *New York Sun* review further articulated of the cast that "Their wit may—in most cases it certainly does—reside in their legs; it never takes up a heavily self-conscious place in their backdrops. They do not stand still to be looked at—they do not stand still for anything on earth. At their best they are, as no white person ever quite is, jazz crazy; they are tom-tom crazy. Through dark blood and dark laughter, syncopation squirms to their fingertips. Every now and then they make the sad mistake of going white; or the worse mistake of indulging in those odd vagaries, which the white mind has fixed as the traditional expression of the colored genius. At their worst they sing mammy songs. And at their best—oh baby, those shuffling feet!"

Blackbirds of 1926 had a six week run in Harlem's Alhambra theatre before it sailed off to Europe. Harper didn't travel along with the company but he did keep in touch with the dainty diva. Harper was optimistic that when her European run of *Blackbirds of 1926* finished next year Florence would let him star her in one of his custom designed nightclub floorshow productions.

Before Leonard Harper could stage Florence Mills in one of his revues the tantalizing fragile songbird of theatre passed away from untreated appendicitis and the entire theatrical community was in a state of sever heartache because Mills was judged to be one of the most distinguished of its stars to ever set foot on any stage. Fans were left with an unsatisfied hollow feeling inside because little Ms. *Blackbird* was supposed to have had a lengthy fruitful career and her early death robbed audiences and colleagues of the pleasure.

Florence was the "Little Blackbird," who sanctioned everyone no matter what their rank in life to aspire and dream beyond their most irrational thoughts as she caroled in her sweet flute-like voice. Flo Mills was the dainty celebrity with the huge image that spawned optimism into everyone's hearts. That the breakable little Blackbird broke and would no longer chirp into the souls of charmed audiences with her signature line *"I'm just a little blackbird"* shattered the theatrical population beyond any printed or verbal explanation.

The Florence Mills funeral was a majestic ceremony indeed as an excess of 150,000 onlookers lined up end to end on the avenues of Harlem to view the gigantic procession. A marching jazz band, flowers galore, numerous cables and telegrams from civil rights leaders and royal dignitaries from the Prince of Wales to master showman Florenz Ziegfeld. Almost everyone in the show world took part in the highly crafted Florence Mills home-going transitional homage. From a passing airplane, one hundred actual blackbirds were released to wing onto 137th. Street while the Florence Mills casket rested underneath an overspread of roses as her remains left the church upon the weeping shoulders of Leonard Harper, Will Vodery and other pallbearers.

Withdrawn from her husband, Osceola Harper discretely sent a floral arrangement, as the tempting flower girls and eye catching honorary pallbearers all chorus girls from Harper's innumerable nightclub floorshows inserted solemn glamour to the service in the flesh.

Following her passing the Florence Mills Memorial Fund raised $5,000 with Harper and his Connie's Inn Revue performing, two shows along with the other marquee acts at the Alhambra Theatre, the Lincoln Theatre and the Lafayette Theatre. The much-lamented husband of Florence Mills, U. S. Thompson was inculpated in the theft of the cash that was amassed for the charitable fund. All the funds that were supposed to be utilized in Mrs. Mills name to erect a home for actors, musicians and anyone connected with the theatre profession went missing. U. S. Thompson also kept for himself the contributed proceeds from the sale of the Florence Mills Dolls, a piece of the Florence Mills Health and Reducing Salon and the light brown Florence Mills skin creams that were meant to turn dark skinned women's complexion into her lighter hue. The scores of supporters and admirers who bigheartedly volunteered their time and offered their hard earned money lost all interest in the Florence Mills Memorial Fund because of Thompson's fiscal shenanigans and abandoned the charitable foundation with the passage of time.

LEONARD HARPER CHATTERED

In an article for the Pittsburg Courier dated Jan. 3 1927 by Floyd Calvin titled: *Man Who Built Reputation Because He Knew How To*

Pick Pretty, Shapely Chorus Girls, Takes Rap At Critics "Explains "Hip-Movement" Dance Which Has Aroused Storm of Protest—-Has Trained Many, Famous Choruses, Harper spoke about the negative protests that came with his work. Harper said "The only people who ever protested against my shows were my enemies. Connie's is one of the safest places in New York for chorus girls. Girls of the revue can't even go out and sit with relatives at the tables without permission, and I rarely grant such permission. This is more than can be said for many of the downtown white clubs. I have worked places where, even with white girls, it was part of the game to secretly countenance soliciting.

Of those who recently protested his show at the Lafayette Theatre Harper calls them "Soreheads" and states that "they have wasted a lifetime of opportunity and as soon as they see somebody else achieving a little success they are ready to try to tear down. The size of our audience proves how well the show is liked. Every time we play they hang out the S. R. O. sign." Mr. Harper is noted for the beauty of his choruses, "I pick girls according to general physical features, smooth skin, and pretty legs and nice hair," he added, "I don't want anybody to think my selections are based on color. I look for beauty I will take in brown girls as quickly as anybody else."

When asked about stage nudity Harper said "I think the stage is well regulated. Some of the same people who complain of what they see in colored shows will pay much bigger prices to see worse in white shows. As far as undressing girls is concerned, if a girl is dark and has a pretty shape why can't we look at her the same as at a white girl."

In his defense of the "Hip Movement" Harper clarified that "the movement is in the same class as the hula dance. I got tired of putting on the hula dance. White girls can't do the hip movement like the colored. I don't know why they can't. I have seen them try. That is one point on which we have them bested." *Variety* wrote on March 9, 1927 in a review of Harper's *4/11/44* that "The average white chorus girl would require a two-day lay-off if they had to hoof (double tempo) alongside those babies."

Harper and his wife Osceola were authored up for *The Baltimore Afro-American* Newspaper August 20, 1927 in a section titled *LEONARD HARPER* by Eva A. Jessye. Jessye marked "I first glimpsed this youthful and prolific producer at a benefit at the Lafayette Theatre. His eyes are his most interesting feature. They are restless, alert and constantly on the move, darting here and there, anticipating entrances, noting errors in the chorus, in general taking a silent but thorough estimate of the entire performance. At this particular show one number was in danger of being completely spoiled by the orchestra, which persisted in lagging two beats behind the dancer."

"Right there, Harper took a hand, or a foot, rather. Seeing the trouble he leaned over two rows of seats separating him from the pit and calling to the orchestra to speed it up, began pounding out rhythm on the floor. Then he (Harper) calmly settled back in his seat and was once more absorbed in the performance. That little incident was full of significance. It bespoke the soul of a creator. Also it showed the spirit of helpfulness, which is not always felt in the professional ranks."

In the *Home Reflects Taste* section Jessye penned "Although this interview began in the parlor, it ended in the most attractive room in the house—the kitchen, due to the unceremonious entry of Madam Harper who caught the unsuspecting Leonard by the ear and lead him to a belated dinner table. Further comment, I fear will be entirely smothered in the odor of fried chicken."

HARPER DID THE SAVOY BALLROOM

Leonard Harper appeared to have run into a professional malfunction when he was signed by Harlem's famed Savoy Ballroom's owner Jay Faggen and manager Charles Buchanan in 1928 to produce specific revue shows. The Savoy Ballroom was a colossal space with a 10,000 foot dance floor which spanned a whole block on Lenox Ave. The interior boasted lengthy walls which were abutted by sets of enormous mirrors.

Charles Buchanan's wife Bessie previously had danced in Harper's chorus lines for quite a few of his staged nightclub and theatrical productions. Savoy manager Buchanan always had a high regard for Harper's works so it was a somewhat quick off the cuff decision for Harper to be beseeched to produce untried revues at the ballroom. Harper brought a specially chosen chorus line calling the girls the "Savoyettes" and they proceeded to work out numbers with Little Harriet Calloway and Alex Jackson's Cincinnati Plantation Band. Collectively they created a sizzling hot new Savoy revue which played two shows nightly on Thursday and Saturday. Harper's conception was to have created the perfect match made in syncopation heaven because the Savoy Ballroom was known as the home of dance lovers. Harper self-assured pronouncement to the press, "Give people what they want, when they want it" would backfire and bite him in the butt big time.

The big jazz band trailblazers that complemented Harper's powerhouse floorshows and Colored Musical Comedies were talents like Chick Webb, Cab Calloway, Duke Ellington and Don Redmond and these same cats were always in hot demand at the Savoy. The live and rhythm grounded butt thrusting big band jazz music became the engine that propelled and stirred common everyday folk to hurdle up from out of their seats and partake by shaking and sweating their money makers on the Savoy ballroom floor. The patrons didn't come to observe a Harper revue show. The essence of the problem for Harper was that most Savoy Ballroom regulars came to dance themselves into a fever with the fun contemporary quasi-acrobatic new dance called the Lindy Hop.

Harper's 1928 Savoy *Revue of Vodvil* went on sufficiently enough generating, measured curiosity but Harper who was now tagged by the press as "the Ebony Impresario" had his sights on considerably more, broader and grander extravaganza prospects on Broadway and dropped the ballroom setting for the time being.

Four years after his first gig there in 1933 Harper reappeared to produce at the Savoy Ballroom again and the previously restrained reaction his *Revue Of Vodvil* received in 1928 was nothing compared to his second outing. Harper's 1933 *Savoy Vanities* production was affected by Harlem's post-depression era blues thus he was able to sign on at rock bottom rates many of the starving out of work singers, dancers and actors who earlier earned top dollar payments. These down and out and broke thespians were enthusiastically full of gratitude for the momentary economic assistance.

By Harper coming to New York to produce at the Savoy at this time was deemed to be a threat to all the other new dance halls who dreaded that they would lose their patronage. Harper's *Savoy Vanities* floorshow had twenty four ravishing chorines, plus Twelve Glorified Savoyettes and Twelve Captivating Harlemaids along with his standard assemblage of variety acts and an augmented twenty two piece snap crackling pop jazz orchestra.

As an added incentive Savoy manager Charles Buchanan decided not to escalate the price of admission for the floorshow and Harper's show played twice nightly to overflowing audiences. Weeknights the ticket price for *Savoy Vanities* was 40 cents with a wardrobe tax of 10 cents and on Saturdays and Sundays the charge at the door went up to a fee of 50 cents, with a wardrobe tax of 20 cents and a government tax of 5 cents. An excessively buoyant Buchanan also planned to sell legal beer as soon as the laws for prohibition were reformed and with Harper's floorshows deposited between the steady Lindy Hop dance interludes the sky seemed the limit for Buchanan.

The four year period between 1928 and 1933 saw a noteworthy historical variance in terms of the way Americans regarded theatrical and dance entertainment within both the black and white communities. This conversion was a foreshadowing of the calamitous episodes that were to appear before Harper occupationally speaking. Harper's life was tightly interrelated and it paralleled his theatrical works which were ever-fluctuating to current events and shifting everyday lifestyle conditions. As the Great Depression played a major financial part in the way patrons night-clubbed the African-Americans who peopled the inner city were embarking on new ways to convey self-pride with a bold aggressiveness in regards to their own cultural freedoms. Part of this self-dignity was realized within the Lindy Hop dance movement scene which embraced regular working folks and a network of acquaintances who engaged in physically social moving and grooving with each other on the dance floor. The Lindy Hop partners appeared as if they had the dance bug on their legs that needed to be scratched so when Harper brought in his Savoy Revue back into the ballroom the response generated little if any excitement this time around.

When the Harper staged *Savoy Vanities De-Luxe* revue was over the Savoy regulars couldn't wait to jump up and shake and bake it on the dance floor. Harper's Savoy presentations moreover invited in more whites and some of the steady black patrons who believed that the Savoy was their private bastion begrudged their downtown visitors because the management pressured them into giving up their good seats. The box office ticket sales at the Savoy did upsurge as Harper's revue went over adequately during the initial first week but receipts plunged dramatically as the week went by.

Harper's *Savoy Vanities,* his second 1933 revue excursion, brought the Savoy Ballroom a dismal catastrophe of a show instead of the Sensational Extravaganza that it was publicized to be. The writer of the *New York Amsterdam News* April 19, 1933 article titled *Harper Revue Not So Hot* suspected that Harper's African-American Musical Comedy Revue flopped in part because the Savoy Ballroom was unable and reluctant to invest in principal talent plus the shape and ingredients of the revue were never focused on recognizing its particular audience's metamorphism and revolutionized personality.

The April 26, 1933 Amsterdam News critique titled *Harper Revue Out at The Savoy-Local Dance Hall Returns to Policy of Presenting Leading Bands* explained how Harper hastily removed his botched *Savoy Vanities* from the Savoy Ballroom and into the Lafayette Theatre after it was utterly rejected at the dancehall. Manager Charles Buchanan replied that he was pleased with Harper's *Savoy Vanities* but described it as being "out of the ordinary" and asserted that he intended for the ballroom to go back to its original form of amusement that served the Negro trade who had always been so unwelcome in all of the other Harlem nightclubs that were owned by whites.

Lindy Hop Royalty and Queen of Swing, dancer Norma Miller said "I was born and raised in the Savoy Ballroom. Leonard Harper created the Jazz dancers. I knew him. They called him a Jazz dance director. He was all over Harlem".

HARPER DID NEW JERSEY

In 1927 Harper "tabbed" off his *Kentucky Club Revue* into Newark, New Jersey's Orpheum Theatre. Newark was just across the Hudson River from New York where lots of African-Americans dwelled and was populated with many of Harper's fans. These Newark citizens withstood a serious starvation for a few nibbles of his speedy choreographed shows, top notch jazz music, and down home comedy routines analogous to the ones that he produced in Harlem. Harper didn't let these rhythm famished New Jerseyites down, and they banqueted on the buffet of rapid footwork, scientifically rustic jazzy music, funny off color jokes and "foreign" variety acts. Harper's Newark *Kentucky Club* showcase consisted of the Three Brownies, Princess Helena, Henry Crackshot, Dorris Rhuebottom, "Jazzlips" Richardson and Ten Charming Girls. The revues were sold out every evening and surpassed all box office expectations at the Orpheum Theatre. Harper was informed that if he ever came back across the Hudson River that "He would need a larger quarter" as his *Kentucky Club Revue* was assessed as a stomping first-rate show.

Newark's overhauled Orpheum Theatre re-opened four years later on September 17, 1931 with a gargantuan Harper revue exhibition titled *Hot Harlem* starring La Mannos and the Parisian Ambassadors, Icicle and Snowflakes and Harper's delectably attired chorus line specially named the Orpheumettes after the theatre. The highlighted solo act was Cora La Redd the illustrious and brilliant talent from the Cotton Club who just happened to be a regularly saluted local product of Newark.

Harper dispensed a nightclub floorshow to New Jersey's Campus Nightclub in 1936. The Campus revue was a fast paced and furiously hot production featuring the fully-grown former Hal Roach, Our Gang comedy juvenile funnyman Mr. "Sunshine" Sammy headlining the cast with his very own adult jazz band. Sammy shared the bill with Slick Chester, the Hardy Brothers from Washington D.C. and the inimitable "Baby White".

CHAPTER FOUR
(1928 to 1929)

HARPER'S *HOT CHOCOLATES'*

In 1929 and in superlative form, Leonard Harper set out to produce his grandest, most theatrical show ever, bequeathing an imprint that still remains with us today. When contemporary audiences see the jovial chubby animated African-American piano playing character actor in a derby singing *Ain't Misbehavin* on the television commercials or in a feature film or while attending musicals like *Black n Blue* and *Ain't Misbehavin* they don't suspect that beneath the surface the creative force and spiritual genesis behind all of those themes and images is Harper. The production of which I write was titled *Connie's Hot Chocolates'* and conceivably in a more racially equitable time, the revue would have been correctly entitled as *Harper's Hot Chocolates'* after its dynamic master stager/producer and the African-American imaginative dynamism behind the piece instead of tolerating club owner and co-producer Connie Immerman's oppressive moniker above the *Hot Chocolates'* heading and Harper's almost nonexistent credit.

For years theatrical academics have written about *Hot Chocolates'* as if it weren't staged by anyone at all or that nightclub owner Connie Immerman had a hand in its creative direction. To set the record straight *Hot Chocolates'* was at that time the sum total of just about everything Harper had absorbed, conquered, performed and schooled theatrically. *Hot Chocolates'* was not only the lifeblood that ran through his organism that constituted his essence but a full view into the window of his entire being. *Hot Chocolates'* was Harper's artistic masterpiece and the African-American Musical Comedy theatrical milestone of which he and his race were delighted to be a part of.

All of Broadway wanted in on *Hot Chocolates'* this new African-American phenomenon to the point where theatrical diva great Dame Ethel Barrymore took on the Blackface role of Miss. Geechee Strumpet the dancing "Negress" in the production of *Scarlet Sister Mary* for the Shubert Brothers.

Hot Chocolates' germinated from the sum total of all of Harper's works from his pickaninny Medicine show performances to his Connie's Inn floorshow revues. He employed the tunefully poetic services of in-house freelance lyricist Andy Razaf. Razaf was the neatly dressed skinny lyricist who possessed a passionate backbone and a steadfast black activist streak that charted him till his passing. Razaf wrote for Harper at the Small's Paradise Club with Charlie Johnson churning out the music and later they collaborated for other nightlife venues. Razaf wrote songs of love, sadness and nightclub life and he additionally conveyed the African-American race's coming unto its own and on occasion his librettos cut like a sharp edged knife. Razaf often masked black rage in his lyrics and used dual meanings with shrouded verses to get his works published and accepted. Even though *Hot Chocolates'* was to be Razaf's first comprehensive big Broadway revue book of lyrics the double entendre rudiments of his writing style were in full force while being mounted as if it were traditional Broadway dribble.

The other built-in ingenious component that completed this staggeringly imaginative trio behind the *Hot Chocolates'* phenomenon was Thomas "Fats" Waller the extraordinarily talented piano player and songwriter. Waller was born and bred as a Harlemite who could play the keys off any piano while jesting and posing with his hilariously flamboyant facial expressions. Previously Harper had outfitted Waller in Arabian Ali Baba regalia and advertised him as the Egyptian Wonder and also had him decked out for appearances at the Kentucky Club and Connie's

Inn in an atrociously miniature Hawaiian outfit with a hefty grass hula skirt. Waller was continually game to amuse audiences as the talented joker with the nimble piano fingers because it amplified his audience amiability and furnished him with bigger gratuities. Beneath Waller's outer exterior as the buffoonish funny man was a somberly serious-minded musical composer who habitually covered up his deep-rooted emotional agonies and suppressed everything with an over-abundance of food and liquor consumption.

Although Waller gave off the impression that he was the happy-go-lucky bad boy underneath the façade was a man who had been uninterruptedly badgered and dragged down by spousal alimony and legal monetary complications. It had been reported that Waller's ex-wife Edith darted thru the aisles at the Lafayette Theatre one evening during one of Harper's shows wearing nothing but a skimpy nightgown. Edith Waller charged the stage while dangling a huge kitchen knife insisting that her panicky ex-husband pay all the back alimony he owed her. As Waller sprinted off backstage Harper tried to make this awkward yet real life turn of events look like an unrehearsed comedy bit that he inserted into the musical on a whim as a humorous spot gag for laughs.

Waller worked for the Immerman brothers in their Harlem deli as a delivery boy supplying sandwiches and prohibited booze to Harlem residents before the siblings obtained enough capital to open up Connie's Inn. Waller got his reputation and initial acknowledgment as a jazz great while performing on the organ at the Lincoln Theatre for Harper's early revue shows playing his own jazzed up style of background supplemental music with the silent photoplays. Waller similarly played for Harper at the Kentucky Club/Hollywood Inn and performed *Senorita Mine* at the Lafayette Theatre to amazed audiences. Together both Harper and Waller previously collaborated with Andy Razaf on a few Connie's Inn nightclub productions. Waller ripened music-wise as the protégé under the celebrated stride pianist James P. Johnson who had been Harper's first musical director when both men traveled in the states and to England back in 1923 with *Plantation Days*.

Waller and Razaf wholesaled their hit tunes on Tin Pan Alley for appallingly small amounts of cash. They were compensated for sums as low as one to five bucks for each song while also being obliged to either give away some or all of their residuals and authorship credits often sharing their credits and profits with white music publishers. The alternatives for Razaf and Waller was to either go along with the iniquitous transactions or go hungry and forsake the music industry altogether. Even Duke Ellington initialed away forty five percent of his proceeds and publishing rights to his manager/booking agent Irving Mills. Irving Mills took the exploitation of Ellington even further by attaching his name to many of Ellington's early copyrights and pocketing an equivalent amount of royalty compensation, while in receipt of contractual credit for music that he didn't craft.

The music and lyrics were often ascribed to the stars standing before the audiences on the stage and or the publishers while impeding the actual African-American songwriters from receiving their applicable credits. The true authors would happily spend their five bucks fee while the white stars and their less celebrated counterparts would effortlessly pull in a $500 to $10,000 profit from their initial investments after making a few minor adjustments and modifications to the compositions.

Collectively the remarkably gifted African-American triad of Harper, Razaf and Waller would for the first time in theatre history prime to craft an artistically and commercially fruitful Colored Musical Comedy piece of work for Broadway known as *Hot Chocolates'*.

THE CONCEPT, THE CHALLENGE AND THE CHANCE

Razaf and Waller coined the music on the Broadway production of *Keep Shufflin* in 1928. James Price Johnson went halves splitting the musical credits with his younger apprentice Waller. Both these piano dynamos jammed for ecstatic *Keep Shufflin* audiences during intermission and it was the equivalent of a breathtaking piano tournament every night with Waller tickling his piano keys while almost tumbling partway off his piano stool. J. P. Johnson was branded to like the taste of liquor as well and if you walked off to go to the toilet thru the intermission pause you forewent your chance to see which playfully drunk piano mastermind could out dazzle the other. Their easygoing inebriation only boosted the impulsive stimulus in their piano rhythm inflections while upraising Johnson and Waller's musical mystique serving as the preamble forecast for Waller's keyboard installations on *Hot Chocolates'*.

For the duration of *Keep Shufflin* Waller made every attempt to dodge his volatile fuming ex-wife and her alimony process servers. Clarence Robinson, Harper's former subordinate and current in-house Cotton Club director was the first to stage *Keep Shufflin* but the minute Harper came in to enhance and perk up the musical the credits were reassigned to him for the staging of the dances and ensembles as Robinson's name was eliminated. Harper joined the *Keep Shufflin* staff to increase the oomph and organize the dancers into moving and grooving with such a mad ferocity that their costumes inadvertently flew off oftentimes dropping onto the laps of lucky audience members. Many a fortunate *Keep Shufflin* enthusiast wound up seizing the free chorus line shoes, belts and headgear costumes to carry home as souvenirs.

Keep Shufflin was executive produced by infamous racketeer Arnold Rothstein as a way to launder his illicit income and gain status in the theatre trade. Rothstein was publicly identified for fixing the Baseball World Series of 1919 as well as his criminal importations of liquor during prohibition. Jack "Legs" Diamond was also brought in as an additional financial sponsor for *Keep Shufflin* when Rothstein became overdue on the payments of the cast and crew salaries coupled with his other copiously unresolved capital conflicts. Rothstein had to eventually shut down *Keep Shufflin* due to his lack of monetary resources.

A frantic Arnold Rothstein struggled to master-mine an illegal drug deal to alleviate his money difficulties and perhaps remount *Keep Shufflin*. During the passage of his drug money arrangement Rothstein organized the headline murder of a Dutch Schultz associate named Joey

Noe. Rothstein was in turn executed at the Park Central Hotel by a cluster of mobsters that included Charles "Lucky" Luciano, Meyer Lansky, Frank Costello and Dutch Schultz. These hoodlums killed Rothstein because the Joey Noe murder was too public. These were the potentially dangerous and seedy state of affairs under which Harper and his fellow talented theatrical pals and associates had to labor under.

The Immerman brothers had always been fans of the collective talents of Harper, Waller and Razaf and what they had crafted with their feverous hot jack jumping works in Connie's Inn and now imparted comparable sentiments for the musical *Keep Shufflin* on Broadway. These former delicatessen proprietors, green-lit the pre-production operations for *Hot Chocolates'* with their personal funds even though existing Colored Musical Comedies on Broadway were considered to be an enormous financial risk with most producers deeming that they were almost always guaranteed failures. Leonard Harper was swift to crack his whip as he retooled his small scaled *Hot Feet* floorshow revue from Connie's Inn for the larger Broadway stage. The title of Harper's *Hot Feet* was replaced momentarily to *Tan Town Topics* then to *Connie's Hot Chocolates'* and was on its way to adapting into one of the greatest nightclub floorshow revues to ever be staged on Broadway.

Let there be no mistake about it Harper's *Hot Feet* was his singular conception conjured up many years before the artistic incubation of *Hot Chocolates'*. The early *Hot Feet* at its most primitive and unsophisticated shape was included in the African American half of *Jimmy Cooper's* formerly all-white *Revue* as a way of multiplying Jimmy Copper's sagging box office sales. But this slick updated recent *Hot Feet* nightclub rendering was a totally different kind of animal, wielding a, ferocity in its artistic distinctions that could conceivably bite you in the ass as you sat in your theatre seat.

Hot Feet now had somewhat of a script and narrative line that interconnected its little fragments, acts and scenes together. *Hot Feet* was also accompanied by gangster Dutch Schultz's illegal cash patronage which afforded the healthy production budget that the company needed to function. An anonymous 1928 clipping titled *Connie's New Music, Lyrics,* read as follows "Connie's Inn's new floor show opened Thursday the 28, in its usual splendor. Other than the beautiful girls and costumes, the outstanding feature is the music by Thomas "Fats" Waller and Harry Brooks, lyrics by Andy Razaf. This production conceived and staged by Leonard Harper, is one of the best pieces of work that Harper has done in years."

New York Show Talk correspondent Maurice Dancer wrote in *Broadway Gets Darker* "Connie's Inn Revue will try to follow in the footsteps of "Blackbirds," which was a floor show at the Ambassadors Club, Leonard Harper the producer, has called the rehearsals too elaborate on his present floorshow to make it a Broadway attraction." Another clipping dated March 16, 1929 from *The Pittsburgh Courier* titled "Hot Feet" stated that "The new revue at Connie's Inn, New York City, which opened last week to a packed house, is the most sensational floor show in the big city. Staged by Leonard Harper, music by Thomas (Fats) Waller and Harry Brooks and lyrics by Andy Razaf, this is the first floor show of New York's exclusive night clubs to be entirely the work of men of color. The Immerman brothers, owners, deserve great credit for having faith and vision enough to have given colored writers a chance to prove themselves capable of equaling and even excelling the work of their white contemporaries."

In the book *Beyond Category* by John Edward Hasse the author inscribed that "Ellington's fourth Cotton Club revue opened on Sunday, March 31, 1929. *Spring Birds,* with a cast of thirty and the Ellington orchestra, again offered songs specially written by Fields and McHugh and with direction by Dan Healy. *Variety* found the show "disappointing," especially in comparison to the nearby club Connie's Inn, but praised, Ellington's orchestra and its "wicked trumpet player" who "heightened the effect to riotous returns." The reviewer speculated that part of the problem with the show itself was that whites created it, while over at the competition, "native Afro-Americans (Leonard Harper, et al.), were primarily concerned in the Connie's floor show."

To get *Hot Chocolates'* prepared for Broadway Harper brought all of the components of his nightclub floorshows together then forged them into its riveting cohesive structure. Since *Hot Chocolates* was to be the grandest Colored Musical Comedy of all time and a large part of the production dough emanated from gangster Dutch Schultz he became the ipso facto executive producer who methodically made lethal warnings against Harper and crew that the musical comedy had better make a profit, or else. During pre-production Harry Brooks was urgently engaged to facilitate the arrangement of selected pieces of music because Waller was doing time in jail for his alimony violations. Waller began to pen songs while in jail but because huge sums of money were on the line Harper and Razaf needed to commence right away. Harry Brooks was utilized until Waller was out freed on bail. Waller alleged that he authored *Ain't Misbehavin* during his incarceration period and that the idea incubated from his reply whenever he was caught doing something wrong or when someone who knew of his troubles inquired about how he was getting along. Razaf disputed Waller's schmaltzy and storybook claims of how *Ain't Misbehavin* was written while in lockup and maintained that the formation of the hit song took place in his attendance while inside Waller's Harlem apartment.

According to the book *Fats Waller* by Maurice Waller and Anthony Calabrese "Early in the rehearsals Harper realized that Ain't Misbehavin was destined to be a big hit, so encored and reprised the piece as often as possible. Harper also determined that a song should be written for the talented Edith Wilson about the woes of being black. The result was, in my opinion, the best Waller—Razaf song ever written. The last line of each verse, a simple repetition of the song's title, is particularly haunting: "What did I do to be so black and blue?"

Harper had a little amusement at Waller's expense during the song writing process by bringing into the studio a nineteen year old Mary Lou Williams who could pass for a ten year old kid. Harper bet Waller that whatever he played or composed on the spot could be replicated on the piano and within seconds by this little girl, honey boogies and all.

Waller a nippy improviser whose spontaneity increased with every shot of gin and puff of his cigar wagered with Harper that there is no way that the little youngster could duplicate his stuff. While Waller bragged to on looking cast and crew members Harper told his chorus line to take a break from going through their paces while the pint-sized Mary Lou Williams commenced to not only replicate the Waller jams on the spot and to the letter, but she also inserted her own particular brand of sugar on the piano keys, ragging and rolling with her unbelievably though undersized finger ticklers. Waller, while paying on his bet to Harper, was compelled to obligingly bow before the new Harper discovery and then raised Mary Lou Williams almost pitching her up into the ceiling. Harper later employed nineteen year old Mary Lou Williams to play piano during his Connie's Inn Revue intermissions and highlighted her act in some of his Brooklyn and Newark productions at a salary of sixty dollars a week.

In *Hear me takin to ya; the story of jazz by the men who made it,* edited by Nat Shapiro and Nat Hentoff jazz musician Mezz Mezzrow remembered the *Hot Chocolates'* rehearsals "Can you imagine hearing Louis Armstrong playing trumpet with Fats Waller at the piano, getting the flavor of the numbers together: The late Leonard Harper (one of the greatest Negro producers that ever lived) calling his chorus to the floor, and giving the routine. Comedians repeating their parts on the side. All the gaiety laughter and enthusiasm."

During the rare instances when the songs for *Hot Chocolates'* were devised without Harper's attendance or supervision the end results were later supplied to him so that he could work out the routines in the flesh on the rehearsal stages with the cast members. Russell Wooding, the musical arranger, was also an integral part of *Hot Chocolates'* victory. Wooding hailed from a background as a United States Marine Band member. After being in New York for just five years Wooding had orchestrated the music for Harper's Connie's Inn floorshow's and Ford Dabney's *Rang Tang Revue* while also musically fortifying Duke Ellington and his Cotton Club Orchestra then went on to orchestrate

Eubie Blake for the duration Lew Leslie's revue production of *St. Louis Blues*. Russell Wooding brought to Harper not only his awe-inspiring musical sensitivity but his divinely jubilant vocal group christened as the Russell Wooding Jubilee Singers.

Dutch Schultz being the unspoken executive producer of *Hot Chocolates'* made his earsplitting presence known at the pre-production preparations while he attempted to pressure Harper and the "boys" to transform the revue into just another one of those run of the mill self-humiliating colored minstrel shows.

Schultz failed to coax the three African-American creators of *Hot Chocolates'* into shifting the musical and specifically their *Black n Blue* number into an amusing black self-loathing song. Andy Razaf defied Dutch Schultz using every bit of the talent and skill that he controlled as a lyricist by rotating the lyrics of *Black n Blue* on its inside out and right side in. Razaf's lines instead brilliantly cultivated and painted a human face on the suffering of African-Americans on the Broadway stage for the first time ever by misleading Schultz and the white audience population into assuming that *Black n Blue* was merely a tune about a self-effacing, grief-stricken, fatality-doomed black girl. Razaf then shock attacked white theatre clients during the climax by having the same unaffected *Black n Blue* routine sung and acted out by Edith Wilson declaring three little words *"I'm white inside."*

Harper enhanced the racial detonation with his staging of the extremely dark skinned actress Edith Wilson who belted out and played her part up to the hilt in the *Black n Blue* segment. Wilson formerly worked with Harper and Blanks in the Town Hall production of *Put and Take* some eight years prior and she was cast with Harper and Florence Mills in Lew Leslie's *Blackbirds of 1926*. Harper formulated the stage idea for *Black n Blue* by heeding back into his past when he danced in Medicine shows that featured a cute jet black lassie in "white face" donning a blond wig and a white dress and bleached undergarments to extract a contrasting distinction to her skin tone.

Wilson warbled and hollered out loud with a behavior designed for maximum stage effect on a massive white bedroom set, with white sheets and white curtains wearing a wardrobe that consisted of a flowing white satin, white on white and seal black skin in a white night gown all in front of dumbfounded audiences viewing the *Black n Blue* number. White on black and black on white as the number increased its dramatic consequence every second as, the gripping tension rouse to its monumental and spectacular upturned wrap-up. Harper's direction aided in the manipulation of the song's final flip flop and racially charged double entendre statement. The disfavored little black woman played by Edith Wilson, had become much more than a racial laughingstock, she was now the mirror image of her tormentor's pathological revulsion. As the disheartened singing black lady was "blue" she carried with her a towering imaginary looking glass that silenced the hilarity as everybody that chuckled at her anguish was now required to take a deeper observation into their own souls and share in her agony because like them she's *"white inside"*.

A livid Dutch Schultz was robbed of his giggles by the skillfulness of the colored men working for him. In Barry Singer's book *Black And Blue-The Life And Lyrics Of Andy Razaf*, Razaf explained from his memories of how Schultz tried to set him up for an possible slaughter at Madame Polly Adler's brothel. The Dutchman hoped Razaf would plunge into a sexual encounter with one of his most favorite and mouthwatering hookers which would then give him license to murder the lyricist. Razaf hip to the Dutchman's game left the brothel un-aroused and still alive.

After its preliminary ten-week pre-Broadway run Harper relocated his *Hot Feet* revue from out of Connie's Inn nightclub into the Windsor Theatre in the Bronx. The label of the show was changed to *Connie's Hot Chocolates'* and he signed up a cast of eighty five while merging in more upmarket production numbers and show pieces during the practice sessions. *Hot Chocolates'* was to be the definitive embellishment of a top notch Harlem floorshow ever mounted for the Broadway stage. After assiduously working out routines in the Bronx the cast hurriedly traveled back down to Harlem for the midnight and breakfast shows at Connie's Inn.

Before *Hot Chocolates'* was ready to be a legit musical theatre attraction for Broadway, Harper rendered numerous cast and bit changes. In the course of the rehearsals in the Bronx as the cast enacted the *Goddess of Rain* number an actual wet rainstorm caused the theatre's roof to cave in. The downpour drenched all the members of the *Hot Chocolates'* company. Harper theorized that these events were a good luck charm and informed the cast that the rain was a sign of good fortune and that the rainfall during the *Goddess of Rain* number had convinced him of *Hot Chocolates'* upcoming Broadway success.

THREE TALENTED TAN-SKINNED CREATORS

As Harper worked out the hard edges of *Hot Chocolates'* at the Windsor Theatre in the Bronx before moving to Broadway's Hudson Theatre the show underwent many changes and transformations. "Snakehips" Tucker an original player in Harper's uptown Connie's Inn *Hot Feet* version of the revue had to leave the show and travel to Europe with Lew Leslie's *Blackbirds* because of a contractual obligation. Harper replaced "Snakehips" with black-faced, bugged eyed "Jazzlips" Richardson, who in his clownish tiny cowboy hat and oil-coat, shook his unbridled rubber legs and jazzy rubber lips like there was no tomorrow and in triple time, no less. Louis "Satchmo" Armstrong who had not yet been introduced to Broadway audiences had just become available because of his problems working on the road under a white conductor who didn't understand or particularly care for jazz. The conductor under which Armstrong worked preferred his music with lifeless repetition, surrounded with unlimbered, starched and non-organic rhythms and he tried to persuade Armstrong to play as he was instructed to, without any spontaneity. Armstrong up and left the gig and his quick exit left him free to sign on to play with Leroy Smith's jazz band in *Hot Chocolates'*, while Harper hired Armstrong's personal band to play for his shows uptown at his other Connie's Inn Revue.

After the late May run-throughs in the Bronx were over, the *Hot Chocolates'* theatrical company moved to the Times Square Manhattan location of the Hudson Theatre smack dab in the heart of Broadway for master rehearsals and its scheduled June grand opening premiere.

Dressed to the nines and smiling proudly, Harper, Waller and Razaf greeted the guests who entered the Hudson Theatre on the opening night of *Hot Chocolates'*. Several of the V.I.P.'s hardly recognized these colored men who were the creative force behind the new musical. Once the curtain went up their names were on the tongues of all rhythm devotees. It was a total blast for 30 year old Harper. As a former pickaninny who danced for pennies, Harper spearheaded the artistic fruition of Colored Musical Comedy Theatre and the nightclub floorshow genre uptown in Harlem, downtown on Times Square, and around the country. Having molded theses productions from his individual artistic assets, Harper and his collaborators, on this opening, night sealed the deal and went legit on "The Great White Way". The weighty and occasionally hilarious 25-year old Thomas "Fats" Waller sandwiched Harper while concealing his piano virtuosity and song writing brilliance. 33-year old lyricist Andy Razaf squeezed in on Harper's other side and completed the welcoming party of this powerfully innovative trio. They looked forward to the new income and were proud of their work on *Hot Chocolates'* but collectively had no idea that their show would make a permanent mark on show business for decades long after they would expire.

Hot Chocolates' possessed all of Harper's signature theatrical fundamentals, burning peppered rapid fire dancing a smoking gospel fashioned chorus, feverish ensemble dance pieces, outlandish adagio movements, uproarious comedy sketches, "transcontinental" Oriental numbers and good looking crooning romantic couples. With getups constructed of satin, formal top hats and tails for the men and countryside gowns for the women all of the *Hot Chocolates'* players sophisticatedly looked the part. The nearly nude magnificent chorus girls in figure hugging, thin mesh mini-skirts with bird feathers around their butts emitted their sexual delectability in unpardonably innovative dance arrangements.

The adagio dancers displayed native American Indian garments and headgear as some of the highlighted players sported southern homestead costumes, bikinis and Spanish matador guises. Afro-wigs and "savage" wild fur bikinis were donned in the *Jungle Jamboree* routine and the eight debonair Bon-Bon Buddies bore elongated faux beards as they beamed and danced hard while a few limited specialty acts performed in blackface.

Some of the tailor made *Hot Chocolates'* set designs were the African jungle motif, a southern steamboat plank scene and a Harlem interior nightclub backdrop that appeared to look just like the inside of Connie's Inn and treated Broadway theatre patrons with a simulated trip up to Harlem. The special treat of *Hot Chocolates'* was the musical insertion of, "The Entre' Acte" with Louis Armstrong playing his trumpet with the house band throughout the intermission, yowling harmoniously *Ain't Misbehavin* from the orchestra pit. Armstrong's distinctive Entre' Act jams offered a marvelously soulful fluidity to a show already busting at the seams with notable entertainment well beyond any reasonable limitations.

Armstrong had a few things in common with Harper, both men were consummate artists in their own right and both of them still retained a hint of "pickaninny" inside their souls. The little southern pickaninny child cropped up and came to life every time Armstrong performed on stage at the Hudson Theatre. Armstrong was the musician who jested, sniggered and shed tears with audiences then threw himself back into his old days as the young musical "pic" whose trumpet did the talking, instantly endearing him to the Broadway public. Armstrong would later come to attribute his domestic stardom to his being cast by Harper in *Hot Chocolates'* and with being afforded the opportunity to sing *Ain't Misbehavin* for a different caliber audience.

Not one to let Armstrong have all the merriment Fats Waller opted to become a member of the cast of *Hot Chocolates'* flabbergasting anyone with working ears during his cameo interlude piano jams by playing the hell out of the musical arrangements. Waller was billed as the soloist for the Entre' Acte with the title of "The Rachmaninoff of Jazz". Although Waller previously declared that he was not an actor Waller did perform in some additional numbers with his co-stars Louis Armstrong and Edith Wilson. The trio were billed as "The Thousand Pounds of Harmony" and tore up their adaptation of *My Man Is Good For Nothing But Love.*

Bill Bojangles Robinson followed Harper's stock cue of jumping from his seat at Connie's Inn and on the opening of *Hot Chocolates'* he sprang from his audience seat and proceeded to implement some of the most mind-blowing tap work ever performed on stage. Ethel Waters, whom Harper considered but was unable to put under contract to appear in *Hot Chocolates'*, convinced him to settle for her consolation prize. Ethel Waters ambushed everyone inside the Hudson Theatre with her unexpected "spur-of-the-moment" unaccompanied recital from her theatre seat. The orchestra fired up the pit and Waters thunder bolted theatre patrons by giving them a chance to indulge in her renown as she processioned up and down the aisles and mesmerized one and all into submissive stupors just like she achieved at Connie's Inn everytime she was a Harper visitant.

During *Hot Chocolates'* opening night in the heart of Times Square, the Hudson Theatre was filled with stars on-top of stars. All of the Broadway glitterati, opera aficionados, affluent socialites and certified vaudevillians, even the thirty Singer Midgets came out to attend the opening. They crammed the Hudson Theatre for one reason alone and that was to see if Harper and company could knock their socks off and kick their hindquarters into a fever with a jamming terrific Broadway version of his Connie's Inn uptown revues. The answer was yes, and not only did he and everyone else onboard deliver the goods, but they wound up surpassing even themselves as *Hot Chocolates'* blasted pungently refreshing inhalations of soulful air throughout the Broadway playhouse and theatre district.

Harper carried out continual adjustments to enhance *Hot Chocolates'* because the tough blood sweating cast doubled the work load by performing at Connie's Inn in Harlem every night, right after the Broadway curtains went down. The exhausting schedule was very demanding on the actors and musicians so Harper brought forth fresh amendments to the show's order, gist and casting to acclimatize the talent and make the operation a little less stressful for everyone engaged. In the 1929 *Inter-State Tattler-Backstage with Stage-Struck* stated in an expose titled *Hotter Chocolates* that in regards to *Hot Chocolates'* "Quite a number of changes with here and there the pruning knife applied has very much altered the original construction of the vehicle."

In November Harper secured the practically unheard of zoot-suit wearing newcomer from Chicago named Cabell "Cab" Calloway to replace Paul Bass. The casting of "Cab" Calloway was based on a recommendation from his sister Blanche Calloway who previously performed in Harper's revues. Both "Cab" and his sister Blanche Calloway toured in a 1925 road show edition of *Plantation Days* which had no Harper participation. Harper featured "Cab" in the *Hot Chocolates'* song number of *Ain't Misbehavin.* He also signed up the ballroom dancing twosome of "Fredi and Moiret" who had just come back to the United States from a European tour. Fredi was the sassy sister of Isabel Washington who at the time was a chorus girl in Harper's Connie's Inn dance line. The adorable and near Caucasian looking dollop of soul Fredi Washington afterwards developed into a bona fide African-American movie star featured in Universal Pictures *Imitation of Life* and other lesser known flicks.

Hot Chocolates' brought in upwards of $12,000 per week on a fixed basis and was one of the few Broadway productions to gross such high averages. No matter how the reviews were spun and twisted all over the place *Hot Chocolates'*, the all-race revue, out shuffled *Shuffle Along* according to the audience members and it was an all-time Broadway blockbuster.

The bonus delicacy to the phenomenon of *Hot Chocolates* was that all of the players in the Broadway production dashed up to Connie's Inn in Harlem after their evening performances were over to further fulfill audiences who couldn't get enough rhythm. At Harlem's Connie's Inn the entire troupe performed in the late night and breakfast productions of Harper's *Hot Feet* with "Two Gala Revues Nightly, featuring PRINCESS VIKANA, Thirty Beautiful Brown-Skins, with Louis Armstrong" during the spring. In the fall of that same year during *Hot Chocolates'* Broadway's run Harper's Connie's Inn production of *Load of Coal* overjoyed privileged audiences with even more swinging grooves and beats. The ambiance at Connie's Inn was altogether different than in the theatre as the customarily white customers gobbled Chinese food, glugged booze and intermingled with a more unsafe, audacious and illicit intimacy.

Load of Coal had Leonard Harper's distinguished and winged striking chorus line and variety acts with some soft shoe, black bottom, love ballads, fortune telling and comedy interlaced into the combination with loads of great musical compositions inlayed with rhythm all over it. *Load of Coal*, as did *Hot Feet* introduced Armstrong to uptown audiences at the Harlem hotspot and he tore the joint apart at every performance. Armstrong's up close medicinal trumpet resonances in Connie's warm venue along with his lively facial expressions was just what the rhythm physician prescribed.

Hot Feet and *Load of Coal* benefited from the use of new material by Waller and Razaf which was written at Razaf's mother's house in New Jersey so as to keep Waller from abandoning his job and ambling back over the Hudson River and into Harlem hangouts. Waller fled from New Jersey back to Harlem anyway and as distracted as he might have been he authored and arranged portions of *Honeysuckle Rose* over the phone in a call from an anxious Razaf who demanded to listen to what Waller had come up with at the bar. Other winning show songs from this dynamic writing duo were *Zonky* and *My Fate Is In Your Hands*. Later Razaf expressed to his wife Mrs. Alicia Razaf-Georgiade "That out of all of the many director/producers that I ever worked with Leonard Harper was the only one who could really best accurately represent the lyrics and fully depict what I had in mind as a lyricist on stage."

Two of these three imaginatively gifted men ill-advisedly were unable to retain most or all of their royalties. Harper and Waller hastily exchanged their rights for upfront cash disbursements, which was all too common a practice for African-American production personnel designated "above the line". Waller was in need of quick cash and sold off his share of what would be worldwide hit tunes that he scripted for *Hot Chocolates'* to Irvin Mills and his Mills music company for a one time flat payment fee of just $500.

The after residual incidents behind production of *Load of Coal, Hot Feet* and Harper's *Hot Chocolates' Revue* kicked up an awfully revolting array of occurrences eleven years after the shows were launched. Waller and Razaf wrote three original songs for Harper's production of *Load of Coal* at Connie's Inn and they were *Honeysuckle Rose, My Fate Is in Your Hands* and *Zonky*. These compositions received satisfactory notice but *Honeysuckle Rose,* which was partially written over the telephone at Connie's Inn, was the only big break out hit song from *Load of Coal.* The unpleasant note behind the tale of the *Load of Coal* and *Honeysuckle Rose* ascended in 1940 when the Twentieth Century Fox Film Company assembled a movie titled *Tin Pan Alley. Tin Pan Alley* displayed filmic depictions of several hit show tunes and by what method they were written. *Honeysuckle Rose* was inaccurately and intentionally portrayed in the film as being written within a jailhouse with white actors playing the authors of the song as prison inmates. Lyricist Andy Razaf's found the film's premise wounding as he crossly posed the question as to why the Fox Film studio had to have white men authoring his and Waller's song in the film and in lockup, no less.

Given all of the racial unfairness in the motion picture industry it would have been a perfect opportunity for Twentieth Century Fox to represent how *Honeysuckle Rose* was truly devised by the dignified and able Afro-American men who actually wrote it. The Hollywood film studio blew its chance to take the high road and chose the unenlightened backward bigoted course instead. Waller nonchalantly chalked up these episodes as just the way things are.

The *Honeysuckle Rose* fiasco ensued in 1940 and by this time Razaf had witnessed many of his fellow sepia talented artists go unnoticed and shoved aside to take back seats as less capable and amateurish whites moved to the head of the line, just because they had the "right" skin color. Razaf knew that the motion picture industry was the West coast playground for affluent white executives whose only use for African-Americans on screen were in minor roles such as devoted mammies, wide grinned and eyeball rolling African savages, unhappy criminals, superstitious religious fanatics, musical entertainers, spare-rib and watermelon eating clowns, or the accepted mentally inferior oaf.

Andy Razaf never worried about being "blackballed" when he spoke his mind over the *Honeysuckle Rose* incident. He had no other recourse but to be opened mouthed since he was unable to sue Twentieth Century Fox for the racial affront due to a contractual accord he signed with the film company for *Honeysuckle Rose's* general usage. All Razaf could do was air his feelings out and baulk to Twentieth Century Fox in an occupational letter. The Fox film administrators giggled at Razaf's written communication and ridiculed him for standing up for his race by publishing his private letter with a very public retort in *Variety*. The Twentieth Century Fox film company's attorney impertinently hurled doubt on the legal rights of a black man north of the Mason Dixon line while hoping to boost his company's film box office sales.

During mid-1929 *Hot Chocolates'* was in full bloom and still continued on with its splendid and outstanding run. Harper faced and attended to a few very restricted back-stage personal matters. For ten years Harper had been covertly financially supporting his first professional childhood fellow "pickaninny" cohort Dave Shaffer while attempting to get him out of prison. Shaffer was carrying a life sentence after getting into some serious trouble in Florida. Harper always felt a little uncomfortable that so much attainment had come to him and that Dave had lived such a problem filled and unlucky existence in and out of jail.

At the time that *Hot Chocolates'* opened up on Broadway Dave Shaffer was released from prison due to Harper's diligent efforts and financial assistance. Shaffer headed straight for New York to thank Harper and in his mind he planned on a theatrical comeback for both of them maybe a *Two Older Clever Pic's Reunion*? But any stage reunion was just not meant to be, as prison life had hardened Harper's old buddy David and the show business faculty that he once bore as an upbeat young child was lost and gone forever. The jailhouse beatings had taken their toll on Shaffer who now hobbled with a game arthritic leg. Shaffer's dancing days were just a heartbreaking memory of the past. Shaffer hung out backstage at Connie's Inn and made himself just a drunken rambunctious nuisance by grabbing on the chorus girls and crying on the floor. As Harper blinked and swiveled, David Shaffer, who shouldered the look of unending disappointment within his eyes, wandered off down the nocturnal avenues of Harlem never to dance, stagger toward, or give a final farewell hug, to his old childhood pickaninny partner again.

The tails and top hat sporting Baby Cox was one of Harper's *Hot Chocolates'* freshest and most sensual artists who was portrayed as dancing "for all the world like a monkey on a stick, doing just the dance grandfather used to sneak off and see at the country fair." In 1928 Miss. Cox scatted, the song *The Moochie* for Ellington and later scatted for Duke on *I Can't Give You Anything But Love* but during her production stint in *Hot Chocolates'* Baby Cox was sued by her white manager Jimmy Cooper. This was the same Jimmy Cooper who exploited Harper's creative designs when he capitalized off of Harper's staging within his *Jimmy Cooper's, Black and White Revue* without sharing or giving credit to Harper for his directorial work.

Cooper desperately wanted in on the *Hot Chocolates'* action in any way shape or form so he sued featured performer Baby Cox for $4,000 pronouncing that he alone paved the way for her in securing the successful role in the musical comedy hit and that he was responsible for coaching Cox. Cooper extended his litigation stating that he sponsored Cox when she was a, nobody and that without his managerial expertise Baby wouldn't have become the recognized star that she was today. Cooper crowed that Baby Cox was still under his indenture for the next three years. Cooper also argued in court testimony that Cox attempted to break her contract with him to join Harper's revue at Connie's Inn nightclub and in *Hot Chocolates'* on, Broadway. Cooper amended his lawsuit to include both George and Connie Immerman as defendants for an additional $20,000. Cooper similarly kvetched that he had a revue of his own that he had prepared for Miss. Cox to be showcased in.

Cox, who just recovered from a nervous breakdown due to her work overload, still had the gumption to counter sue Jimmy Cooper, stating that he paid her only seventy five dollars and that she currently earned $115 in Harper's show. Because of Cox's believable statements and the sympathy from an understanding and a conceivably smitten judge the court quickly threw out and dismissed Cooper's lawsuit as frivolous. Jimmy Cooper was very fortunate that he lost the case because if he had won the legal proceedings Dutch Schultz the executive producer of *Hot Chocolates'* was waiting in the wings to take matters up in his own hands gangster style. Schultz would have made certain that Cooper's final resting place would be under the waters of a Hudson River pier for meddling with his box office returns.

Harper continued to be bogged down with a few more problematic concerns as a number of the more oddball *Hot Chocolates'* cast members sparkled under the limelight. One optimal specimen was the abnormal conduct exhibited by blackface comedian and dance phenomenon Amanzie "Jazzlips" Richardson who costumed in a waggish hat that was too small for his head and also donned a tiny bow tie and frock coat. Mr. "Jazzlips", with his quadruple jointed legs and jaws, obtained glowing reviews for his excitedly bizarre *Hot Chocolates'* "Jungle Dancing". The *Evening Graphic* defined Amanzie "Jazzlips" Richardson as being "blacker than a rent collector's heart" mythologizing that he "came out on stage unheralded by any blare of trumpets and stopped the show deader than a press agents gag." With his charismatically incessant habit of using incorrect grammatical inflections "Jazzlips" confessed to journalists that he is "not so good in the readin', writin' and rithmatic areas" and that he "neber eber had a right ejumacation".

After enjoying such a breathtaking *Hot Chocolates'* opening night Harper adopted to elevate "Jazzlips" by billing and upgrading him into the ranks of a featured player, moving his dressing room from the fourth tier to the ground floor nearer to the stage. "Jazzlips" was uneasy by the relocation and didn't want to change a thing saying "Not for mine" in a 1929 article titled *Jazzlips Won't Leave His Attic Dressing Room* "Jazzlips" expressed his doubts by asking the reporter "how high is up?" then declared "All of my life, I have been even lower than the ground floor. I have been a snake charmer in carnival pits, a vaudevillian who dressed in basements and I prefer to stay where I am."

"Jazzlips" refusal to switch his dressing quarters proved an inconsequential annoyance for Harper because he was to be arrested backstage and charged with the crime of "illegitimate parenthood." When "Jazzlips" was taken to the Court of Special Sessions he was found guilty and ordered to pay $15 a week child support to his ten year old son "Amanzie Jazzlips Junior". Little "Amanzie Jazzlips Junior" worked for Harper beforehand along with his momma in *Harper's Kentucky Club Revue*. Little "Jazzlips Junior" and his mother Mama Anna Mae "Jazzlips" Fritz appeared at the legal proceedings where "Jazzlips" Richardson pledged to the judge that he would pay the child support and the five hundred dollars bond right away. "Jazzlips" didn't show up at the court to post the bond or make the child support payment that he promised and was instantly rearrested and enforced to secure the cash on the spot or else not be permitted to return back to his *Hot Chocolates'* duties and amaze electrified enthusiasts.

The up and coming Louis "Satchmo" Armstrong derived the full benefits of his new found fame as a bona-fide superstar with his lady fans, but not before entreating that they sign one of his many dozen sexual intercourse consent forms that he concealed within his pockets. The ladies were required to autograph his sexual guarantees before any consensual hanky-panky got underway and Armstrong even obliged his wife to sign them. Armstrong's wife Lillian Armstrong signed the "Permits" that gave her hubby the right to "lasciviously party" with any girl that consents. Armstrong additionally had his current girlfriend Miss. Alpha Smith who play acted like his true wife in public sign the understandings. Alpha Smith became Armstrong's actual third wife almost a decade afterwards but Lillian in all probability was the one behind these sexual guarantees/permits because she was in fact much more of a business manager than a wife to Armstrong. Lil Armstrong in her functions as Armstrong's manager/parent and guardian was a solid self-determined woman who cavorted around on the side with other boyfriends herself while wedded to Armstrong. Lillian Armstrong was keen enough to foreknow the impending difficulties for Armstrong realizing that he entertained many sweethearts and maintained numerous sexual and quasi-matrimonial relationships which might make him the target of an unlimited number of breach of promise or conjugal sex lawsuits.

AN UNDYING BROADWAY INSCRIPTION

Hot Chocolates' was such a smashingly colossal hit on Broadway that a brand new fashion craze arose for women on the Great White Way and it was the *Hot Chocolates'* styled nylon stockings described as being in a delightful warm shade of tan. The Rogers Peet clothing company distributed and promoted a tan wet-proof overcoat for both men and women using the *Hot Chocolates'* slogan in the show's program advertisements stating that "Hot Chocolates are warming on chilly days—so are our Scotch Mists, the smart wet proof overcoats."

Quite a few of Harper's attractive *Hot Chocolates'* chorines were able to earn a little extra money from being associated with the show as they modeled in, advertisements for hair straightening products. The fortunate actress's also got additional personal publicity endorsements with a few sentences about their private backgrounds that were incorporated within the "La-Em-Strait" hair dressing for stubborn "Colored" hair ads. La-Em-Strait was priced from 25 to 50 cents and it assured to make a "Colored persons hair stay back and look smooth like silk, without the grease". Most of the Harper girls never used any of these products even though it was given to them for free. Harper and *Hot Chocolates'* were mentioned in at least eight separate hair relaxation cream advertisements.

Dolly McCormick, one half of the sister duo known as the McCormick Sisters who were featured in *Hot Chocolates'*, was signed to model the "Black and White Peroxide Vanishing Cream" because she was so fair skinned and cute. The snow-white cream was not only supposed to make one's skin lighter but keep the skin soft and smooth and Dolly's prettiness was endorsed as the evidence of a "Glorious Complexion". These avowals were touted in many of the African-American newspapers. The Black and White peroxide beauty cream syndicate not only promised that the skin cream would make Negroes whiter complexioned but it purported that it could open up the doors to exclusive society circles while identifying the buttery skinned Dolly McCormick as a "young social leader" because the cream "leaves only a thin film which guards against the darkening and coarsening effects of the sun and wind while removing the dirt."

The McCormick Sisters were Panamanian immigrants and even though they were young they owned a stage presence reserved only for theatre veterans having already danced in loads of Harper's theatre and nightclub floorshow productions before their employment in *Hot Chocolates'*. Harper showcased Dolly in the specialty *Goddess of Rain* dance number early on, but she had been eradicated and made to return back to the chorus line because her enactments were deficient in "the dash and verve" departments which was essential in carrying out a lead spot in a show filled with so many blowout talents.

It was a good thing that Harper downgraded Dolly because he replaced her with the outwardly uninhibited Louise "Jota" Cook, a Baton-Rogue, Louisiana native. "What she (Jota) did with her stomach, would make you seasick" said Ray Nance the *Hot Chocolates'* trumpeter and part time dancer as written in linear notes by Martin Williams for the *Souvenirs of Hot Chocolates'* archival original cast album. Dolly boasted the extra ability of being able to play the violin but it was not utilized in her *Hot Chocolates'* stage interpretations. While back in the chorus line Dolly executed a sizzling semi-nude dance number which triggered quite a positive analysis and stimulation even though she was no longer highlighted in her very own solo number.

Dolly's sister Pearl McCormick performed as an adagio dancer and was decked out in a Native American Indian getup in *Hot Chocolates'* giving the impression to all who witnessed her that she was a little more gifted than her sister. Sister Pearl also costarred in a supporting role with an all-African-American cast in the first entirely black talking picture drama concocted by a white company titled *The Scar of Shame*. The feature film concerned itself with the "scars" of being either a dark or light skinned African-American living in a world that had been unconstructively provoked by white racial pigeonholing and the inner indignity that it produced on the fatalities of racial preference while sensationalizing the complexities of identity problems. Pearl's role as a featured actress in *The Scar of Shame* was a direct result of her illustrious notices in *Hot Chocolates'*.

The McCormick Sisters resided with their parents and Dolly continued to arduously hustle as a chorus line dancer for Harper at other venues well after the *Hot Chocolates'* run. Sister Pearl McCormick married Charlie McClane the lively manager of the Royal Theatre in Philadelphia deserting the stage life to become a proper wife but was drawn back to perform years later for a brief period. After her stunted stints as a featured theatre player Pearl headed back down to Philadelphia for good where she frequently passed for a Caucasian woman vanishing from her race whenever she could get away with it. Assuming the nondiscriminatory special privileges not afforded to African-Americans Pearl McCormick was able to shop in any store she liked without having to enter through its back doors. Pearl was also able to touch the merchandise without being required to purchase it beforehand and she relished the white privilege of being able to sit in the front of the bus when she went out to dine in some of the Caucasian only dining establishments.

James Baskette, one of the introduced players from *Hot Chocolates'*, gained national fame years later by playing the adorable Uncle Tom known as "Uncle Remus" in the 1946 Walt Disney feature film *Song of The South*. James Baskette got a default honorary Academy Award for his performance as *Uncle Remus* while many African-American organizations such as the N.A.A.C.P. asked that Negroes boycott the film because *Song of The South* boosted the Remus character as just a "one dimensional white loving servant." Baskette received his honorary Oscar from Hollywood posthumously after his death which occurred two years after *Song of The South* was released.

Eddie Green the *Hot Chocolates* alumni and author of *A Good Man Is Hard to Find* (1918) redeployed in the 1930's into the behind the scenes area of show business as a colored film company entrepreneur and producer. Green's enterprise was known as "Sepia Arts" and it specialized in movie shorts. During the early 1950s Eddie Green procured the character of the lawyer Stonewall in the racially provocative *Amos and Andy* television series.

Edith Wilson went from singing and acting in Harper's first staged Afro-American Broadway protest number *Black n Blue*, to being the model shown with the big white teeth and the red kerchief on the Aunt Jemima Pancake mix box. Edith came to enjoy her eighteen years as the famous Quaker Oats company persona of Aunt Jemima the hospitable motherly pancake flipping Mammie with that tasty home cooked breakfast meal for the master and his family. When the black civil rights movement came into play Wilson was driven out as the house Negro slave-cook and throw back to the days of "happy' captivity. After several effective "Black Power" protests the Quaker Oats pancake mix, corporation finally converted to using an illustration of the contemporary sendup of Aunt Jemima which is reflected on today's breakfast boxes.

Hot Chocolates' musical recordings were generated at assorted locations during the year 1929 when the musical revue was mounted. Many original cast members from *Hot Chocolates'* contributed along with Duke Ellington on piano and his band with Sonny Greer drumming on recordings such as *Snake Hips Dance, Jungle Jamboree,* and *That Rhythm Man* a fox trot tune from the show. Ellington was otherwise busy composing music for the Broadway musical *Showgirls* starring Harper's dance apprentice Ruby Keller and the flagrant black slang vocal copycat Jimmy Durante. *Showgirls* shut down after 111 performances.

Conceivably for legal purposes Ellington switched the names of his band back and forth for the *Hot Chocolates'* soundtracks from the Harlem Foot Warmers/Stompers to the Memphis Men and then to the Jungle Band. Ellington happened onto the *Hot Chocolates'* scene because he was in association with Irving Mills who owned the Mills Music Publishing Company the man who purchased the majority of Waller's songs from the hit show at a giveaway fee of $500. Mills Music made an economic killing off of the catalogue of Waller's *Hot Chocolates'* theatrical scores which included *Black n Blue, Jungle Jamboree* and *Ain't Misbehavin*.

The heartfelt and rough-edged *Hot Chocolates'* recordings consisted of Louis Armstrong singing and playing it down home style on *Ain't Misbehavin, That Rhythm Man* and *Sweet Savannah Sue*. Thomas "Fats" Waller executed lite-fingered piano solos on *Ain't Misbehavin* and *Sweet Savannah Sue* while Edith Wilson sang her own original rendition of *Black n Blue* and *My Man Is Good For Nothing But Love*.

Sending A Wire which was a droll sketch with comedian Eddie Green sold as a single on the Okeh Electric Record Label for seventy five cents. *Sending A Wire* was a respectable addition to the *Souvenirs of Hot Chocolates'* cast album not for the reason that it was uproariously funny but because it gave a feel of the outdated Colored Musical Comedy genre. The *Hot Chocolates'* recordings were released as singles during their period then were later jointly assembled for a cast album titled *Souvenirs of Hot Chocolates'*. The LP is on file at the Smithsonian Collection Recording Project. The music publishing division of the *Hot Chocolates'* title's currently earns additional monies from the retailing of its sheet music, revised recordings and celebrity cover versions through various music labels.

In 1929, the same year as the opening of the Broadway show, cast members from *Hot Chocolates'* kicked off the foundational start of Roseland Ballroom's tenth fall season by participating in the evening's special entertainment. A month later Harper brought the *Hot Chocolates'* gang featuring composer Harry Brooks on the piano up to Harlem's Rockland Palace for the Apex Beauty Pageant. Universal News Reel filmed the whole event which was projected worldwide. Leonard Harper and Andy Razaf were the judges in the Apex Beauty Pageant which asked the question "Who is The Prettiest Girl in the East?" Harper additionally had the *Hot Chocolates'* cast perform the same year for the Manhattan Elk's Lodge Number 45's benefit at the Alhambra Theatre with W. C. Handy cooking up a torrid cornet solo. Other guest artists on the Elk's fundraiser listings were Peg Leg Bates, the Blackbirds, Izzy Ringgold and the "Tan Town Nightingales".

Off-shoots like contemporary musicals such as *Ain't Misbehavin* and *Black n Blue* have preserved the spirit of *Hot Chocolates'* and kept it alive in other configurations and embodiments for decades after Harper's version of the revue closed leaving an ongoing testament of *Hot Chocolates'* creative impact and enduring artistic legacy.

Harper's *Hot Chocolates'* enjoyed 219 performances at the Hudson Theatre from June 1929 to December of that year, before the Immerman brothers opted to take the revue on the road. According to show business specialists, had the Immerman's not been so impatient with their schemes for more immediate dollars and if they hadn't been so zealous to tour out *Hot Chocolates',* the revue could have played on Broadway well into the 1930s. Connie Immerman and Leonard Harper squeezed all that they could out of their hit show and toured it out for years first transporting it uptown to the Lafayette and then all across the country. The acts were in a constant state of transformation but nobody cared as long as the show was entertaining. Harper even split up the acts in the revue so that audiences would have go see the first act of *Hot Chocolates'* one week and then they would have to return the next week to purchase tickets to see the second and final act at an additional cost.

Harper shipped out his Connie's Inn version of *Hot Feet* at the same time that his 1929 *Leonard Harper's Revue* and *Get Hot* were on tour.

Both *Get Hot* and *Leonard Harper's Revue,* were comprised of many of the same *Hot Chocolates'* cast members. All the revues were structured with identical replicating fundamentals knocking off some of the same exact *Hot Chocolates'* numbers higgledy-piggledy together in altered scenes, occasionally with slight revisions that concealed any indication of a past show's resemblance.

When the *Hot Chocolates'* production journeyed to Maryland the cast size was increased to 150 talents and it featured Thomas "Fats" Waller on the piano. Once on the Maryland stage the producers used encouraging press and print excerpts inside their poster notices which declaimed the following *The New York Herald –Tribune, in an editorial dated October 18, {1929} which mentioned "Hot Chocolates," and then went on to say: "The Negro is not merely a vaudeville joke, and not merely as a highbrow cult he has arrived. "Hot Chocolates" embraces the finest colored talent ever assembled on one stage, bringing to the foreground artists that will make future Negroid history."* The exceedingly entertaining *Hot Chocolates'* musical revue stuffed with breakneck rhythm dancing went on generating merriment in the hearts of audiences all over parts of America well into 1932. Louis Armstrong came to headline a 1932 *Hot Chocolates Homecoming Edition* and the revue attracted capacity hordes and big box office cash everywhere it was staged. Harper's *Hot Chocolates'* was revived briefly in 1935 and then was never to reappear again.

On the domestic front, Harper's relationship with his wife Osceola slowly drifted toward a nonexistent pretense. The tremendously over worked and wearied Harper came to his apartment and straightaway plunged onto his bed and snoozed for hours. None of Harper's emotional, romantic, and sexual requirements were met at home any longer.

While at work many of the striking and voluptuous chorus girls tried to gain Harper's approval and interest. After a while he gave up fighting off these luscious high steppers by giving in as he was unable to forbid his secreted cravings any longer. When Harper wasn't staging he regularly wound up thoroughly throwing in his towel to the world of sensuous titillation. Osceola being his devoted and caring wife eternally had a place in her heart for him which made it unproblematic for her to overlook his trysts. Harper nevertheless still loved Osceola, just as he prized his mom and brother, but Osceola's domesticity could not compete with the radiant young females that rhythm tapped with an overabundance of bouncy seductive vigor on his dance floors. As an alternative for the lack of genuine affection he began to over eat Osceola's meals and it started to show.

The instinctual aromas that emanated from a featured dancer or chorus girl's perspiration combined with the pleasing floral scents of their perfumes turned Harper on. Harper became crazily aroused with the same matching exuberance that he felt from producing his revue shows only this time it was erotic and he whiffed those fluids as often as he mounted a show. At night while backstage in his office forming and conjuring up new ideas after everyone had left the theatre, an aspiring chorus girl would slink coquettishly into his dark workspace asking for guidance. She might request his views about dating or ask him for some professional advice by bringing up the subject about something minor like how are the other dancers able to keep the feathery costumes or tassels from falling off during a performance. Being very generous to his cast with money Harper might receive a special thank you gift for allocating a healthy cash advance in a time of need. Harper strayed and it became just part of what went along with the territory, when one was at the pinnacle of their game theatrically.

In 1929 Harper batted an eye and just about all of his great undertakings from uptown to Broadway and even his touring productions collapsed and, crumbled away to be disremembered with the arrival of the October 29th economic breakdown and the start of the Great Financial Depression. Author Langston Hughes wrote that "The depression brought everybody down a peg or two. And the Negroes had but few pegs to fall." The once affluent whites no longer found it fashionable to slum uptown and watch the merry "darkies" make spectacles of themselves in revues as they knocked back whiskey and wolfed down

Chinese or soul foods because they now had to watch their decreasing bank accounts, wallets and hollow pocket books.

As written in the book *Harlem The Making Of A Ghetto/Negro New York 1980-1930* by Gilbert Osofsky. Mr. Osofsky wrote "The Great Depression brought an abrupt end to the concept of a 'New Negro' and the image of Harlem as an erotic utopia. A nation sobered by bread lines no longer searched for a dreamland inhabited by people who danced and loved and laughed for an 'entire lifetime.'" The show folks like Harper and his ilk strained to keep up a false front with grinning faces as they championed the value of their craft. The situation was so problematic and dismal that many lost hope. A large quantity of regular theatre goers could no longer purchase a ticket to see a show.

Langston Hughes sorrowfully stated that "most Negroes were out of vogue" and it hit every African-American square in the face. Many of the talented white New York producers and directors trekked out to Hollywood to create motion pictures and the movie studio bosses never even contemplated calling on Harper or any other African-American director to work their magic in the motion picture industry.

Instead, the Hollywood producers made deals with directors like Busby Berkeley because he was an "All-American director" with the correct skin color.

Leonard Harper and Osceola Blanks. *Harper & Blanks* (The Smart Set Couple) United States Passport Photos before sailing off to London, England to perform in *Plantation Days*, 1923.

LEONARD HARPER

Leonard Harper Press Photograph. 1924.

Leonard Harper System Broadway Dance Studio advertisement. 1924.

Interior The Nest Club 1920s. Courtesy Schomburg Center for Research in Black Culture Photographs and Prints Division, New York Public Library, Otis Butler.

Harper's *Tan Town Topics* advertisement. 1925.

Leonard Harper and the Famous Plantation Beauty Chorus in *Blackbirds of 1926*. N. Y. Public Library/Lincoln Center for the Performing Arts, White Studios. Billy Rose Theatre Collection.

LAFAYETTE THEATRE

7th Avenue and 132nd Street

Telephone 1811 Morningside

ONE WEEK BEGINNING MONDAY, SEPTEMBER 5, 1927

Leonard Harper
Presents the King of Dance

BILL (BOJANGLES) ROBINSON

In a Spectacular Revue

The Pepper Pot

WITH

Billy Higgins — Madeline Belt
Joe Byrd — Smokey City 4
Ernest Whitman — Mary Perval

The Fastest, Merriest, Peppiest Revue of Them All

In Addition, Two Great Photo Plays

Mon., Tues. and Wed.
Buck Jones
in
"Hills of Peril"

Thur., Fri., Sat. and Sun.
"COLLEEN"
with
Madge Bellamy

No Advance in Prices   Midnight Show Friday

Harper's *Pepper Pot Revue* featuring Bill "Bojangles" Robinson and the Harper Chorus Line. 1927. Harperettes and Bojangles perform Dance-Offs and the chorus girls duplicated his patented tap steps, phrase for phrase and pitter for patter. Audiences went wild.

Harper's *Kentucky Club Revue* advertisement. 1927.

Harper's *Hot Chocolates'* "Jungle Jamboree" scene featuring Louise "Jota" Cook (bending over on left) and Baby Cox (standing center). 1929. N.Y. Public Library/Lincoln Center for the Performing Arts, White Studios. Billy Rose Theatre Collection.

Backstage at Harper's *Hot Chocolates*' with Louise "Jota" Cook in 1929 with an insert of her likeness painted on *The Exile* movie poster 1931. N.Y. Public Library/Lincoln Center for the Performing Arts, White Studios. Billy Rose Theatre Collection.

Inside view of Harper's Floorshow at Connie's Inn. 1920s. Helen Armstrong Johnson.

CONNIE'S INN

presents Leonard Harper's
NEW SUMMER REVUE

"HOT FEET"

2 Gala Revues Nightly 2
featuring
PRINCESS VIKANA
30 Beautiful Brownskins 30
LOUIS ARMSTRONG
AND ORCHESTRA
"You'll Want to Dance"
7th AVE. at 131st ST.
Reservations Suggested
Phone Harlem 6630

Harper's *Hot Feet* at Connie's Inn advertisement. 1929.

Leonard Harper (center) leading the Hal Bakay Funeral Cortege with George Immerman (to his left) and Sam Wooding (to Harper's far left) on 7th. Ave., Harlem across the street from Connie's Inn and the Lafayette Theatre. 1931. Inter-State Tattler.

Harper's *Cream-Colored Creole Revue* Cosy Grill nightclub program. 1932.

Fannie Pennington at 21 years old in Asbury Park, New Jersey. 1935.
Grant Harper Reid Collection.

Harper's *League of Rhythm Revue* at the Apollo Theatre poster. 1936.

Leonard Harper (center) in-house Apollo theatre producer looks on in Apollo theatre office as Eddie Green (left) signs a motion picture distribution deal. Jimmy Marshall (seated) manager of the Apollo accepts the contract. September 30, 1939. *Chicago Defender*.

CHAPTER FIVE
(1929 to 1935)

'HOT HARLEM' GOT FROSTY

Harper's *Hot Chocolates'* was "tabbed-out" in countless versions and editions shoving off to tour around the country for roughly three years after its initial Broadway run. Harper then went on to stage the dances and supervise the prototypical casting of a new-fangled updated 1929 version of *Plantation Days* with his former producer/manager Maurice L. Greenwald. The 1929 adaption of *Plantation Days* rambled on a Southwestern road tour for a good twenty weeks. Harper also helmed a special Harlem floorshow for the Smalls Paradise Club Room titled *The Versatile Revue* starring Bill Bojangles Robinson and Harper's Brown Buddies came on board for a broadcasting carnival revue that also featured Small's Paradise specially skilled terpsichorean dancing and singing waiters and it was all the way "rhythm a la mode".

For most of the top talents of the post-Harlem Renaissance era and the aftermath of the 1929 stock market crash an earnest artistic fruition came into existence. Black culture was voiced without all the urgency and hype of having to play into the hands of the compensating Harlem Renaissance customer's entertainment requirements. They were able to explore and exhibit their creative impulses from a much more maturely measured and seasoned perspective.

In January of 1931 Harper personally performed and highlighted many of the acts for a Gala Urban League Benefit then later that same year he moved on to do a show titled *Creole Jamboree* at the renowned Harlem Opera House with the shockingly sidesplitting blackface comedian Pigmeat Markham and Twelve Dancing Haperettes (the legendary chorus line Harper named after himself). All through this same period Harper produced at Connie's Inn and he did a revue titled, *Spades are Trumps* with "Fats" Waller banging the music out as Harper performed as a featured entertainer with a full cast of other gifted revue artists.

In mid-February of 1931 Frank Schiffman, owner of the Lafayette and Lincoln Theatre's, notified Harper that he had made an arrangement with major African-American motion picture filmmaker Oscar Micheaux. Schiffman administered their new film company and both men wanted Harper to direct some scenes for what was be the first all-Afro-American Talkie motion picture. According to the publication *Blacks in black and white: A Source Book On Black Films* by Henry T. Sampson, at the time Oscar Micheaux was the top African-American filmmaker in the country and previously from mid-1920 on Micheaux had been in contact with Harper and fellow producer Irvin C. Miller because Oscar Micheaux sought to produce and direct short African-American musical pieces with jazz and dance artists and with two of the nation's most prominent black directors. The talks between Micheaux, Harper, and Miller went nowhere because Micheaux didn't have any cash in his budget. Micheaux realized that it was crucial for him to acquire the leading available African-American talents for his films and he hoped that he could acquire them through directors Harper and Miller.

During the past decade white film companies such as Vitaphone began snatching up and courting top African-American on camera talents like Ellington, Armstrong, Bojangles, Waller and Eubie Blake. The white firms paid good money for these African-American stars to perform in their short movies and they could afford it because they controlled the distribution system in their white theatres. These white theatres banned Oscar Micheaux's African-American films from their movie houses and thus he couldn't find the money to hire many of the top African-American artists because his profits from audience revenues were always so dismally depleted. The Caucasian theatre's illegitimate prohibition against Afro-American independent films made it challenging for filmmakers like Micheaux to compete budget wise and this was a reoccurring problem that dogged Micheaux throughout his entire career.

Due to budgetary limitations Oscar Micheaux was driven to restructure his film company. Micheaux was desperately in need of an infusion of funds so he contacted Frank Schiffman. Schiffman became the vice president and his theatrical business partner Leo Brecher was jobbed as treasurer with Micheaux retaining the title of president of their newly established "Fayette Pictures" company labeled after the Lafayette Theatre. For their new venture Micheaux and Schiffman immediately leased out the Metropolitan Studio which was the largest independent film production faculty on the east coast and located just over the Hudson River in Fort Lee, New Jersey.

Leonard Harper was on board to direct and stage the dance and ensemble scenes for Fayette Picture's first motion picture titled *The Exile-The First Mighty Modern All Talking Epic of Negro Life*. The Harper on screen credits were, "Dances and Ensembles Staged by Leonard Harper." Micheaux found Harper's services indispensable with the thinking that Harper's nightclub ensembles alone would draw in the white audiences and lure his Broadway, *Hot Chocolates'* fan base. Micheaux also presumed that Southern and non-New York State whites would be attracted and curious to catch sight of what a real Harlem nightclub would look like and wouldn't mind viewing it all from the sheltered comfy and distant environment of a local movie theatre. Patrick McGilligan wrote in his book *Oscar Micheaux: The Great And Only: The Life Of America's First Black Filmmaker* that, "He (Micheaux) splurged on the singing-dancing sequences, bringing Leonard Harper and Donald Heywood to Fort Lee to stage the film's cabaret interludes, and to help out with *Darktown Revue*, a short subject to accompany the feature."

Micheaux directed and produced *The Exile* with his all African-American cast while Harper staged the film's able line up of veteran singers and dancers amassed from his various floorshow productions. *The Exile's* female chorus line were all clad in flimsy feathered get-ups and were credited as "Harper's Chorines" and "Harper's Connie's Inn Chorus" and the girls danced it up like a hurricane. Harper also staged the beautiful Louise "Jota" Cook from *Hot Chocolates'*. "Jota" Cook master-pieced her oozing sexy "belly muscle" dance and Roland Holder was featured in tails and a top hat tightening up a specialty tap dance routine as if he was dialoguing in an omnipresent language of his own by the pliable use of his body and feet instruments.

Reviewers assumed that *The Exile's* sensual African-American dances would never get past the censors but the dances did in fact get past the blue pencils. Patrick McGilligan documented in his tome *Oscar Micheaux: The Great and Only: The Life of America's First Black Filmmaker* that "Leonard Harper's tap-dancing chorus girls took over here and there, exploding before the cameras with their big smiles, slivered outfits, and long legs. Nothing in Hollywood movies compared with the "Hot Chocolates" at their hottest: Micheaux knew he'd have to shuffle this very sexy footage when facing the censors later."

What the censors found objectionable in *The Exile* was the racial theme of the film. *The Exile* was about modern northern Negro life and starred a light, near white skinned, looking sepia lady who fell in with love an African-American man. Micheaux's lead actress looked so white that many Southern audiences miscomprehended the film to be about an interracial love story which was categorically a no-no at the time. White audiences bristled when they watched what they thought to be one of their own female Caucasoid brood interrelating with African-Americans on the screen. Micheaux had the reputation of being obsessed to the point of fanatical fetishism with the subject matter of light butter skinned African-American people. The high yellow skinned female lead of *The Exile* not only looked the part but her character believed that she was a Caucasian lass, and these scenes infuriated two white women members of the Pennsylvania Board of Censors. These board members banned and discontinued screenings of *The Exile* and their actions prevented Micheaux from releasing and circulating the movie to screens outside of New York State proper.

The censor's disapproval of *The Exile* due to its racial content didn't seem to be the central difficulty or defect of the movie instead it was its run-down budget quality with its incessant soundtrack snags and pitiable untrained acting. *The Exile* premiered at Frank Schiffman's Lafayette theatre after two unalike live staged Harper revue productions showcased. Harper's productions were titled *Blue Rhythm* and *Hot Rhythm*. Micheaux was known to publicize his productions to excessive degrees and the Fayette Film Company did bang-up ticket sales after Harlem was saturated with superb colorful posters, pictures and show cards. *The Exile's* legendary and foremost color poster had a painted representation of Miss Louise "Jota" Cook the "Oriental" dancer, who was featured in *Harper's Hot Chocolates'*. The actual photo of "Jota" Cook that was recycled for the Micheaux advertisement was a painted replica of a still backstage snapshot from Harper's original 1929 *Hot Chocolates'* publicity unit.

Because of Schiffman's and Micheaux's solid and well-oiled hype machine advancing *The Exile*, initially the film boasted a healthy box office. *The Exile* similarly triggered a hubbub as it was the first entirely African-American spawned talkie that flooded audiences with blackspeak while thematically zeroing in on the subject of northern blacks and how Americans grappled with the highly charged skin tone dissimilarities within the Negro race. *The Exile* as a feature production gave black audiences who already had an ever rising awareness a quick kick in the butt and a statelier sense of self-respect not only because it was a talkie film but because it was assembled by members of their own race.

Micheaux moreover directed a short filler film at the time which screened along with *The Exile* and it was titled *Darktown Revue* and while the images were crisp and the soundtrack was suitable the director didn't apply any camera movements. *Darktown Revue* was fundamentally a showcase film featuring and juxtaposing highbrow and low brow African-American entertainers. *Darktown Revue* interspaced the

Eurocentric bourgeois class of Negroes singing semi-operatic classical tunes juxtaposed between the buffoonish Jigaboo-Niggerish comics who get insulted when offered a job, category of Colored personalities. One of the songs featured in *Darktown Revue* was called, *Watermelon Time*.

The twin category depictions of the Negro race in *Darktown Revue* further underscored the existing 1931 schizophrenia of post-slavery African-Americans trying to figure out how to best distinguish their recently freed status as they struggled to realize the American dream. The film short begged for answers to the internal question of "how does the African-American race that was stripped of their legacy want to be perceived in America?" If African-Americans went totally "European" and turned their backs on their heritage to fit into American society they might very well be abandoning their African roots. Or should they stay in the post slave mode?

There was a great deal of good will between Frank Schiffman and Oscar Micheaux throughout the making of *The Exile* because these men assumed that they had a hit movie on their hands. Frank Schiffman while in pre-production on *The Exile* inadvertently integrated the white owned Frank's Restaurant which was a highly regarded Harlem 125th Street, eating establishment. Frank's Restaurant was in the middle of Harlem yet the white owners and the wait staff refused to serve and acknowledge African-American customers. Schiffman brought Micheaux into the restaurant against its policy for a business lunch and when the waiter declined to accept Micheaux's order Schiffman simply instructed the attendant to bring over two lunches for himself and when the cuisine arrived he handed one of his plates to Oscar. The manager of Frank's didn't know what action to take because he certainly couldn't toss out the great Harlem theatre owner Frank Schiffman who also happened to be a regular customer. Micheaux ate his meal and both men refused to leave the restaurant until their business discussions ended.

The relationship between Schiffman and Micheaux quickly got mucky when *The Exile's* box office receipts didn't live up to their expectations and dropped off after its opening evidencing that the picture would become a financial failure. Micheaux was ordered by a Supreme Court Judge to give a detailed accounting of his expenditures for the Fayette Motion Picture Corporation after Schiffman suspected him of cashing more than $3,500 worth of checks belonging to the company. Furthermore Micheaux was accused by Schiffman of clandestinely copyrighting the script of *The Exile* in his own name, even though the film's draught was adapted and based on Micheaux's book *The Conquest*.

Micheaux was subsequently arrested and held in jail with a $500 charge for petty larceny from the accusations pursued by Schiffman that Oscar was guilty of the illegal and personal usage of their film corporation's money and for cashing Fayette company checks without the proper authorization. Micheaux in turn incriminated Schiffman saying that he called an underhanded meeting with stockholders comprised of prominent African-American actors in an endeavor to remove him as president of the Micheaux film company. Micheaux further charged Schiffman of inadequately financing *The Exile* thus causing him and the project to set off on the threshold of bankruptcy. Oscar Micheaux was never able to overcome the opposition that he had to withstand as he sought to obtain nondiscriminatory equitable distribution deals for his films from the white motion picture industry.

In May of year 1931 the Immerman brothers proved to be hard-hitting cookies when it came to business as they and Tommy Rockwell, Louis Armstrong's former manager, charged Armstrong in court of not being wholly "loyal" to them contractually. They wanted Armstrong to remain on the ever continuing *Hot Chocolates'* touring gravy train, which they depleted all the artistic life out of. Armstrong had other plans and decided to go it alone as an independent artist without a managers' input or any performance limitations. Armstrong hastily left for a quick unplanned national tour with a pickup traveling jazz band.

Harper's attitude of George and Connie Immerman altered as he started losing some of the admiration that he once had for them. He never got over how Connie Immerman forced him into casting only light skinned women while banning his dancers of a darker hue in his Connie's Inn chorus lines. Harper also reminded himself with great irritation about the time when the Immerman brothers sought to doublecross him by sabotaging his floorshow at Ciro Terranova's nightspot. They snitched and dropped a dime on Ciro's outfit to police authorities by informing them that racketeer Ciro Terranova didn't have a dance license. The Immerman's appeared to give the impression that their booked talents were their personal property and their latest revolting legal incursions against Armstrong didn't prove otherwise.

In September of 1931 Harper kicked off a successful production run across the Hudson River in Newark, New Jersey. He was hired to produce at the recently renovated Orpheum Theatre. Unfortunately, just two months after the Orpheum opening on November 7, 1931, tragedy struck one of his show personalities. Spencer Williams an in-house songwriter for Harper who had just completed some lyrics and music for Harper's *Pepper Pot Revue* which was scheduled for a Smalls Paradise Cabaret opening in December killed a fellow Connie's Inn employee. Hal Bakay an affable twenty one year old character actor was gored to death by Williams. Williams and Bakay quarreled over a salacious sexual slur that was aimed towards the ravishing and stunning Miss. Consuelo Harris, one of Harper's pet chorus line dancers at the Inn.

The derogatory slight concerning Miss. Harris came from Williams and the strapping Bakay did the gentlemanly thing by stepping in to lessen the tension by standing up for and siding with the disrespected Miss. Harris. A confrontation ensued at a theatrical party taking place at Big John's apartment which was a popular rendezvous that Harper's performers often used to relax and unwind. Big John's was located within walking distance from Connie's Inn. The thirty nine year old Williams jabbed a seven-inch blade into Bakay's chest and then went into hiding for five days. The well liked Bakay perished in Harlem Hospital due to paralysis of the intestine and pneumonia. After giving himself up to the police and being locked up and arrested without bail on the murder charges, Williams still maintained his innocence. Death threats were made by members of the nightclub community that if Williams was cleared of the murder rap and got out of jail he better not dare try to walk the streets of Harlem again or "he will be taken care of" street justice style.

Leonard Harper, George Immerman, and Russell Wooding headed the funeral cortege along Seventh Avenue to Saint Luke's Hall for the service and they marched past Connie's Inn where the butchered Master of Ceremonies Bakay was employed. At the flanks of the hearse were pallbearers "New Orleans" Willie Jackson, Zudie Singleton and "Snakehips" Tucker with an all-inclusive Connie's Inn troupe behind them, shadowed by the trio Three Little Words.

The presentation that murderer Spencer Williams carved out the music for was Harper's New Edition of *The Pepper Pot Revue* for Small's Paradise and it went on anyway without a hitch. Harper had his chorus girls fit together a prop house on stage right in front of audiences during the *Building a Home* song and dance sequence and the Harper Chorines were described as "youthful, supple and easy on the eyes, girls who dance and wiggle with grace and abandon."

January of 1932 begot Harper to stage an All-Sepia floorshow titled *Harlem Nights* at the Canton Inn in Brooklyn, New York. It was the first time Bronze talent had broken into the typically all white nightspot. The floorshow was billed as the "Grand Premiere of The Greatest Colored Revue in Town."

Harper supplied a comparable nightclub floorshow revue for the Cosy Grill located in Montreal, Quebec, Canada. The Revue was titled *Leonard Harper's Original Cream Colored "Creole Revue"* and it played three shows nightly. The cast was comprised of Pearl Baines, Margaret Simms and Babe Wallace who fronted in specialty numbers like *Red Hot Harlem, Rhythm of the Tambourine, Borneo* and *Minnie the Moocher's Wedding Day*. There was the customarily solid chorus line of Harper's plenteous physique vibrating honey-babes and they were credited as the "Ladies of The Ensemble". The music was catered by Eddie Perkins also known as the "Professor of Jazzology" and his Cosy Grill Orchestra.

1932 Harper shouldered freelance directorial assignments at innumerable far-off spots from the outer borough of Brooklyn, to Midwestern cities like Chicago. The concluding part of January 1932 had Harper staging and producing the First Annual Dance for the New York Branch of the National Association for the Advancement of Colored People's entertainment committee at the Renaissance Casino. With the support of the Columbia broadcasting company he offered the Mills Brothers as headliners who were radio's latest African-American vocal sensations.

Correspondingly highlighted on the N.A.A.C.P. show were the amateurs of Mrs. Laura Jean Rollock who hailed from Brooklyn acting in a musical comedy revue skit called *The Lincoln Settlement Follies*. The young dancing beauties of *The Lincoln Settlement Follies* were comprised of actress's from various New York City churches. The additional popular entertainment artists in the first N.A.A.C.P appeal were professionals from Harper's Connie's Inn Revues such as the Sepia Songbirds who sang *It Looks Like Love* and Connie's Inn soloist Mary Ellis who elicited inspiring reactions from all who showed up when she belted out *Sleepy Down South*. With over 1,200 guests filling the Renny Casino the initial N.A.A.C.P. event was a terrific victory. The donors and members of the N.A.A.C.P. danced with each other during intermission and, following the Mills Brothers performance.

According to a *N. Y. Amsterdam News* article titled *Theatre Owner Talks to Garvey* in the month of February 1932 Frank Schiffman owner operator of the Lafayette theatre departed for a Jamaican vacation. After Schiffman arrived in Kingston, Jamaica he touched base with none other than Jamaican Councilman Marcus Garvey who operated an outdoor theatre. Garvey who was a United States exile resided on the British controlled Island. Frank Schiffman was asked by Garvey if he might be able to acquire some musicals from America for his island theatre similar to Harper's migratory "tab" productions. Schiffman assured Garvey that he would look into the matter but because of the exorbitant costs of transporting the acts and setting up production operations in Jamaica Schiffman quickly dismissed the concept.

Once Schiffman got back to Harlem he decided to do some spring cleaning at his main showplace and shelved Harper's Revues at the Lafayette for the summer. The Lafayette theatre showed movies while interior renovations were being conducted as a replacement and Harper found work elsewhere with little trouble.

HOLLYWOOD HERE WE COME—NOT!

Harper along with the rest of the Harlem village got hoodwinked by a white California swindler named Sunshine Scoville in February 1932. Mr. Scoville appeared in Harlem alleging that he was from the Gold Coast of California and announced that he was "known from Montreal to Texas and from Manhattan to Hollywood." Scoville maintained that he would furnish an authentic film contract to the most talented colored gal in the city. The prize-winning colored beauty was to be selected by the general public who attended his contest which would take place at the Rockland Palace in Harlem. Sunshine Scoville imparted that he was looking for the colored damsel who possessed the most beauty, poise, charm and personality and exclaimed that he would bring her to Hollywood where he promised that she would become a famous movie star. Scoville recruited the services of many prominent Harlem menfolk such as newspaper representatives, nightclub producers and theatrical managers to tally-up the ballots and gage the audience applause before he would announce who would be the "Miss Colored New York" victor. This competition was a fantasy dream come true for the lucky young local colored woman who might be chosen and destined to secure the trip out to the west coast.

Harper believed that he had the winner of "Miss. Colored New York" in Consuelo Harris the "copper-colored, bewitching chorus" girl who had become one of his favorite Connie's Inn dancers. Harper individually coached Consuelo and procured newspaper notices for her with photos showing her off in a bare suggestive feathered Indian costume. Miss. Harris was Harper's image of what a velvet brown beauty looked like and he expressed that he had faith that Consuelo Harris was qualified to be the beauty selected to collect that indispensable piece of Hollywood paper from west coast Hollywood administrator Sunshine Scoville and Harper labeled Harris his "It" girl.

Consuelo Harris was the lady whose good looks involuntarily precipitated the attack at the party which, lead to the demise of actor Hal Bakay last year. Harper said of Consuelo in the *Inter-State Tattler* that "she is one of the most beautiful girls in New York." Harper's participation in Scoville's film contest gave much more credibility than the fraudulent Sunshine Scoville or the bogus "Miss. Colored New York" competition should ever have merited.

A dishonest local Harlem shutterbug got mixed up in the "Miss. Colored New York" contest by falsifying and using an unauthorized I.D. This picture taker pretended to be the official photographer to at least 200 susceptible young females who yearned to be contestants. The photographer's lies about being the authorized snapper permitted him to charge the ladies six dollars to shoot their certified "Hollywood" prints for the contest. This neighborhood trickster received his payments from the aspiring and gullible "starlets" while never putting any film in his camera with not a single print to submit. The photographer's desertion left a significant majority of the "Miss. Colored New York" contestants and their families embittered about the event. Hardly, nobody flocked to Scoville's beauty match and the box office take was a paltry thirty seven dollars with the interior of the Rockland Palace nearly vacant aside from the 100 girls who entered and got suckered into Scoville's hoax.

Sunshine Scoville's devious plan to scam the Harlem community went up in smoke because of a smalltime neighborhood crook who beat him to the punch by pilfering the unsuspecting beauty pageant contenders with nonexistent photographs. Scoville earned little money from his ticket sales and high-tailed it out of Harlem with none of the plunder that he was hoping for. Not a single young lovely obtained a Hollywood film contract and the unfortunate aspirants were deserted with their same unattainable dreams of a wonderful new livelihood in Hollywood.

Harper found consolation and sanctuary away from the Hollywood Movie Ball disappointment with a completely brand new Colored Musical Comedy. Harper's spring revue smash hit of 1932 was titled *'Hot Harlem'* with music and lyrics by Razaf, Waller and Spencer Williams. The extravaganza swanked a fluctuating cast and boasted a few middling popular hit songs like *Stealing Apples'* and *Do Me A Favor Lend Me A Kiss*. Don Redman and his Columbia Broadcasting/Connie's Inn Band supplied the music and the Mills Brothers topped the bill for some of the performances with Blanche Calloway enrolling with the cast of fifty when the revue departed from Connie's to go on tour. Midway through the second edition of *'Hot Harlem'* Harper attached a stirring new number called *Evolution of The Negro* and actress Glennie Cheesman executed a *Frankenstein* monster number that turned out to be a highlight of the show.

The Immerman brothers had to grapple with some very perilous and scary gangland troubles in the course of the lucrative exhibition of Harper's *'Hot Harlem'* revue. Mobster wannabe and punk upstart Vincent "Irish Baby Killer" Mad Dog Coll schemed to kidnap Connie' Immerman as an affront to Dutch Schultz in an attempt to get a piece of the Dutchman's Harlem numbers and nightclub rackets.

Coll made an attempt to abduct Connie Immerman during an evening performance of *'Hot Harlem'* but managed to snatch George Immerman, Connie's sickly brother instead. Harper and the cast and crew of *'Hot Harlem'* as well as the floorshow patrons ducked for dear life during Coll's onslaught on the nightclub. Mrs. Immerman, the mother of Connie and George, set up the ransom payment with the police for her son's release. Mrs. Immerman constantly cautioned her sons about the rough hoodlums that they would have to contend with owning a nightclub but her sons never paid attention to her until now because this time they were scared to death.

Mad Dog Coll brought an unscathed George Immerman back to Connie's Inn eager to collect his ransom money. The police waited on the street and inside the club for Dog's drop off of George and a big shootout ensued with George nearly getting shot by the crossfire. Mad Dog fled Connie's Inn without a cent of the ransom money.

The Immerman brothers pledged to their mother that they would ease out of the nightclub business for good. When Harper got wind from the rumor mill of the Immerman's plan to close up Connie's Inn instead of getting the information directly from the brothers he began to develop strong doubts about his role in their future plans and his standing within the famous Connie's Inn nightclub institution.

'Hot Harlem' sooner or later set off on a road tour and the first stop was Hurtig and Seamon's 125th. Street, Apollo Theatre. The official title of the show remained *'Hot Harlem'* but to lure in new spectators the production switched titles calling itself *Connie's Inn 1932 Revue*. Most of the original cast members were onboard but the popular Mills Brothers had departed from the show. Harper expanded the revue to include a gigantic "Dynamite Burlesque" production number. The "Dynamite Burlesque" swelled the sum of the cast to a total of 110 people comprised predominantly of desirable girls. Harper's sought-after chorus girls were termed Cyclones and the Dynamite Burlesque was thought to be the most lavish and bountiful revue ever staged with ticket prices ranging from twenty five cents to one dollar and fifty cents. The *'Hot Harlem'-Connie's Inn 1932 Revue* was transported into B. S. Moss' theatre on Broadway for a Second Edition with a totally fresh cast later on in the same year.

Respecting their mother's biddings, that they were serious about getting out of the treacherous nightclub world, the Immerman brothers withdrew from the Harlem nightclub business. Mrs. Immerman's argument for her sons to leave the nightclub scene was effortlessly achieved as Connie's Inn profits fell down severely during the depression. Connie and George intended to go back to the Broadway area, like they did with *Hot Chocolates'* three years earlier, anticipating that the move would ease their mother's qualms with a new location away from the immeasurably unsettled Harlem.

Harper's new *Ace in The Hole Revue of 1932 of High Yaller Gals* for Connie's Inn was in the mix and the production was transferred directly to the Central Theatre on Broadway and Forty-Seventh Street. Harper's *Ace in The Hole of 1932* crowed a cast of sixty and featured both the shockingly delightful "Snakehips" Tucker and the irregularly amazing "Jazzlips" Richardson along with Baby Cox all performing elaborately staged somewhat-sexualized rhythmical body contortions to the music of Benny Carter's Hot Cha-Cha Orchestra. Watching the chorus line dancing in the show was like observing a speeding locomotive and the girls seemed as if their rear and pelvic regions were let loose off of a highly motorized electric body shock machine. *Ace in The Hole of 1932* also featured the girls portioning up some extreme speed rope skipping while concurrently tap dancing from curtain rise to the finale.

The faultfinders were of the opinion that the elements of Harper's *Ace in The Hole of 1932* revue had been visited before in many of his other shows and though it pleased some of the audience members they would have liked for him to dispense with something a little more fresh and different. During its initial week the audience count for *Ace in The Hole of 1932* was measured as adequate and that was a generous approximation. Maurice Dancer who authored the *Harlem By Night* gossip columns indicated "We pass the Central, where Connie's Inn attempted to invade Broadway for a summer's run with Leonard Harper's "Ace In The Hole" revue from the popular Harlem nite-club. After much ballyhoo, slightly draped sepia beauties, white robed colored doormen and putting the first colored girl in their cashier's cage, with Baby Cox, "Jazzlips" Richardson, Margaret Simms and the Four Bon-Bon's, from their successful "Hot Chocolates" revue, this revue only lasted two short weeks… now the Central is going white burlesque again."

The Immerman brothers, having miscarried on Broadway with the poor notices from Harper's *Ace in The Hole of 1932,* elected to open up a booking agency for African-American acts in the Times Square area with the expectations of developing an entirely different type of downtown trade.

This subsequent booking agency undertaking by the Immerman's to get a toehold on Broadway was a mistaken effort that in due course went belly up. The Immerman brothers carried on operating Connie's Inn in Harlem while they explored other downtown commercial possibilities.

Harper's occupational disappointment with the Immerman brothers magnified. This state of affairs was exacerbated due to the unknown future of Connie's Inn's as a nightclub and the fact that the Immerman's had not let Harper in on their future plans which directly affected him. Harper had been their key in-house producer/stager, whose masterpieces achieved distinction and prosperity, but the brothers took him for granted and left him out of the loop as they plotted and planned their next course of action. Connie's Inn would have been little more than a saloon with music and wouldn't have occupied its astronomical status on the entertainment map had it not been for Harper's floorshows.

Harper hankered for new artistic challenges after conquering Broadway three years earlier with *Hot Chocolates'*. At thirty-three years of age with parts of his interior makeup having never been explored because of his tough work schedule the romance that he once shared with his wife Osceola had mutated into a creature of mere dehydrated marital obligation. Though Harper was encircled by many workmates and colleagues in the theatre sphere he discovered himself to be inadequate personally and professionally, without any tangible channels for emotional expression and these, long time buried intimate blockades were on the threshold of detonation.

Harper quit his job at Connie's Inn in October 1932 and it was reported in the gossip columns that "he didn't leave with a happy handshake" when he resigned. College educated director Ted Blackman was employed as the Immerman brother's new in-house producer to succeed Harper. Blackman, while a contemporary of Harper's and a fine producer/director in his own right, didn't have that extra specific captivating showy aptitude that Harper generated. According to *Pittsburg Courier* theatre evaluator William Smith on October 1, 1932 "the Immermans were frantically searching for a successor to Leonard

Harper and Maurice Dancer suggested Ted Blackman." Maurice Dancer was the Harlem gossip reporter who noted down the *Nite Life Shadows* and entertainment news pieces for *The Inter-State Tattler*. Harper believed that Maurice Dancer had double crossed the line as a journalist because he had no business enmeshing himself in the occupational affairs of Connie's Inn and then writing about it in his gossip column. A slight resentment was fostered against Maurice Dancer by Harper because of his meddlesome interference and press accounts

Teddy Blackman's new Connie's Inn show was titled *Harlem Hotcha* and he did a satisfactory and adequate chore at taking the place of Harper. Connie Immerman assisted as the stage manager/co-director while sourcing many former Harper talents. The decent notices for *Harlem Hotcha* broadened Harper's overall edgy feelings of angst as he questioned his dispensability. Harper paid for a boat ride for some of his friends and showbiz associates to acknowledge and express his thanks for their past efforts expounding to his grateful guests that his signature floorshow productions would have been nothing without their contributions.

Harper vacated his gig at Connie's Inn the same year that he brought his *Savoy Vanities* variety/floorshow into the Savoy Ballroom. Harper's *Savoy Vanities* royally bombed because the patrons wanted to take part and Lindy-Hop leap and step on the ballroom floors for themselves. Harper was stung when some of the intoxicated Savoy customers mocked his show out loud as he strained to pinpoint why *Savoy Vanities* was so disappointingly received. He wondered if he had lost his directorial golden touch. This existing deep deficiency of professional self-assurance was a major turning point during this phase of his life.

HARPER ROMANCED YOUNG FANNIE PENNINGTON

With some of Harper's current productions receiving poor appraisals and walking out on his mainstay at Connie's Inn and with his wife continuously imparting an evil eye in his path whenever he came home he initiated a dogged hunt for an outlet to lessen his present state of agony. Harper obtained contentment in the flowering arms of young Fannie Pennington. Fannie, being fifteen years Leonard's junior, was an aspiring and motivated wannabe showgirl dancer at the time they encountered one another. Fannie, the striking high yellow rubenesque looker, had a history of being awestruck by powerful men of authority such as ministers and politicians. For Harper, the big time director/producer, meeting Fannie was like hitting the jackpot. Equally Fannie and Harper had their rearing in the Baptist/Christian faith as a shared attachment as well as their inherent charismatic dispositions.

Fannie Pennington was born and raised in New York City and from nigh infancy was an enthusiastic member of the Abyssinian Baptist Church. Her papa Matthew Mark Pennington was a native of Macon, North Carolina.

Fannie grew up with the young Adam Powell Jr. and she recalled "It was at one of those Baptizing Sundays that I first remember Adam Powell Jr., who was about thirteen years old, Adam was wringing out his father's robe. He was a tall, skinny and good looking kid who wore knickerbockers." In the early 1930's Fannie decided to run off from her family church for the show business profession. Conceivably Fannie was influenced by the Abyssinian Baptist Church's various art and drama ministries or maybe the handsome underdeveloped and semi-roguish rule breaker Adam Powell Jr., who without approval often slipped a young Fats Waller into the church to practice on the organ. Fannie also attended Bible study with Duke Ellington's sister Ruth Ellington in the Abyssinian Baptist Church's, "Young Thinkers" Sunday school class which was instructed by her buddy the charming Adam Clayton Powell Jr.

Fannie's dad was a cab driver who was familiar with the women who worked at the box office at the Lafayette Theatre and he would often bring his impressionable and unseasoned daughter to see the Afro-American Musical Comedy shows for free. Fannie aroused her memory about how her father adored the *"Bon-Bon Buddies"* the male dancing troupe from *Hot Chocolates'* who sported elongated over-the-top beards. "Papa took me to see Leonard's *Hot Chocolates'* when the show came uptown to the Lafayette."

Another persuasive foundation for Fannie's showbiz inducement came about when she befriended and moved in with the Moses sisters. For a transitory extent of time Fannie dwelled with the very fashionable, curvaceous, captivatingly and ultra-appealing Moses sisters. Lucia Lynn Moses was the principal star of the feature Sepia movie The Scar of Shame and was judged to be America's most stunning African-American star. Sister, Ethel Moses was termed "the Bronze Venus" and for a stretch she performed and danced in Harper's *Keep Shufflin* as well as his Connie's Inn and Ubangi Club floorshows. Sister Ethel Moses starred in many Oscar Micheaux directed films and was "sometimes touted as the Negro Jean Harlow," for her leading lady stints as author Donald Bogle stated in his book *Tom's, Coons, Mulattoes, Mammies, & Bucks*. The other Moses sister was Julia and she was an equally adorable professional dancer and her mannish partner/lover Miss. Camille carried out a little amateur talent managing on the side, amongst other things.

Fannie plunged right on into the wild world of entertainment by relocating into the Harlem apartment of a second entertainment family. Fannie resided with her new chums the vivaciously agile performing McCormick Sisters of the Cotton Club, Connie's Inn, *Hot Chocolates'* and *The Scar of Shame* motion picture fame. *The Scar of Shame* was the white produced African-American premised motion picture. The Afro-Panamanian-American Pearl McCormick and her younger sister Dolly stayed with their parents and brother and sister and were glad to welcome Fannie into their household. Fannie and all of her girl-friends were considered to be the glamour girls of Harlem at the time of its post Renaissance era.

Fannie wished to become a dancer on the stage and screen just like all of her girlfriends. Once she was introduced to Harper her head illuminated like a row of flood theatre lights overflowing and glowing with pipedreams of becoming a big performing star. Fannie recalled how she met Leonard Harper "I met Harper in 1931 or 1932, by being around the theatre with some friends we went out a couple of times. I went to see all the shows and I used to go to places where they sold whiskey but that was around the time when they made it legal. I became friends with Andy Razaf too he was a nice man but was always by himself."

The Harper-Pennington romance consisted of them going to Italian restaurants like Harlem's Domenick's and to the Coney Island Amusement Park. They once traveled to Pompton Lakes in New Jersey to observe a Joe Louis boxing exhibition. Fannie fell in love with Harper not only because he was so nice to her but because as she professed "he treated people nice, pleasant" while opening up a completely new world to her a life of dazzling lights and big metropolitan show business. Fannie said "Harper, I was fascinated by him, being a dancer."

While Harper found Fannie entrancing he wasn't taken enough to relinquish his obligation to his discontented spouse Osceola. Harper's self-inflicted part time dreary enslavement to Osceola became the very reason why he was able to easily wander away from her without regret. Young Fannie the susceptible wannabe hoofer with stars in her eyes and an uninhibited gene had allowed herself to be lead on in Harper's emotionally tart game. Whenever Harper returned to his household cage Osceola was either glaring vacuously at the wall or wickedly eyeing him and it heightened his surreptitious need to be with someone more engaging.

Osceola's concerned mother appeared in New York for a brief visit because she intuitively had trepidations about her daughter's wellbeing. When Harper's mother in-law arrived he was able to alleviate her worries by being a most cordial host. Harper, Osceola and the mother in-law hit the Harlem theatrical party and nightlife scene big time. Osceola's mother returned home persuaded that everything was fine in regards to her daughter who still seemed to be won over by Harper's believable off-stage act.

1933 brought about not only the end of prohibition but official end of the great depression for some Americans. Harper co-choreographed and staged the *Stormy Weather Revue* in collaboration with Dan Healy and Elida Webb at the Cotton Club. This staged edition of the *Stormy Weather Revue* was mounted a good ten years before the movie version was shot and released. The staged *Stormy Weather Revue* had a three month run at the Cotton Club before going out to tour across the United States.

Associate Pastor of the Abyssinian Baptist Church Adam Clayton Powell Jr., who was known to be a regular club goer side, stepped away from the African-American stuffy society class and its world of available tea sipping young Gay Northeasterner debutantes who pursued him whenever he was required to appear at their events. Pastor Powell strategized his marriage to the flaming hot divorced and distinctively high spirited Harper Connie's Inn and Cotton Club showgirl Isabel Washington. Even the pressure of a fractional excommunication from Abyssinian Baptist church for young Adam by his exacting dad the Rev. Adam Powell Sr. didn't sway young Adam away from his anticipated nuptials to Isabel. She was a divorcee, a showgirl who danced in revealing outfits and a Pastor's wife no-no.

The minister and the showgirl made news headlines which gave rise for a much weightier toleration of theatre and nightclub types by church goers. The gap was now formally bridged between the African-American church going public and people of the nightclub/show world. Years later, Pastor Adam Clayton Powell Jr. who also acted in an early church drama titled *Wade in The Water* would become the sanctioned Negro's Actors Guild's Chaplain. These noteworthy undertakings by Pastor Powell validated his potent support for performers and the recognition of them as being fellow children of God servicing followers of the Lord by providing entertainment and it was a belated yet much needed and well acknowledged blessing for the formerly pariah thespians of the Harlem community.

Connie's Inn shut down in the springtime of 1933 and its closing harvested a mute retribution for Harper. The nightclub's collapse confirmed to everyone that Harper's attachment as its producer/stager was at the root of the club's enormous success all along. Harper's resignation at Connie's Inn had all of Harlem and Broadway whispering about his absence being a causative component to its downfall advancing his legendary reputation as a master nightclub floorshow producer. That liquor could be bought and sold legally all over speeded up the ruin of many nightclubs and speakeasies while it eradicated the aberrant elements that went along with them. The venturesome appeal of the nightlife still carried on but with a hobble.

Fannie disclosed her meticulously shielded new surprise to Harper making it known that she was pregnant with his child. That Fannie was with his child freaked him and coarsened his wife Osceola's hostility because someone other than she was producing an offspring for her husband, a task that she was incapable of doing. Woeful with the agony of a damaged marriage and a broken heart Osceola now had something new to add to her list of sorrows.

Fannie asked Harper for nothing now that she was with his child attesting to her tough streak of self-independence. She came to perceive Harper as personally puny and as a matter of fact didn't want to be bothered with him anymore now that the child within her was her sole priority.

HARPER "DUFFED" HARLEM FOR CHICAGO

Harper duffed Harlem absconding from all of his personal and career difficulties when he accepted the proposition to become a full time non-exclusive producer/stager for racketeer Alfonse "Scarface" Capone's Chicago Grand Terrace Cafe nightclub known to night owls as "The Cotton Club of the West". The Grand Terrace was stationed inside of Capone's Grand Trenier Hotel. Once Harper arrived in Chicago it took little time for him to transform Chicago's "Windy City" into America's top nightclub and Afro-American Musical Theatre showplace. Harper, with the swiftness of light, whipped those high mid-western winds into the capitulation of the rhythm. According to the July edition of the

Baltimore Afro-American newspaper's *Downtown in Chicago* section "Harper is so popular that he's asked to assist productions and (other) producers."

Al Capone was a silent backer of Owney Madden's Cotton Club in Harlem and had been a longtime admirer of Harper's works which also played in Capone's Chicago located Plantation Club. But by the time the Capone organization secured Harper as the producer Capone himself was doing his first year of hard federal lockup time for tax evasion.

The Capone Grand Terrace Cafe deal was for Harper to produce on a non-exclusive basis at the highfalutin night spot. The Harper contract was set up by Capone's nightclub manager Ed Fox and the Capone crime family acting boss mobster/accountant Frank "the Enforcer" Nitti with crime underboss Tony Accardo looking over everybody's shoulders. Harper produced at other nightspots anywhere he wanted in Chicago and for other parts of the country as long as he brought in the goods at the lavish Grand Terrace Cafe. While Harper produced floorshows for the Capone/Nitti organization in Chicago he also created theatrical productions for the Balaban Brothers at their Chicago based Regal Theatre.

Harper's supervisor at the Grand Terrace Café was Frank Nitti who at the time implemented a very diabolical and effective unlawful shakedown of the Balaban/Katz Brother's theatrical business generating even more ill-gotten and untaxed currency for the Capone group. Harper's audience at the Grand Terrace Cafe were all white with a small number of African-American pimps who were permitted inside the club to set up bizarre and venturous erotic and narcotic events for some of the affluent Caucasian clients. With twelve chorus girls and twelve show girls in the line-up Harper worked his charm by satisfying Capone's many associates, guests and the general public every time they entered the Grand Terrace nightclub.

Right off the bat Harper was tested by backstage complications with one of his principal cast members at the Grand Terrace Café. The second week of June in 1933 Harper staged his first big floorshow for the

Capone outfit starring Valaida Snow the former precocious little diva girl from Harper's past. The spoiled Valaida Snow used to travel on the road with father John Snow's troupe the Pickaninny Troubadours during her and Harper's childhood pickaninny days. John Snow billed his daughter as the "Great Valaida Snow with her Violin and Bow" and it went to her head. The gifted feisty adult mood swinging Valiada Snow was prone to intolerably stormy temper tantrums. Valaida played a mean coronet a-la Louis Armstrong and her instrumentals were major crowd pleasers as she always knocked audiences dead.

Valaida was staying in Chicago with her husband Ananias Berry of the dancing crew the Berry Brothers who also performed in Harper's Grand Terrace revue as did Earl Hines with his band handling the musical chores. Harper's dance staples Meers and Meers and abdominal dancer Louise "Jota" Cook from *Hot Chocolates'* with a few of his reliable Harlem showgirls joined in with some mid-western additions on the spectacle's lineup.

This specific Valaida Snow program already had been overseen by Ed Fox of the Capone run operation well before Harper came on board. Once Harper took the reins, he and Ed Fox dismissed most of the stage talents including the objectionably self-engrossed Valaida Snow because she acted as if she could not be supplanted. Snow's warranted sacking took place during "a theatrical blood, letting," according to Rob Roy journalist for *The Chicago Defender*. In Roy's June 17, 1933 article titled *Big Shake Up In Grand Theatre/Valaida Snow is Dropped In The New Deal* Valaida "is said to have sought Mussolini powers over things in general at the café." Another June 6, 1933 *Chicago Defender* press article, titled *Valaida Now In The East For A Rest* stated "Valaida Snow, singer and producer of floor shows at the Grand Terrace café in Chicago for the past several months, who was replaced by Leonard Harper at the spot is here now en route back to New York. Miss Snow refuses to comment on the story appearing in the West that she had been dismissed by the Grand Terrace management."

Harper had no option but to terminate the other cast members along with Snow because she had poisoned and indoctrinated the whole on stage lineup against him with her unnecessary ultimatums and it was his onus to shepherd the floorshow without any insubordination. Valaida Snow had been handled like an empress for most of her life and she had come to expect nothing less than getting her way all the time and couldn't relate to people unless they were kissing her ass. Harper retained only two performers from the original floorshow. The hasty canning of the cast and the many creative revisions had everyone realizing that "Mr. Harlem Renaissance" himself was in their city and was prepared to do business.

As a momentary inhabitant of the "Windy City," Harper was able to get familiar with his mother Sarah once again. Gene Harper his struggling and unemployed brother still dwelled with mother Sarah and had a little daughter of his very own named Eugenia Jean Harper. Eugenia lived with her dad and Grandmother Sarah and all of them received supplementary support from Harper's monetary magnanimity.

On September 18, 1933 Leonard Harper's daughter Harriet Jean Harper was born in New York City. The legal birth name of his baby with Fannie Pennington was Harriet but they rarely used that designation instead the delightful little girl was known as "Jeanne", "Jeannie" or "Jean" Harper named after movie star Jean Harlow.

Grandfather Matthew Pennington believed that he was blamable for Fannie's rebellious activities. To make up for the absence of her maternal mother who left him Matthew brought little Fannie to all of those productions at the Lafayette Theatre while employed as a cab driver and he speculated that these early influences caused Fannie to wander recklessly away from the church and into the arms of Harper the theatre man. Matthew "Pop-Pop" coached his granddaughter Harriet Jean to memorize the Lord's Prayer as soon as she learned to talk and the child loved to recite it for all who listened.

Harper had no credible justification for not being in New York City at the time of his daughter's birth as substantiated by his numerous production excursions all throughout the same time period. He journeyed to Harlem from Chicago in the spring of 1933 to direct *Savoy Vanities* for the Savoy Ballroom. The Savoy Ballroom was in trouble as it had to confront new uptown competition from the Dixie Ballroom on 125th. Street, and Seventh Ave. which had its grand opening on March 2, 1933. Harper was implored to return back to Harlem by the owners of the Savoy to make sure that the Dixie Ballroom opening was a catastrophe. He found the time to hire and train twenty-four gorgeous girls, twenty-two male syncopators and two Red Hot dance bands with an all-star entertainment squad for his *Savoy Vanities* Grand Inauguration Deluxe Revue Extravaganza yet he couldn't find the time in the fall of that same year to embrace his wee toddler daughter, hold her in his arms, and kiss her like most doting daddies would do.

According to the theatrical gossip column *Going Backstage with The Scribe* which was contained in the *Chicago Defender,* "(Harper) took off by plane for New York where he was booked to stage the opening floor show to accompany Cab Calloway back into the Cotton Club he set a new record for long distance shows staged in one week. Harper had just witnessed the opening of the show at the Grand Terrace here, which he produced with a combination of Chicago and Harlem talent." This 1933 Cotton Club show that Harper flew to New York from Chicago to choreograph alongside Dan Healy was undeniably a smashing accomplishment which showcased not only Cab Calloway, the Nicholas Brothers, Avon Long and Fannie Pennington's comrade and hang out buddy the knock-em-dead dazzling movie icon Ethel Moses. Ethel wiggled in this Cotton Club floorshow in a *Show Girls* number with two other women and the three of them were considered "delectable parcels of femininity" while they sauntered on the dance floor with large fans to conceal their nudity.

Theatre critic Billie Rowe wrote that Harper produced a show titled *Get Lucky* in 1933 which occurred the very same year Harriet Jean was born. *Get Lucky* was an all-star Western revue featuring Timmie and Freddie a duo brought to Harlem from Chicago by Harper. In October of the same year of 1933 the month after his daughter was conceived he found the time to travel back to New York once again to produce an all-white novelty floorshow on Broadway at Delmonico's. The nightclub was newly operated by Al Delmonico whose family owned the swanky Delmonico Club on Fifth Ave. Harper signed "Noma" the legendary stripper and fan/balloon dancer to headline the floorshow. The revue didn't have an exclusively all white cast even though it was billed that way. At first peek the high-lightened copper-tinged Noma was so flaxen skinned that she fooled everyone into thinking that she was white.

Fannie resided with the stylish singing and dancing McCormick Sisters and their parents at the time of her daughter Harriet Jean Harper's birth and she assigned dancer Pearl McCormick as her baby's Godmother.

Meanwhile in Chicago Harper's mother Sarah insisted that he bring his newly born daughter Harriet Jean to live with her so that she could raise the little girl with Eugenia Jean his brother, Gene's child. Mother Sarah meant well but was excessively maternal and failed to comprehend that Leonard's daughter also had a devoted mother and other family members who had already been nurturing her on the other side of her lineage.

RHYTHM FOR SALE

The winter of 1933 not only brought about the end of prohibition but it was also the year in which Harper staged *Rhythm For Sale* at the Grand Terrace Cafe with musical associate Andy Razaf who professed to be in Chicago just for a vacation with his new writing collaborator the white British ex-vaudevillian composer Paul Denniker. Just like Harper both Razaf and Denniker lodged in their own excessively plush suites at the Hotel Trenier known as the most luxurious hotel to ever cater to African-Americans. These three squires hung out with black beauty business entrepreneur Madame C. J. Walker and her daughter A'Lelia Robinson Walker at the hotel's extravagant banquet room feasting with other thriving African-American elites. In March of 1934 the

Chicago Defender reported that "Harper pays less attention to his chorus girls, now that he's a big Producer". Although Harper was not a chronic drinker he was able to sample his first glass of high-priced sparkling champagne thanks to Capone underboss Frank Nitti. The bubbly was a notably big step up from the traditional speakeasy brand of cheap gin.

One adjustment that Harper was required to institute into *Rhythm For Sale* was the insertion of patron dancing during the intermission. Harper appeared to have understood his lessons from the Savoy Ballroom debacle that he must permit floorshow customers to do a little dancing with each other between sets. He had no choice but to apportion time for the audience and let them cut the rug.

If You Can't Get Five Take Two, No More Thrills, and *Show Me Your Qualifications* are the titles of some of the original tunes specially written for, the show. *Rhythm For Sale* had a sluggish start because of the numerous personnel changes one crucial example was that Earl Hines the nightclub's musical conductor was on the road so Harper had to hire Carroll Dickerson and his orchestra to fill in. Continued cast alterations were critical as Harper had to eliminate all of the components that bogged down *Rhythm For Sale's* opening.

Once *Rhythm For Sale* officially unbolted, critic Earl J. Morris of the *Pittsburgh Courier* asserted the floorshow to be "one of the finest revues in the country-fast, peppy and highly sophisticated." *Rhythm For Sale* played to a full capacity house every night until the summer of 1934.

Harper was able to employ many imported Harlem talents and by using his influence he summoned up some of his big name performers like "Sunshine" Sammy, Baby Cox, the Midnight Steppers, the babyish Nicholas Kids and his Twelve Harperettes. He also employed local Chicago favorites like Della Collins "The Human Violin" who doubled as a dark skinned Mae West impersonator with a blonde wig. It was said that "Della got the Mae West hat, eyes, staff and hips." Rumba Queen Elizabeth Kelly and the Five Racketeers were among some of the many regional variety acts who shared the bill in the *Rhythm For Sale* revue.

"The 'Ol King" funnyman Billy Mitchell a comedian who impersonated Bert Williams' style of jesting was one of Harper's set fixtures at the Grand Terrace Café. 'Ol King' Mitchell introduced the creator of the Shim Sham Shimmy dance Mr. Leonard Reed during *Rhythm For Sale's* kick off. Leonard Reed spoke to Melba Huber on January 1, 2003 for the *Dancer Universe* magazine and said that "The greatest choreographer of my time was Leonard Harper and for five years of my choreographed shows, I stole everything I could that Harper did." Reed also composed a letter regarding Harper stating "My first job with Leonard Harper was at the Lafayette theatre in Harlem in 1927. It was a revue he produced called *Sundown Revue* with Garland Howard. I was featured with Madeline Belt. My next appearance was in 1931 at The Grand Terrace in Chicago in a production called *Death of The Blues*. To my mind in his day, Leonard Harper was the best producer I ever knew about, Black or White. I might add that had he been White, Hollywood would have jumped over a lot of other producers to get him. Connie's Inn would not have been without him."

Harper was coerced into bringing back the bothersome and self-captivated Valaida Snow for several more revues around Chicago town. He had no choice but to summon her reappearance because Valaida was an audience favorite and a crowd pleaser and her skills were eternally in demand by her faithful groupies. This time around Valaida was easy going and less demanding to work with as the trials and tribulations of her life in the fast lane had humbled her considerably. Harper retrieved another personal favorite the adagio, ballet, tango, waltz, jazz, bolero and ballroom interpretive dance act of Norton and Margot. Norton was the son of dancers Lopez and Lopez and Margot S. Webb studied to be a French teacher only to fling away all of her linguistic lessons for the wonderful world of dance.

The comely Margot S. Webb of the distinguished "Norton and Margot" dance team warmly recollected about dancing for Harper "Leonard Harper was a great producer. His shows were always fantastic. He was a perfectionist. I worked for him as far back as 1932, first as a chorus girl and later as a featured act, 'Norton and Margot.' I was in high school when I first met him. He was always kind and patient and helpful to young girls and boys in his shows. When Norton and I started traveling as a team, he always helped us get engagements. We worked with Mr. Harper in 1934 and 1935 at The Grand Terrace in Chicago with the Earl Hines band. We also worked with him at the Apollo (New York) and some of the theatres on the "Black" circuit. Leonard Harper never received the publicity due him in his many years in show business. He was an exceptionally, talented person." Margot Webb had a minor discrepancy with one of Harper's costume and choreography ideas because for a short period he made her outfit up as a dancing French bar waitress. Webb didn't very much like having to be thrown about crossways on the stage every night in an undersized snug outfit capped with a French beret. Margot was immeasurably much more of a classically educated dancer than that, having studied with partner Norton under Monsieur Demax.

Harper was encouraged to reproduce some of his earlier trademark Colored Musical Comedies that were launched in New York like his fast-moving *Pepper Pot Revue* and mid-westerners ate it up. Music wise some of Harper's floorshows were listened to every night over the Columbia Broadcasting System from radio station WBBM/Chicago. Harper branched out to produce in other Chicago theatres and nightclubs like the Oriental Theatre and the "Black and Tan" interracially mixed Midnight Club. The Regal Theatre served the purpose as a parallel venue to exhibit his cleaned up nightclub works for the general public just as the Lafayette Theatre had for him in Harlem. Regular African-American people now had access to his revues outside of the segregated nocturnal nightclub environment.

Once staged at the Grand Terrace Hotel and in the Regal Theatre, Harper was able to disperse his revue's to go on the road with headliners such as the Nicholas Brothers, Mabel Scott and the McKinney Cotton Pickers in his *Pepper Pot Revue*. His touring adaptation of his *Grand Terrace Revue* was dispatched with Earl Hines, Valaida Snow, "Sunshine"

Sammy, the Midnight Steppers, the Harperettes and a whole host of others. One week after Harper's arrival at the Regal Theatre *Chicago Defender* critic Rob Roy wrote "Truly, the Regal has seldom seen such a well-balanced, jazz crazed, dance wild, production as it offers this week."

In May of 1934 Harper made another spree back to Harlem from Chicago, not to see his one year old daughter Harriet Jean or his wife Osceola but to produce a show with his former assistant Clarence Robinson, who now had a magnificent reputation in his own right almost equivalent to Harper's. Robinson was currently the in-house fulltime stager for the world renowned Cotton Club. The Harper/Robinson production that they join forces on was for the Apollo Theatre and Thomas "Fats" Waller was on the top of the bill with shockingly humorous blackface comedian Pigmeat Markham, the riotously senseless John Manson and a slew of other blackface jokers along with Robinson's revue cast of fifty. Harper and Robinson both shared the "Dances By" credits on the African-American Musical Comedy.

One of the real reasons behind why Harper trekked to Harlem and took the gig at the Apollo Theatre was because Frank Schiffman, owner and former employer at the Lafayette Theater, was surreptitiously scheming to take over part of the Apollo Theatre's operations. Schiffman and Harper were on the verge of making a move on the Apollo Theatre's owners and management. The present owners of the Apollo Theatre were Hurtig and Seamon along with Sidney Cohen and the three of them had incurred an outstanding debt of $60,000.

Morris Sussman the manager-at-large of the Apollo Theatre secured the capital to pay off and buy out the outstanding $60,000 past due note. Part of the transaction was for Sussman to acquire the Apollo theatre from his former superiors and previous owners Hurtig, Seamon and Cohen. In January of 1934 Sussman opened up his version of the showplace. Frank Shiffman and his partner Leo Brecher planned to shut down their cash losing Lafayette Theatre in a few months and continued to mount their productions, from their Harlem Opera House located on Harlem's main through-fare and commercial nub, 125th. Street.

Schiffman confidentially informed Harper that he and his partner Leo Brecher intended to make a deal with Morris Sussman because he was only an administrator and not a theatre owner. "Sussman's way over his head with a theatre like the Apollo." Schiffman divulged to Harper that it would be just a matter of time before Sussman would need the assistance of an experienced theatre owner like himself and a seasoned producer like Harper to run a theatrical business like the Apollo. Harper let Schiffman know that "he's in."

Frank Schiffman was a clever, ferocious and super-crafty entrepreneur who situated himself in close proximity to both Sussman and the Apollo Theatre by overseeing Sussman's new theatrical tasks from out of his neighboring Harlem Opera House offices. Schiffman waited it out until the gullible Morris Sussman got into financial difficulty. Schiffman moved in for the kill offering to lend a "helping hand" with a co-ownership deal while presenting the Harper/Robinson and Fats Waller's showcase which opened up at the Apollo in June and played for one week. Harper returned back to Chicago with all of this information about Schiffman's impending designs for the Apollo Theatre stored in his head.

Harper's tempo palpitating *Rhythm For Sale* maintained its run at Chicago's Grand Terrace Cafe and a few months later Harper, Razaf and Denniker teamed up once again to begin work on a new Harper floorshow. Razaf and Denniker were commissioned by Ed Fox at the Grand Terrace to write the lyrics and music for a new rupturing of footwork floorshow extravaganza titled after the Windy City itself *Chicago Rhythm* for a fall/winter debut at the tremendously hot nightclub.

CHICAGO RHYTHM

On August 4th, 1934 Harper staged a Midnight Benefit Show for the N.A.A.C.P. National Defense Fund starring the scorching fan dancer and strip artiste Sally Rand. It was a huge show for Harper to handle because he was missioned to direct all of the floorshows acts which included all of Chicago's, other nightclubs. He had to incorporate revues from the Sunset Royal nightclub, the mid-western Cotton Club-the Grand Terrace Cafe, Dave's hotspot, the Morocco, the Midnight Club, the Talk O' The Town, Shelton's Grand, the 205 Club and the Panama Club. The saving grace for Harper's loaded assignment was that all of these nightclubs were filled with stunning chorus girls. Harper was the stage director for the entire cast of entertainers and a seven piece orchestra was commandeered by Will Vodery as the musical director. Legendary circus animal hunter and collector Frank Buck who was known for presenting untamed wild beasts that he fought to death in his *Wild Cargo* and *Bring Em Back Alive*" documentaries was on the bill reciting spellbinding stories of his adventures with the ferocious animals. Noble Sissle and other lesser acts seamed the audience with twelve of Harper's regular Grand Terrace Cafe talents such as Valaida Snow, Alma Smith, Billy Mitchell, Norton and Margot, Mantan Moreland and George Dewey Washington.

The box office for *Chicago Rhythm* was so healthy that it played well into year 1935, cramming in thrilled audiences at every showing. The column *Going Backstage with The Scribe* likened *Chicago Rhythm* to Harper's co-production involvement with the *Stormy Weather Revue* which previously played New York's Cotton Club. *Going Backstage with The Scribe* imparted that "Not even the 'Stormy Weather' revue that played the Cotton Club out-distanced this one much, save for the appearance of Ethel Waters and Cab Calloway's band."

In the latter part of November Harper produced dual Chicago children's charity shows at the Regal Theatre for Bud Billiken's Aid foundation. One of his productions stemmed from the Grand Terrace Cafe and the other was generated from his current nightclub floorshow at the Midnight Club lead by white showman Jimmy Noone and his Victor recording orchestra. The Bud Billiken charity event was underwritten by Robert S. Abbott the African-American owner of the *Chicago Defender* newspaper and the establishment gave away fifteen free turkeys during a Thanksgiving contest for the best juvenile amateur dance competition winners. All of the 3,000 disadvantaged children that turned up for the Bud Billiken charity got free bags of goodies that year. The generous occasion had the judiciously low admission price of ten cents for the youngsters and twenty five cents for grownups.

In December of 1934 Harper, Razaf and Denniker teamed up once more and crafted an all Caucasian casted show at Chicago's white patronized Club Royale. Joe Lewis the white humorist who went by the moniker the "Clown Prince of the Night Clubs" headlined in Harper's *Royale-Frolics* musical revue. It was Harper who facilitated Joe Lewis' stage comeback after he was declared all but washed up, stuck in the past, and incapable of adjusting or freshening up his material. Under Harper's guidance Lewis was able to work his physical style of comedy such as his fly squashing bit. While at the Club Royale Harper also coached all of the nice looking, white Club Royale girls on how to tap with sepia styled rhythm. The *Royale-Frolics* revue also co-starred the charming blonde singer Etta Reed and the act Mary, Buddy and Dick who tapped to the tuneful number, *Three on a Match* and "Giggles" Regan who cackled melodies from out of her oral cavity instead of singing them. Some of the Razaf, Denniker songs performed in the *Royale-Frolics* were *Shim Sham Shimmy, Melody in Blue, That's What I Think about the South, Nudist* and *Cellophane.*

While Harper's *Chicago Rhythm* was still running at the Grand Terrace Café in 1935 he was also able to take his flashy and tight production of *Red Pepper* to Cleveland's Cotton Club and it was said to be one of his sharpest floorshows ever. Harper transported some of his newly unearthed Chicago performers with his Mid-West chorus girls to Cleveland with him to work the *Red Pepper* revue as Razaf and Denniker traveled down to handle the music chores. Back in Chicago Harper's *Chicago Rhythm* at the Grand Terrace Cafe was pronounced by critic Rob Roy of the *Chicago Defender* as being, "a musical caviar," one of the new songs written by Razaf that accompanied a burning dance number was titled *That's The Jungle In Me.*

Mother Sarah Harper was still on her son's case because she still wished to her see her new granddaughter Harriet Jean Harper. Harper became increasingly fatigued by his mother's relentless expressions of misery over it.

As the spring of 1935 drew near a very remarkable conversion transpired at the Grand Terrace Café, in April the nightclub shut down for several weeks purportedly to recognize the Lent religious sacraments. This closing allowed Harper the time to set up a completely new floor-show with the expectation that the Cafe would soon be opening back up. During this interruption interval Harper sensed that things were not the same within the Chicago nightlife landscape and although he couldn't pinpoint what it was he still perceived a major unnoticed shift was on the horizon.

From Harlem Frank Schiffman apprised Harper that the transaction between him and his associate Leo Brecher to secure Morris Sussman's stake in the Apollo Theatre had been successful and that Sussman had been let go. Harper was asked by Schiffman how quickly he would be able return to Harlem to inaugurate the new bigger and better Apollo Theatre that he "inherited" from Sussman. Former Harper protégé Clarence Robinson was the theatre's interim in-house producer but Schiffman was not particularly satisfied with his work feeling that even though Robinson was competent he still preferred his dependable Leonard Harper who he also believed did a more superior job at stirring and enthusing audiences. Harper let his mother know that he was planning to return to Harlem. Mother Sarah begged and demanded that he take her with him to Harlem so that she could be nearer to her other granddaughter Harriet Jean.

Harper instantaneously duffed Chicago to, return back to Harlem leaving his mother and her, never-ending badgering back in Chicago. Harper had one thing on his mind and that was to become a smashing success as the main in-house producer of Frank Schiffman's new Apollo Theatre. Harper had an extensive history at Billy Minsky's Little Apollo Theatre as it was a first sojourn for many of his touring productions and he also maintained an office downstairs in the nightclub basement club below the 125th Street Apollo. The nightclub back then was called Joe

Ward's Swannee Club and Harper created floorshows for Ward's club as well.

The period of Harper's arrival to Schiffman's newly owned Apollo theatre was described by Frank's son Jack Schiffman as the foundation of the Harlem Heyday years as the theatre was chock-full of major stars and behind the scene stage talents. Jack warmheartedly called to mind "I remember Leonard Harper very well and that he was a good looking, brown-skinned man. He was also one of the most talented of black, producers of his era."

A few months after Harper had left Chicago for Harlem, it was conveyed by Earl Morris in his August 22, 1935 *Pittsburgh Courier-Grand Town-Day and Night* column that, Chicago was not fairing very well. Morris wrote "I remember a time when Leonard Harper could offer a, chorus girl forty smackers a week. Now a girl is subject to all sorts of things in order to eke out a living. There are plenty of cafes, which are nothing more than brothels. Girls are expected to be a little more than a hostess." Mr. Morris' contention was that the Chicago nite-life scene required some sort of dire, urgent and drastic theatre and nightclub reform due to "the practice of chiseling, cheap theatre managers" and he ended his piece with "there would not be so many vacant seats in theatres and clubs if the management would wise up to the fact that you cannot get the best talent for cheap wages. You have to give the public something for their money now. The public is not so easily fooled as in days gone by. It must be the real McCoy." Right after this September article was published Grand Terrace manager Ed Fox visited Harlem and pleaded with Harper to return to Chicago to produce another floorshow hoping for a much needed nightclub revival.

Manager Ed Fox had altered the Grand Terrace Café nightclub's entry policy so it could compete with the other hotspots. By abolishing the cover charges and reducing all of the other prices he figured that he could draw in the patrons from the other shoddier and less swanky South Side Chicago nightclubs. Fox's strategy was to make everything more reasonably priced and it worked. The Grand Terrace Cafe started snatching away a good deal of the business from the other competing Chicago nightspots.

Although Harper was absolutely entrenched in his work in Harlem he nonetheless grudgingly consented to reappear in the "Windy City" once again for Ed Fox but for only very brief extent of time. When Harper concluded staging his last Grand Terrace Cafe floorshow and was about to return to Harlem and start his production callings at Apollo Theatre Ed Fox and Frank Nitti tried to make it problematic for him to depart by pledging him a significantly larger financial take. Harper rejected their generous offer by making a point that he had other contractual obligations in New York. As a good faith gesture he propounded to prepare and practice a specialty line of Grand Terrace Café chorus girls in Harlem to be dispatched out for the Chicago nightclub. The Grand Terrace Café always treated Harper admirably when he was under their employ plus he didn't want to get on the cruel side of these fellows.

Ed Fox made a second pressurized duty call to New York in a futile effort to induce Harper to travel back to Chicago, once again. Fox begrudgingly accepted Harper's terms and took him up on his suggestion to work with the girls in New York and send them off to Chicago without him. Harper trained the chorus line in New York close to his new Harlem dance studio. He coached the young women for ten weeks as Ed Fox remained in New York to monitor the rehearsals. Once the chorus girls got their routines up to Harper's standards they traveled to Chicago with Fox and all parties were satisfied.

Harper was finally able to totally dedicate all of his time toward the revitalization of Frank Schiffman's new Apollo Theatre. Harlem's huge show business population both on the theatre stage and in the nightclub settings braced themselves for the onslaught of much needed African-American Musical Comedy rhythm and amusement stimulation Harper style. Right after Ed Fox arrived in Chicago with the Harper trained chorus line, the Capone family gangsters unloaded their financial interests in the Grand Terrace Cafe as well as the Trenier Hotel and new proprietors took over.

CHAPTER SIX
(1935 to 1937)

UNSEEN PRODUCER/DIRECTOR

Harper arrived to this post-Renaissance Harlem where some politicians voiced out and pandered on about making the required changes to improve the state of African-American New Yorkers. The people of Harlem craved for employment opportunities and were tired of being padlocked out of the workforce. What the people of Harlem additionally hungered for was a setting where they could escape from their existence. A fast moving, funny, African-American Musical Comedy Theatrical show and a speedy moving lively nightclub floorshow revue was just what the doctor ordered. Harper returned back to fill this prescription and medicate the community that helped make him. Harlem's new audience now owned a tough fought bourgeoning awareness of racial dignity.

Harper's apprentice from days gone by, Clarence Robinson, attempted to vacate his position as the outdated Apollo Theatre's momentary in-house stager by acting on his anticipated withdrawal as soon as he was informed that Harper would return from Chicago to become the new permanent production chief. Robinson hoped to leave Frank Schiffman high and dry during the short-termed Harper transitional phase as a way of saving face occupationally. Robinson fabricated a yarn that he was going to Europe to stage a show yet he lingered on and resumed his work at the Apollo for the few weeks before Harper's arrival.

Robinson's high stepping chorus girls were called the "Rockettes" and they were ousted by Harper's assemblage of "16 Harperettes", "Harper's Apollo Beauty Chorus," "Harper's Dancing Dolls," "Harper's 16 Lovely Brownskin Gorgeous Cuties" and "Leonard Harper's Prize Chorus". Clarence Robinson later became part of a cluster of supplementary stagers that rotated in the producing chores beside Harper at the world famous Apollo Theatre.

In the early years Harper had churned out many shows at the old 125th Street Apollo Theatre and had also staged musicals when it was known as the Hurtig and Seamon Burlesque House prior to Mayor Fiorello LaGuardia's shutting the old Apollo stage down due to public indecency. After his acquisition, Frank Schiffman was spending large sums of money to refurbish the Apollo theatre which prided itself on its 1500 seats, four floors and thirteen dressing room accommodations.

After Mayor LaGuardia had the "Tree of Hope" chopped down in front of the Lafayette Theatre, Frank Schiffman was able to secure the illustrious oak tree stump from dancer Bojangles Robinson who contributed it to him at the Lafayette Theatre. Schiffman carried the "Tree of Hope" stump with him to his new Apollo theatre. The Apollo Theatre performance acts got accustomed to rubbing the tree stump for good luck just as they did during the Harlem Renaissance when it was located on the Seventh Avenue thoroughfare. Schiffman, the biggest employer in New York of an African-American offstage workforce, had big plans for his new showplace and scheduled forty two shows a week and six shows a day trusting that Harper would have all of the 1500 seats filled.

Harper's charge at the Apollo was to slickly interlace all of the variety acts within the assorted productions. He had to make sure that all of the featured acts that came on stage between the dancing chorus girls and boys and comedy skits meshed together with the specialty numbers. This alone was not enough as Harper had to also make sure that everything seemed novel, glitzy and rousing. Harper was also accountable for choreographing his signature chorus line of girls and boys with breathtaking firecracker perkiness during every show and have them live up to their reputation as the best damn chorus line in the world. Most importantly "The Harperettes" must open with a lighting start then fill in the "dead" spots and close the show with a stirring finale. A number of the more dynamic Chorus girls were jobbed to play minor roles in comedy skits and on rare occasions assist with the live animal acts. Sometimes these spicy terpsichorean cuties would have to make up or copy dance routines on the spot in seconds. The late great Leroy Myers of the famous "Copasetics," the league of topnotch Tap performer's whose task was to reawaken the dance, said of Harper "He was one of the greatest and the most closely associated stage producer with the Apollo theatre".

Later on Frank Schiffman engaged other first-rate dance directors who had hitherto either created musicals for and under or with Harper like Clarence Robinson, Charlie Davis and Addison Carey. With four principal acts per-production and at least seven sub-structural acts as stuffing, the contracting of additional producers was a no brainier for Schiffman. This forthcoming action also lessened Harper's workload significantly allowing him the ease and opportunity to work in other nightclubs and theatrical venues energetically.

In July of 1935 Harper was one of the dance directors for the *Cotton Club on Parade 26th Edition* which unbolted at the original Harlem Cotton Club. Harper also took on additional producing assignments at the downtown Broadway Connie's Inn location where he directed both the spring and fall editions of *Connie's Hot Chocolates'* with co-director Teddy Blackman. Occupied as he was, he still found the time to produce and stage brand new floorshow revue spectaculars at the Smalls Paradise Club and the Ubangi nightclub.

The visiting bands at the Apollo had to acclimatize with pit seats that were much too miniature for their meaty hindquarters. During some of the first Harper productions Schiffman was compelled into detaching the undersized seats after a number of the band members found their behinds wedged between the arm rests and had to be pried out by the stage crew. Harper, ever the improviser, had the big bands play right up on the stage while sitting on transportable upright chairs. Schiffman's cost cutting on the tinier new seats for the orchestra backfired and he was goaded into purchasing larger seats to accommodate the more portly of the musicians.

At the Apollo's backstage entry doorways on 126th street was a small area where genial gatherings of theatre people and their followers coolly grooved together, gambled, played basketball, discussed politics, imbibed, got high and goofed off between stage stretches.

Many well-known big shots made unexpected backstage visitations when Harper returned to helm the Apollo Theatre's 1935 Grand Inauguration Premiere. The exciting and amiable Louis Armstrong would drop by because he had gone head over heels in love with his future wife and Harper Apollo chorus line dancer Lucille Wilson. The effervescent and happy eyed Lucille Wilson did a turn as a dancer in one of Lew Leslie's *Blackbirds* and was presently one of Harper's chestnut skinned Apollo Harperettes. The skin pigmentation prerequisites and restrictions for Harper's chorus girls had slackened off noticeably as many African-Americans embarked on the extended cultivation of racial pride demanding that all shades of their race be recognized and treated as full-fledged American citizens.

At twenty four years old it was Lucille Wilson who helped fracture the color line for chorus girls when she was hired by Harper to dance in one of his *Cotton Club on Parade* dance lines. Wilson also happened to be a good chum of Fannie Pennington the mother of Harper's daughter Harriet Jean Harper. Fannie and Lucille were former classmates having both attended Harlem's all girls Harriet Beecher Stowe Junior High School named after the author of *Uncle Tom's Cabin*. When Lucille hooked up with Armstrong he often drove both Lucille and Fannie to Yankee Stadium to check out the Bronx Bombers. Quite often Armstrong would emerge from the backstage street during one of Harper's Apollo showcases popping out of his shiny car with chocolate chip cookies and flowers under his arms for Lucille.

Both Harper and Schiffman got to work preparing for their immense *Apollo Theatre Grand Inaugural Week Leonard Harper Stage Production.*

Schiffman signed up Lillian Armstrong and her band. Lillian was the first and "every now and then" wife and business consultant of Louis Armstrong. Frank didn't have to shell out too much money for Lillian and he was nevertheless able to get the Harlem crowds to squeeze into the theatre because he duped ticket purchasers into thinking that Satchmo Armstrong himself was either coming to make a cameo appearance or that he had something to do with the orchestration of his wife's band. A few of the suckers who trampled into the Apollo like sardines also assumed that Lillian must be just as brilliant a musician as her husband. Mrs. Armstrong did swing in tuneful smartness during the Apollo Theatre's *Grand Inaugural Week Leonard Harper Stage Production* opening and the customers got their money's worth. Lil Armstrong hoggishly held onto most of the disbursements that was supposed to be payment for band while she compensated the ensemble personnel with a measly five dollars apiece nightly.

HARPER DID THE UBANGI CLUB…TOO

It was the summer of Harper's first year at the Apollo and he was taken into service to produce nightclub floorshows at the Ubangi Club. On July 23, 1935 he went to work hard and fast and opened up with a brand new floorshow. The Ubangi Club was located in the same basement space that Connie's Inn occupied on Seventh Ave. between 131st and 132nd street and was named after Africa's Ubangi River and the Congo tribe which inhabited the area. The Ubangi Club had an integrated multi-racial and gay accommodating open door policy which at long last welcomed the African-American inhabitants of Harlem. During the post-depression years the Ubangi Club had no option but to initiate an unrestricted access policy as most of the affluent whites no longer found the pastime of slumming up to Harlem for hot jazz, risqué shows, soul cuisine, drugs or anything exotically black interesting enough or worth the cost of admission anymore. Uptown club owners were financially driven to allow anyone that paid cash inside of their clubs no matter what their race or sexual preference. Stately African-American Harlemites who were only allowed in as nightclub food and drink servers, custodial staff members or entertainment merchants were now accepted inside the club as patrons.

Now that little "Sunshine" Sammy was fully grown up at the ripe old age of twenty three years the former *Our Gang* juvenile star was able to persuade Harper to cast his practically teenaged twenty year old cute as a button wife Annette McAbee as a "Ubangi Club Girl" chorus line member. Harper advertised the precocious diminutive Annette "as the tiniest chorus girl to ever perform on stage". As usual "Sunshine" Sammy had just as much backstage drama behind the curtains as Harper had him provide on stage to his audiences. Sammy's public fights with his young bride were salacious and they took on deep sexual inflections. The turbulent marital problems Sammy had with Mrs. Sunshine Sammy were extra sour because Sammy's father who also acted as his manager joined in the skirmish mix. Daddy Morrison resented his daughter-in-law's participation in Sammy's affairs. Papa Morrison also conjectured that Annette's manipulation would wreck the career schemes that he had for Sammy's future with his jazz band. Most importantly the teensy and sensuous Annette endangered Daddy Morrison's arrangement to uninterruptedly jockey in on his son's economic gravy train.

Andy Razaf penned the majority of the music librettos for Harper's *Ubangi Club Follies* in 1935. The following year had Andy Razaf and Harper working with some very able collaborators such as Paul Denniker, Alex Hill and Fats Waller. These talents together all inscribed and created the music for Harper's 1936 Ubangi Club smash revue titled *Round N Round In Rhythm.* Selected listings of the memorable tunes from the *Round N Round In Rhythm Revue* were the songs *Beautiful Legs* by Waller and *My Joe Louis of Love* by Denniker sung by the sinuous torch songstress Mabel Scott.

Earlier Harper appointed a former dancer named Llewellyn "Lew" Crawford as his assistant. Lew Crawford was one of the Bon-Bon

Buddies in Harper's 1929 *Hot Chocolates'* and was placed on call for twenty-four hours and seven days a week now that his boss was back in Harlem and based at the Apollo theatre and in serious need of an around the clock subordinate. Llewellyn was later bequeathed with the designation of Harper's officially sanctioned secondary at the Ubangi Club.

Pearl Bailey's elder brother Bill Bailey was another highlighted player in several of Harper's Ubangi Club Revue's. At the Apollo Theatre Harper/Schiffman promoted Bill Bailey as *Bojangles the Second* or, the *Junior Bill Robinson*. Bill Bailey was a warbling, tambourine spanking and tanked-up unconventional tap dancing showman years before the Lord put a cap on his whiskey bottle, sobered him up and summoned him to be a caroling and boogying minister just like his father.

Harper was able to rotate unyielding sexuality mores in the opposite direction and backwards then inside out and gyrate them, 360 degrees theatrically speaking while working at the Ubangi Club. Harper casted a "fella" named Toni Stuyvesant and he utterly mystified Ubangi Club regulars who thought that they were in a *Ripley's Believe It Or Not* because Mrs. Toni was so convincing as a woman that he/she was touted as the act that performed "things you can't afford to miss." Harper also had casted Gladys Bentley the delightfully voiced Harlem fixture as his Master/Mistress of Ceremonies. Gladys was the deliciously charismatic near 300 pound overweight lesbian male impersonator who was constantly decked out in full formal male "butch" attire.

By far the most dazzling and outrageous gay act that Harper presented at the Ubangi Club, were the jazzy jigging Ubangi Club Boys and their dance parade. The Ubangi Boys were not simply openly gay but they were six lavender lads who flaunted their sexuality and partner partialities with a relentless and shamelessly frisky audaciousness. Harper was even able to farm out his merriment loving, hammy and flirtatiously flamboyant Ubangi Club Boys for road trips to other theatrical venues and they sashayed and shimmied in their loose satin pants and teasingly suggestive outfits all the way into the laps of delirious if not red and blue in the face nightclub audiences. With names like Fifi and Clara Bow what would one expect from these secret men of the, twilight. The press asked "Take three guesses, were they girls in slacks or boys in sashes?"

The particularly well liked Fannie Pennington had countless personal acquaintances that she hung with such as the enticing dancers Edna Mae Holly and Cleo Hayes. Cleo was branded as a snazzy dresser and "Mississippi's gift to Harlem". Both Edna Mae Holly and Cleo Hayes were featured entertainers in Harper's Ubangi Club productions.

The compellingly fascinating and bracingly forthright dance artist Cleo Hayes evoked the period when she worked for Harper "I met Mr. Harper and started working for him at the Grand Terrace in Chicago then, I came to New York City when he became the main house producer at the Apollo Theatre. I worked for him at the Ubangi Club on Seventh Avenue too. Mr. Harper was a producer who could put together the whole show. He would tell the dance captain how to stage the dance steps, but the show was his total creation. He conceived the whole production, band, comedians, sets… Mr. Harper, he could dance he didn't have to depend on the girls to work out his routines like Clarence Robinson and the others. They would show pictures. To Mr. Harper, it was not a plaything it was a business. He was paid to produce, that was his living. He did everything with his feet. Hard stomping dancing, he worked hard shows. I thought, Mr. Harper was a P.I.A. (*"Pain in the Ass"*). I can see him right now with his little fat stomach sticking out. Mr. Harper wanted things done his way."

As Cleo Hayes indicated, at this juncture in his life Harper was by no means the skinny high bounding quick footed boy of his formative years as all those generous servings of fried soul foods prepared by Osceola that he devoured revealed itself on his belly. In 1941 the Ubangi Club closed at its Harlem location and resurrected itself in the same year on Broadway and Fifty-Second, Street only to finally close down for good.

FANNIE AND POCKET-SIZED HARRIET JEAN HARPER

When Harper returned to Harlem to help open the new Apollo Theatre a soft spot in his core that he never knew existed awakened and he became sparked whenever he interacted with his two year old daughter Harriet Jeanne-Jean Harper. He was profusely spellbound by his sweet offspring. His daughter had triggered his delayed and inactive fatherly instincts to finally kick in.

Fannie Pennington resided two blocks west of Harper and Osceola's Harlem apartment building. Fannie's apartment building was also the home of two of the most magnificent looking African-American women on the planet the Moses sisters who were also featured in many of Harper's Ubangi Club floorshow revues. Ethel Moses was the most entrancing of the three siblings and the one who owned a deep husky voice and she lived elsewhere. Harriett Jean harked back to her youth as a laughing toddler when all of the Moses sisters bathed and combed her hair something they often did. Julia Moses along with Miss. Camille her loving gay companion and sister, Lucia Moses babysat Harriet Jean for Fannie even taking the cheerful little moppet on lengthy sightseeing bus rides.

Harper would pick up his little daughter from Fannie's house and take her on tender and passion filled jovial walks through the neighborhood park and he paid attention to Harriet Jean as she recited The Lord's Prayer something she loved to do for all of her family members. Harriet Jean remembered affectionately that at just two years old she asked her father for some "appetite" leaving him befuddled until he figured out that she was really asking for "applesauce." He purchased ice cream for her in its place. After dropping Jean off at Fannie's apartment the memory of his little daughter's adorable innocent love for him frequently brought Harper to tears. Harper tried his best not to let Osceola know too much about his daughter and Fannie but because they lived in such close proximity it was impossible for her not to have some knowledge of it.

Harper spoke to his mother Sarah detailing his close bonding encounters that he underwent with his daughter. He told his mother about how pleasing it was for him every time he escorted little Harriet Jean to the playground and described his quality time with her expecting that Mother Sarah would be delighted now that he was behaving like a mature dad. Instead his reports of Harriett Jean harvested the reverse outcome in Sarah and tore away at her heart. Sarah Harper broke down whenever her son informed her about Jean Harper and she got down on her knees and begged God for the day to come when she might be able to help raise her new granddaughter just as she did with Leonard's brother, Eugene's little girl Eugenia Jean Harper. Harper comprehended the consequences of his actions, that it was a grave misstep to converse about his daughter with his mom, but it was much too late. Mother Sarah passionately and endlessly demanded that he move her to Harlem from Chicago so she too could get with her new granddaughter Harriet Jean.

In 1936 Harriett Jean Harper was three years old and the acting bug had bitten her mother Fannie Pennington. It was only a matter of time before Fannie would try to make a go of it on stage under the bright footlights what with all of her showbiz friends and having a daughter with the man who ate, slept and perspired Copper Colored Musical Comedy and variety floorshow revues. It was a gutsy and emotional decision for Fannie because her sister Amelia had gone into show business as a dancer and died on the stage floor at 16 years old in 1931 due to a ruptured appendix. Fannie recalled "For a time I left the church to try show business. I went on tour as a dancer and I danced upstate New York. But my feet hurt and that life was not for me. I went to a few little places to dance, but I didn't like it and I wasn't much of a dancer. I did clubs and theatre up in Boston, New York State, Philadelphia and one time they were supposed to go to Pittsburgh, but it was too far from home, so I quit. I went with Dolly and Pearl McCormick (*Hot Chocolates'* dancers). Pearl was my daughter Jeannie's godmother. Later we traveled with a dance group and we danced one time in Newark, New Jersey in a theatre. The whole black variety show went with us. A Black & Tan show, the white show came on first, and then we came on. I had a lot of friends in it and I was hoping that I could be as good as they were, but I wasn't. My heart wasn't into it like the other girls and I wasn't much of a dancer. They turned out to be Cotton Club dancers. I wasn't in it that long. I worked downtown in a club called the Kit Kat."

Fannie performed in the Kit Kat Club which was owned by suspected goon Julie Podell, who didn't want African-Americans patronizing his spot. The club was full of hooligans and the New York State Liquor Board padlocked its doors because they peddled and provided whiskey after prohibited hours. On the evening that the Liquor Board closed the nightclub down, more than one hundred African-American entertainers, cooks, waiters and service people were hurled out onto the sidewalk and out of employment.

Fannie ruminated about her brief spell on stage "Yeah we did two or three little numbers and we had a tap dancer and a comedian. In 1936 I would go up to the White Tower Lodge in Pleasantville, New York. That's when I became good friends with Elvira "Baby" Sanchez (Sammy Davis' mother)." Baby Sanchez was Sammy's very well kept Cuban-American mother who in fact came across looking many years younger than her talented young son.

The White Tower Lodge was one of the nightclub resort venues where Fannie performed during 1936 and was defined in their publicity material as "The first of its kind to throw open informal doors to out-of town pleasure seekers." Fannie's suitor at the time was Ray Scott who managed the White Tower Lodge. The Lodge was an excellent get-away place for New Yorkers who desired to escape the City because it was just seven miles beyond White Plains, New York amidst the backdrop of millionaire estates. The White Tower Lodge featured a huge lawn garden, tennis courts, wide croquet court and loads of country flowers for all the city folks to enjoy while they forgot all about the concrete sidewalks of New York.

The Master of Ceremonies at the White Tower Lodge nightclub used to traffic his miniature piano from table to table just like the one

Fats Waller used years ago in Harper's floorshows at the Kentucky Club/Hollywood Inn. Quite a few of Harper's celebrity and semi-celebrity cast members traveled up to the White Tower Lodge resort for the evening shows to relax and get away from it all. It was reported that after she finished her own late night Manhattan nightclub café performances Billie Holiday scuttled up to the White Tower for their distinctive weekend break of day breakfast presentations.

According to Fannie "when Joe Louis won a prize fight against a white fighter one of the white drug store workers from across the road came into the lodge yelling "the Nigger won, the Nigger won." The White Tower Lodge was charred to the ground by intolerant and green-eyed white upstate New Yorkers who begrudged the inflow of African-Americans in their countryside hinterland and detested the reality that some Negroes were prosperous and accomplished. The Caucasian upstate residents could not tolerate the fact that African-Americans were allowed into such a charming vacation resort.

MOTHER HARPER RELOCATED TO HARLEM JEAN HARPER LEFT FOR DOWN SOUTH WHILE-FANNIE'S ON THE GO

Jean Harper recalled her pure formative years with fondness "at the age of two and a half years old I was put on a train by my grandfather Matthew Mark Pennington. The decision to send me to Macon, Georgia at such a young age was made by my mother's side of the family, so I could have a proper Christian upbringing. Perhaps because my mother was young and single at the time or it could have been because my father, nightclub producer, Leonard Harper's mother Sarah (my grandmother) was interested in taking me away from New York to Chicago to live with her and my mother's side of the family feared I would never be returned. In any event it was at the time of the beginning of World War Two and all of our working parents sent a lot of us children down south to live with our grandparents or other relatives."

For Harper these times were exceedingly challenging for him emotionally and he finally gave in to his mother's plea to relocate her to Harlem. A 1936 press clipping in the *Chicago Defender* read *"Leonard Harper is playing host to his mother, Mrs. Sarah Harper and his young niece, Eugenia Harper and has set up a nice apartment for them in Harlem."* Harper brought his mother and niece Eugenia to New York from Chicago by train and moved them right into Fannie Pennington's Harlem building. Fannie ever the ferocious independent was still moderately fond of Harper but had simply moved on in her life having never besought a dime from him. Fannie's intentions for a life in show business were in full swing and she was now miles away from little Jean for brief periods of the time.

When Fannie was away struggling to make a name for herself on stage her dad Matthew "Pop-Pop" Pennington was the one who actually reared his granddaughter. Matthew, the dedicated Abyssinian Baptist church official, along with the remainder of their enormous God fearing clan never accepted Fannie's theatrical objectives.

Harper muddled matters further for himself by carrying his three year old daughter to his apartment causing a dreadful squabble with wife Osceola. Jean remembered "There was a lady sitting in the living room and she looked mad and mean. She said to my father 'So this is Jean.' They went to another room and argued some more. I wanted to cry."

Matthew Pennington and his daughter Fannie were reasonably distrustful of Sarah Harper moving into the same apartment building as Jean so they rapidly formulated a plan to transport the little girl down south to North Carolina to live with other family members.

Fannie reminisced "Papa always taught in Sunday school, he was an Usher, Sexton and a Trustee, Papa never came to my shows. I'm sure he didn't like me trying to get into show business, but he, never said nothing." Matthew wanted his granddaughter, now known as Jean, to be nurtured in a wholesome Christian atmosphere far away from razzle-dazzle inducements of the stage.

The closest thing Jean Harper ever came to any stage during the course of her life was singing in the choir section of the Abyssinian Baptist Church with its Gospel Choir. Harper was saddened when he got wind of Jean's southern move because his innocent daughter was the only individual that didn't place demands on him.

Sarah Harper was now living in the same Harlem building as Fannie but without Jean and they often dropped in on each other. Fannie revealed "Sarah Harper was a nice lady and I remember her other granddaughter Jeannie Eugenia, because she used to sing in the courtyard downstairs."

Harper authorized his assistant Llewellyn "Lew" Crawford to reach out to Fannie with a job hiring offer for her to perform at the Apollo Theatre as a way of throwing her a bone and getting into her good graces again. Fannie was no longer attracted to the stage and definitely not interested in working under Harper's direction. With that decision she effectively renounced her dreams of ever becoming a chorus line dancer for good and secured a job at Harlem's fabulous Palm Café also known as "Harlem's Home to The Stars". First she was at the cash register then moved up the ranks to become a barmaid surrounded by the same theatrical showbiz and gangster types she supposedly just left behind.

As for mother Sarah Harper she didn't stay in Harlem too long after becoming conscious that she would never get to meet and abduct her other granddaughter Jean. Mother Sarah ultimately moved back to Chicago after accepting that her splintered delusions to raise her famous son's little girl as a member of the Chicago Harper clan would never come true.

Harper saw his daughter from time to time after she grew up and moved back to Harlem. Even though their get-togethers were brief and scarce both he and his daughter were pleased to be in the company of one another. Jean called to mind that her father would always give her money whenever she went to visit him at his modest central Harlem dance studio. Jean recalled the large studio being in a brownstone with all of the rooms filled with huge mirrors. She admired his prominence in the same way that she marveled at her mother's attractiveness and popularity. Jean occasionally dropped in on her dad at the Apollo Theatre with her girlfriends because it was on the way to the Lowes Victoria movie theatre. One of Jean's teenaged pals Betty Saunders remembered Harper standing in front of the theatre wearing very polished big wing tipped shoes and fine clothes "and as he gave Jean money he looked like a pimp."

In Congressman Charles Rangel's book with Leon Wynter titled *And I Haven't Had A Bad Day Since: From the Streets of Harlem to the Halls of Congress* the ace politician inscribed of Fannie's bartending days fondly "I still joke with her about how so many years after our Jocks days, she found Jesus and I found Congress." Fannie who always regarded the Abyssinian Baptist Church as her spiritual family joined many of the church clubs and volunteer groups while she took work as a part time barmaid at Jocks and the original Red Rooster. Fannie also became deeply immersed in the equal rights movement while working out of the Democratic Club with Congressman Adam Powell and many of New York's political elite.

Fannie Pennington never set foot on the theatrical stage again but in 1952 she did join a Harlem social club called "Bel-Viv" with the Adelco Theatre Award founder Vivian Robinson. In 1973 Fannie was on the "Friends of Josephine Baker Committee" along with Honi Coles, Harold "Stumpy" Cromer from "Stump & Stumpy", Josephine Primice, bandleader Teddy Hill, Hazel Scott and other showbiz notables. This esteemed committee welcomed the world famous Josephine Baker and her International Revue featuring Bricktop with the George Faison Dance Experience back to Harlem from Paris for an uptown midnight show.

As things turned out, Ms. Pennington's decisiveness to decline Harper's proposition for her to dance in the Apollo Theatre chorus line was spot-on. Harper might have attempted to procure the benefits of being her boss by misusing their past personal association for his own see-sawing individual esteem issues. The other good reason Fannie's pass on Harper's Apollo deal was the correct one was because of what he was to initiate on the amorous front while he was producing his *Round N Round In Rhythm* floorshow at the Ubangi Club.

Round N Round In Rhythm was reportedly the speediest and most jazzed up show of the season. Harper's eyeballs darted just as rapidly as all those quick dancing feet on stage as he maneuvered in the direction of one of his previous chorus girls who emitted all of the poise, pizzazz, and pungent pottage he craved. His gesticulations to seduce this, endearing lass were more fast-moving than the nippy winks of his eyes. Harper took on a new girlfriend and she was one of the Lang Sisters. The Lang Sisters were part of a trio of three young women that only the previous year had graduated from the Harper chorus to form a variety tap dancing trio of their own. The Lang Sisters were not actually blood sisters and their chief was twenty four year old Marion Worthy and the other two members of the company were twenty one year old Ludie Jones and twenty three years old Peggy Warton.

All of the Lang Sisters lived with their parents at the time of their origin and they were high-grade enough to play the Radio Keith Circuit and the Paramount Theatre where they opened for the Leonard Harper produced Louis "King of the Trumpet" Armstrong production. Along with a host of other variety acts, the Lang Sisters went on to tour with the Armstrong revue. Peggy Warton was the frisky one of the bunch and she was also the brand new girlfriend of producer Harper. Peggy had a nickname for her new man she called him "High-Top," in private and when socializing with intimate friends. The relationship was like a brief fling or a short but delightful vacation.

Ludie Jones one of the Lang Sisters summoned up the past "Harper staged my group the Lang Sisters Trio when he helped produce and kick off Louis Armstrong's new all African-American production at the Paramount Theatre on Broadway. It was wonderful, a great big stage that moved. It was the first ever appearance of an African-American show at the Paramount under a new policy. We were not real sisters, the name Lang just sounded right. Harper was like our tutor and he had us doing fast kicking and high-stepping routines in flash, bellhop, porter and night robe costumes. Harper dated one of the girls in our act her name was Peggy Warton. Mr. Harper would later make Peggy an official Harperette. We also worked for him at the Ubangi Club and I danced for him with the Apollo Theatre Chorus line, too." The third Lang Sister, Marion Worthy, later left the trio to perform solo in one of Harper's Apollo Theatre Revues.

THOSE FABULOUS HARPERETTES

On March 21, 1936 *The Baltimore Afro-American* newspaper's *Stage-Theatrical World-Screen* section printed a large set of photographs under the title *Stars of Tomorrow-Twinkle Today*. The montage of images consisted of Leonard Harper seated on the edge of a stage encircled by his Harperette chorus line. At both sides of this picture are magnified close-up headshots of each girl along with their names and nicknames below their likeness. Above the photograph of Harper and sandwiched between the highlighted designation the line read: "Leonard Harper, the Flo Ziegfeld of Harlem, who has discovered and trained more beautiful girls than any other producer, is seen with a bevy of his Apollo chorines." Below the photograph of Harper and his name the byline read: "Above is a group of the Apollo Theatre Chorines who are rounding out their second year under the deft hand of Leonard Harper, Harlem's ace producer and discoverer and trainer of talent. These young women, from all sections of America, comprise his number one unit. He has six such groups, which are kept constantly working in the Apollo and theatres in Philadelphia and Washington. One group remains at the Ubangi Club. Out of these groups he involves the stars of tomorrow. These girls do a new show every week, 52 weeks a year, and are always ready with new routines when the program changes."

In the aforementioned *Stars of Tomorrow-Twinkle Today* photographic layout Harper seemed awfully jolly, comfortable, and in his element as if he didn't want be anywhere else than with all of his lovely young dancers that were encasing him. The girls in the photo seem similarly as ebullient as they cozied up to their boss.

The Harperettes and the Apollo Theatre Chorus line were swappable augmentations of Harper's imaginative concepts and according to Jackie Lewis Parton one of his dancers "Harper didn't talk to us chorus girls anymore instead he gave his orders through his assistants." The Apollo Theatre chorus girls were at the top of their game at this time in history and they were all in fine and great shape. If one surveyed a little closer beneath the surface their undisclosed inner work related irritations would be apparent. A consciousness was beginning to set in with these gradually maturing ladies and it was about time. Father time was catching up with them as they started grasping the idea that they weren't receiving the full monetary recompense for their talents that they so richly deserved.

It wasn't the 1920s anymore and some of the girls were now full grown women who were starting to fret about their futures. The Apollo Theatre was a secondary phase in terms of stage occupational highpoints for many of these dancers with their initial Connie's Inn, Cotton Club and Grand Terrace Café days being the first glamour chapters of their careers.

If something went askew with an act in a stage comedy spot at the Apollo, Harper's job was to save the show by hurriedly propelling his showgirls from behind the curtain to perform in a mixed assortment of dance routines in various tight-fitting outfits. He would dress them as Drum Majorettes, Spanish Maidens or Cowgirls to inspire sexual fervor within the male audience members and fuel the faraway and romantic fantasies of the ticket buying females.

Another reason why things were not all that "honky-dory" for the Harperettes was that the experience of bigotry and ghettoization barred them from contracting continual work on "The Great White Broadway Way." Only the extremely light skinned Afro-American girls who could effectively camouflage their racial selfhood by passing for white could procure any semblance of regular Times Square employment. Most of these multi-talented Afro-American girls were able to execute much more than just dancing because they were required to. Not only were some of these gifted young women able to rock the roll and belt out a tune they all were also able to dance with prohibitive punts and eye catching footwork. When these ladies participated in comedy skits their prankster roles were so convincing that audiences presumed that they were certified humorists. Alas the only way American audiences could enjoy their wonderful stage gifts was to come uptown and see them either at the Apollo or during one of Harper's nearly passé Harlem nightclub cocktail floorshow revues.

The complications that the chorus girls had to cope with were compounded by the fact that their salaries were so low and it resulted in many of them having to struggle just to get by from week to week. It also took a terrible toll on their performances and deposited extra hefty burdens on their psyches. In 1936 columnist and stage critic for *The New York Age*, Alfred A. Duckett wrote of the advancing lack luster and fluctuating presentations and overall shabby state of the Harperettes in his *Seeing The Show* column. Duckett said "Perhaps we are too harsh on the Harperettes but the thrill is gone. When they drift across the stage in the same old bored manner, we find ourselves concentrating on the details of the scenery. We must say that a rather good job is done by creating atmosphere."

THE WORLD FAMOUS APOLLO THEATRE…Y'ALL

Harper began to question his status in theatre and had to handle the reality that he was no longer the thin and slim performer who merrily sang and danced about the stage. He begrudgingly glared into a backstage mirror and was no longer able to favorably reflect upon the twinkling images of the glory days of his ancient Connie's Inn, Cotton Club and Chicago's Grand Terrace Café floorshows.

Harper was beginning to recognize that the Apollo's audience's gradual boredom of his formulaic comedy, acrobatic and novelty-specialty acts also included his celebrated yet distressed chorus line. The primary draw for the Apollo customers had increasingly become the big band-jazz acts like Ellington, Armstrong, Basie and the up and coming Ella Fitzgerald. Like most people do when their status is uncertain Harper began to display hints of anxiety. Although he was satisfied with his work at the Apollo and the Ubangi Club and proud of his downtown Cotton Club revue as well as his scaled back production work at Small's Paradise Club the shift in audience discernment stalked most of his jubilation with an ill-omened whiff.

It was commonly known among show business circles just how autocratic Schiffman was in terms of deal making. For instance Schiffman had decreed that any acts that played in Harlem's Alhambra Theatre located just around the corner from the Apollo would not be able to play in his theatre. Schiffman contracted Blanche Calloway to get back at her brother Cab Calloway because he performed at the Alhambra. Blanche even received top billing with Schiffman labeling her the "Queen of Hi-De-Ho" even though compared to her famous sibling she was deficient in the talent department. Schiffman also banked on the idea that gullible African-Americans would pay top prices and wait in droves to see the cut-rate sister Blanche expecting that the crowds would mistakenly believe that the same talented Calloway blood flowed through her veins and that she would give a show as equally robust and enjoyable as her brother Cab.

Schiffman's blackballing of acts that performed at the Alhambra succeeded in most instances even though big names like Ellington did whatever they wanted to and were never intimidated by him. Schiffman was never the less triumphant enough to ultimately drive the Alhambra theatre into locking its doors and ending its live theatrical operations. The Alhambra was compelled into restricting itself into operating just as a full time motion picture theatre house with RKO.

Things did not always go Schiffman's way for instance when he signed the big African-American Hollywood movie star "Stepin Fetchit"

He had no alternative but to give into Fetchit's outrageous requirements if he was to secure the actor who made a name for himself on the silver screen by portraying the lazy-good for nothing stereotypical Negro. Fetchit insisted on a Chinese collapsible serving tray, a Chinese tea wagon and an Asian tambourine to go along with his precondition for an all Chinese appearing chorus line and faux Chinese looking singers dressed in his mandated Chinese wardrobe disregarding anything remotely Afrocentric.

Frank was also known as a very benevolent fellow at times making numerous no interest loans to a few of his down on their luck talents that performed on his stage. But they had better pay back on time or else they would have to face the nasty, ill-tempered side of Schiffman. If an act didn't pay back their advance they would get an I.O.U. after performing instead of a paycheck on their next performance payday. The exclusion to this rule was Big Mama Bessie "Queen of the Blues" Smith who never put up with any of Schiffman's cunning bookkeeping or payroll gimmicks. Full-sized Bessie would get into chaotic drunken eruptions inside the Apollo theatre lobby if she didn't collect her salary or an upfront advance before she was to step on the stage. Schiffman always yielded into Bessie's demands because he was deathly afraid she might sit on him and wrap her humongous arms around his head and cause him to suffocate.

Like the time when she appeared in *Leonard Harper's League Of Rhythm Revue* in 1935 once Mama Bessie Smith got her money, she always gave the much appreciative Apollo audiences a tear inducing, piss in your bloomers show of a lifetime while she tore up her numbers and broke down the blues.

Schiffman's notorious financial sleight of hand subterfuge with his talent contracts where he would actually pay an artist only fifty dollars then alter the contract to reflect a much higher payment such as $100 was a technique that he started at the Lafayette theatre. His artists would never grumble about getting the lesser earnings because they knew that they could bring the fake $100 contracts and shop their wares in downtown playhouses with expectations of garnering higher performance wages.

If an act flopped or was roundly jeered off the Apollo stage by the disorderly assembly they got a callous dead embrace from Frank Schiffman backstage. Hugging was his inimitable way of banishing the dreadful entertainers into their own theatrical graveyard without them knowing it. The acts that got squeezed by Schiffman never walked out on his stage again.

Harper was well aware of just how shrewd Frank was from their old Lafayette theatre days and would stand in his Apollo theatre office quietly taking notice. Harper observed as Schiffman booked the bigger name acts during the weeks that the welfare checks were distributed. For now Harper was protected from getting one of Mr. Schffman's famous hugs.

Harper and his fellow show folks were in high spirits about the planned inaugural of a new uptown reworking of the Plantation Club in Harlem because it meant more work for them and also it opened up the prospect of a revitalization of the Harlem Renaissance. Harper had prior difficulties with a previous Plantation Club launching when an entrepreneur named Oscar Ruby sought to unveil his rendering of the club off of Lenox Avenue and 126th Street.

At the outset Mr. Ruby gave the impression that he was doing everything properly. Firstly, Ruby hired Harper to produce the floorshow revues then he commissioned top notch interior decorators to install beautiful wood flooring along with his purchase of classy chairs, tables, mirrors and drapes. Oscar Ruby wanted his new Plantation Club to have a stringent private membership only policy with a handpicked clientele of only the most affluent of New Yorkers gaining entrance while he promised to put over 100 black people to work as stage talents, doormen busboys and toilet cleaners.

With all of the currency Ruby had to throw around for his new undertaking he made the grave blunder of not including protection payments in his budget to keep the many criminal organizations that were flourishing in Harlem off of his back. During the Plantation Club's decorating process thugs made an evening visit and chopped up his dance floor and orchestra platforms then shredded apart his beautiful piano with ice picks, axes and crowbars. Ruby's new electrical equipment and pricy mirrors were demolished as well. The exquisite new paintings that he bought and was so proud of depicting scenes of the Southern African-American way of life were slashed and torn from their frames and all of Harper's new chorus line costumes were slit and sliced to ribbons. Even the rumors that the Immerman brothers were silent partners with Ruby couldn't halt the attack. Without kissing the pinky rings, of the Harlem mobsters Oscar Ruby pigheadedly still opened up his Plantation Club and on the second day an investor with the club named Harry Block was murdered. This time Ruby and everyone else involved got the message that this attempt at opening a new Plantation Club in Harlem was kaput.

The original Cotton Club closed its uptown doors in February of 1936 and opened its Broadway version in September of that same year at the very location that Broadway's Connie's Inn had just been padlocked. The Broadway Cotton Club proved to be another short lived novelty site for whites and sightseers to experience a Colored floorshow without having to trek up to Harlem. After four lean years of struggling to stay afloat the downtown Cotton Club was also shut for good.

On December 12th 1936 Bojangles Robinson celebrated his fiftieth anniversary at the downtown Broadway version of the Cotton Club and Harper was a guest. At 3 p.m. on the same day before Bojangles had his Cotton Club party New York's Mayor Fiorello LaGuardia came to visit him in his Harlem apartment. One could only imagine what it was like for Mayor LaGuardia to have driven past the barren area on Seventh Ave. where he so callously had the "Tree of Hope" amputated. Mayor LaGuardia also schemed for the shutdown of the Savoy Ballroom because of the barrage of objections from his prejudiced constituents about blacks and whites who enjoyed dancing the Lindy Hop with each other as mixed race couples. LaGuardia ultimately closed the Savoy Ballroom because of the mixed race dancing and socializing.

CHAPTER SEVEN
(1937 to 1942)

HARPER DID THE *DOWNTOWN* HARLEM UPROAR HOUSE

Theatrical entertainment proprietor L. Jay Faggen was one of the two financial backers of the Savoy Ballroom which was Harlem's response to Broadway's Roseland Ballroom. Faggen had been a longtime aficionado of Harper's. Harper's floorshows for Faggen's new downtown Harlem Uproar House, which they termed "Revusicals", were filled with lots of low cost titillating burlesque strip-tease stylized numbers that intertwined throughout and within the acts that were filled with layers of hot singing, tapping and bucking splits. The Harper sets were comprised of jungle habitats, island witchcraft voodoo beaches and Asian and uptown street scenes that were also part of the nightclub's exotic anywhere but downtown New York artistic getaway themes. Harper with his Harlem Uproar House "Revusical's" followed the quick invented pattern of "newsreel theatre" by offering a ninety minute program that included his signature floor burning fast dancing chorus lines with the music of two orchestras that played live rhythm constructed jazz compositions for six shows each night.

The quandary that the Harlem Uproar House bumped into was that Harper included not only mixed black and white race acts but that some of the jazz band members were of dissimilar racial configurations as well. As the year 1937 moved on toward the winter so did Adolf Hitler and his wicked armed forces of Nazis who advanced on Europe to fulfill his personal desire for world domination.

While the majority of Americans disputed Hitler's homicidal exploits and declarations about the superiority of the Aryan-Indo-European race there were a number of illiterate "Uncle Sam" styled bigots who abided by his demonic statements and activities. With Hitler's upsurge these ugly Americans were empowered and encouraged by his provocative anti-Semitic and anti-darker race Nazi points of unreason from abroad. These home grown crackers occasionally stormed into engagements and such was the ill-fated case for the Harlem Uproar House which became a target of its own awkward place in time as the extremists who called themselves the "Night Riders" submitted to Hitler's immoral instructions and took it out on the nightspot by destroying the property.

Harlem Uproar House owner Jay Faggen got a phone call warning him against hiring a black and white swing band because too many white male musicians were looking for work on Broadway. The "Night Riders" broke into the club and demolished musical instruments, stands, chairs tables and other furniture then smeared the place with ink. They left a huge swastika painted on the dance floor with an inscription warning the club not to hire the racially mixed jazz bands. Many of the musicians feared for their lives.

Harper reappeared at Small's Paradise and this time it was to become the nightclub's key in-house producer after owner Ed Small's grumbled to the press in a piece titled *If There Were More To Watch, There Would Be More To Work*, that not enough African-Americans were frequenting his joint. Ed Small's believed that the Afro-American nightclub goers were waiting for white people from downtown to come up to Harlem and formally validate his club like in the good old days of the Harlem Renaissance. Small's worried that if he didn't drum up business "toot-sweet" he might have to shut down his hot-spot due to a lack of incoming cash. To quote Ed Small's from the aforesaid press item "If there were more to watch, there would be more work. I could put more of these girls to work if Negroes would patronize their own nightclubs. They are waiting for the whites to do it and the whites aren't coming uptown to Harlem anymore."

Ed Smalls trusted that Harper could single-handedly fetch the white late night crowd from downtown and have them coming back uptown to cram the seats in his diminishing nightclub and this in turn would cause the local Harlemites to flock inside of his mixed race hangout once again. Harper always inculcated to his Smalls' Paradise chorus lines and dance staff to adhere to the dictum "Watch my swing and watch my rhythm" so bringing the master floorshow producer into do what he did best was logically a no brainier for its owner. Small's hunch was right, local African-Americans were being encouraged to see a Small's Paradise Harper nightclub floorshow along with white customers and it was a slight affirmation that equality was on the horizon for some members of all races.

St. Claire Bourne the sports and entertainment reporter for the *New York Amsterdam News* wrote an article dated October 2, 1937 titled *Small's Offers Speed, Rhythm In New Show* about Harper's new Small's Paradise revue titled *Harlem Jamboree*. Bourne wrote the following "A capacity crowd, including a very liberal representation of whites, was on hand to greet the rapid-fire revue with wall-shaking applause which was deserved. The new vehicle which will delight Harlem stay-out-lates during the coming season is the work of Leonard Harper, with music by Edgar Dove and arrangements by Billy Grey and speed combines with dazzling flash to make it a show well up to the standard which has maintained the Paradise as one of the most rock-ribbed ramparts of the Harlem Dawn, Patrol."

Harper's Small's Paradise staged production of *Harlem Jamboree* had a corps of light-footed singing and dancing waiters who exhibited "first-class" tray spiraling. It's hard to believe but the wait staff didn't drop many portions of chow or whiskey on the customer's happily bobbing heads or laps. The *Harlem Jamboree* acts performed on a small stage and they consisted of Margaret Watkins a transplant from Harper's Chicago Grand Terrace shows, Leon Hill a poor man's facsimile of "Snakehips" Tucker who had since passed away, and Alice Porter a songster who harked back to the good old days of Harlem yore. Oran "Hot Lips" Page and his twelve-piece band offered up the music along with twelve other variety attractions.

The jazz bands that accompanied Harper's revues during this particular period at Small's Paradise had names such as Sausage or Ikky Meyers and his Tramp Band. Though these schooled jazz musicians were humorous and hammy in their performances with homeless "Hobo" stage theatrics, audiences weren't the least bit fooled and recognized that beneath all the jesting the bands were made up of dynamic musicians who conquered the musical sounds of Ellington, Waller and Armstrong with crude buckets, simple kazoos, outdoor washboards, and household broomsticks.

Broadway producers started flocking uptown and spending time in Harlem all over again as they came to gaze at Harper's feverishly snappy Small's Paradise floorshows. Harper dressed his chorus girls as firecrackers in skimpy bikinis with headgear that gave the impression that every time the ladies shook their rear ends the lids of their fused topped bonnets were about to explode.

Many of Harper's initial Apollo theatre shows were standing room only as Harlemites congregated to see sidesplitting corked up comedians Pigmeat Markham and John Mason. These uproarious men ran about the stage in blackface rotating their colossal eyeballs and flapping their animated lips. Markham was either being chased by a ghost or an ominously relocating tombstone in many of his priceless skits. You had to be there to understand what is was like to see big man Markham doing the new dance steps he created and staged with Harper called *Truckin* with Harper's new chorus called the "Truckin Maniacs". Actually Harper introduced *Truckin* six years earlier at Connie's Inn as confirmed by renowned columnist Walter Winchell and Harper featured it in the 1935 *Cotton Club Parade*. During the early years the Apollo Theatre authorized Harper to structure goliath production routines around his dancers who employed jerky body refractions and unlawful rhythm timed leg struts.

Comedians John "Spider Bruce" Mason and Dusty Fletcher performed their popular *Open the Door Richard* skit about an inebriated tenant trying to get in his apartment on a ladder without waking up the landlord who was trying to collect the back rent he was owed once awakened. Mason also executed his individual signature bit where he got his African-American wife pregnant who delivered one black child and one white baby. Mason's character begged the hospital staff to bill him only for the black child.

Life imitated art when comedian John "Spider Bruce" Mason launched his Bar-B-Que and Chicken Loaf eatery on West 126th Street one block up from the Apollo theatre. During the restaurant's profile-raising grand opening, Mason barbecued and fried food for the sexy Harperettes. While scrambling at his counter Mason wore his outrageous blackface makeup and with his wide spacious fanatically blinking eyes "Spider" said in his mindless waggish voice "I'm just trying to fatten up these glamour girls, with this good food" as he mugged it up with his greasy fried food. With an oily spatula in his hand "Spider Bruce" puckered up not to bite the spare rib but to lean over the counter to bite and look up the dresses of the amused tiny skirted dancers.

All sorts of solo dancers from handicapped hoofers to the circus novelty categories performed in Harper's Apollo showcase productions just as long as they had that spirited rhythm element. Take for instance the man who pirouetted on top of his homemade xylophone and wowed audiences with not only his dexterity but with the soulfulness of his tunes.

The one and only "Porto Rico" a former stagehand used to sprint out on stage and shout poisonous swearwords at deserving unqualified acts while running them off stage with a large hook or waving a gun or other clown props at them to leave. Years later "Sandman Sims" continued to badger abysmal Apollo theatre acts in the same fashion that Porto Rico did but with more dancing in his repertoire. Sandman Sims carried on his career by sourcing from Harper's 1942 dance invention from *Harlem Cavalcade* titled *Pushing the Sand* which became a popular sand dance sequence long after the Apollo Theatre's Golden Age had come and gone.

The in-house dance choreographer to Motown Records performance artists Cholly Atkins told of his obtaining his very first start after being employed in 1932 by Leonard Harper at the Apollo Theatre in his autobiography. Cholly Atkins' book is titled *Class Act: The Jazz Life of Choreographer Cholly Atkins,* by Cholly Atkins and author Jacqui Malone. Cholly danced for Harper when he was part of the sensational talented acrobatic dance threesome called the Miller Brothers and Lois. Cholly and his trio were put on the Apollo theatre bill as a second act under Ella Fitzgerald and her band in 1941 and the trio later performed under Harper's staging in Ed Sullivan's 1942 *Harlem Cavalcade* during its Broadway and Harlem run. Harper choreographed the Miller Brothers and Lois to "prance fearlessly and well on dizzying contraptions" in *Harlem Cavalcade* according to *N. Y. World Telegram* critic John Mason Brown. Harper also had them hoofing on-top of three miniature stages which gave the impression of enormous brick construction blocks not unlike what audiences would see at a three ring circus and they performed with unbelievable, agility.

Cholly stated in *Class Act: The Jazz Life of Choreographer Cholly Atkins* by co-author Jacqui Malone, that "One of those times when I was lying around, starving to death, Maggie lined something up for me at the Apollo with producer Leonard Harper. She told him, 'Why don't you get Cholly Atkins to do a couple of chorus line numbers for this show?' Mr. Harper asked me to do a special number to a tune called "Every Tub," with headliner, Count Basie's band. You talking 'bout swinging! That was the first piece I choreographed at the Apollo. Then Mr. Harper got to the place where he'd just call me up, 'I'd like you to come do a number for me, man.' These were spot assignments. I'd go in there and he'd give me forty or fifty dollars for one piece, which was a lot of money at that time."

Indications that the Apollo Theatre was a swinging rocking and rolling rhythm musical mecca during the years of Harper's regime are in Jesse Stone's accounts in the Nick Tosches book titled *Unsung Heroes of Rock' n' Roll: The Birth of Rock In The Wild Years Before Elvis.* Jesse Stone was in on the early evolvement of the birth of "rock n roll" and produced Ray Charles and the Drifters for Atlantic Records. Stone was also known as the down home blues and rhythm songwriter who penned and composed two of the first great rock themed hits *Shake Rattle and Roll* and *Money Honey*. Jesse Stone also co-wrote the music with James P. Johnson and Dan Burley for Leonard Harper's 1941 Apollo Theatre production of Abram Hill's *'On Strivers' Row'* and he composed the music for *Sensations Of 1943* which was to be Harper's very last floorshow at Murrain's uptown nightclub.

Jesse Stone stated in Tosches section titled *He Who Controls Rhythm* "I started working for the Apollo Theatre. This was right after it had been turned over from being a white burlesque house. I worked for Leonard Harper, staging shows, composing songs, writing jokes and routines and such for comedians—Pigmeat Markham, Dusty Fletcher, Sam Theard. Acts came in, did a week, then they'd be gone. I filled in missing parts for musician's arrangements. I'd add a trumpet part that was missing, a couple of saxes or something. When I started at the Apollo, I was making $15 a week. By the time I left, I was making $300." Duke Ellington got Jesse Stone his first job at the Cotton Club in 1936 and Ellington even hooked Stone up with a Harlem apartment just a few buildings away from where he used to boarder with the Harpers on Seventh Ave.

Blackface Negro comedians deteriorated artistically during this period because of the humiliating "Cork" makeup, full-sized lip gestures with the sluggish spinning of the eyes and the continual practice of using the word Nigger as part of their stage routines. Apollo owner Frank Schiffman annoyed by the constant complaints from the N.A.A.C.P. and from his audiences barred the use of the word Nigger on his stage. Frank set off the expulsion of the blackface comedy acts and it was only on the rarest of occasions when a blackface comedian could surface on his stage.

As distinguished dancer and Apollo Theatre manager Honi Coles put it in *That Vaudeville Style: A Conversation with Honi Coles, Running With Ghosts* by APF, author Mel Watkins "Most of them were totally natural, what you saw on stage was the same thing you saw on the street. Stepin Fetchit didn't consciously make fun of black folks; he was acting out his sense of what black folks were about. It wasn't a matter of doing an impression of a black man, that's the way it was. At that time that's all a black man could do; he was either a waiter or a porter, or in some subservient position. Mantan Moreland also-with the buck eyes, gleaming teeth, running away from ghosts-there was some truth to that."

A lot of time-worn "Corked-up" comics felt naked without the blackface makeup and with the Apollo Theatre audiences unable to view their painted embellished lip and eye movements and with Schiffman's restrictions their livelihoods came to an end as comedians. Only the most decidedly proficient and malleable of the former professional blackface jokesters were able to outlast the cultural revolutions of their stage inventory.

Many white talents as well as their agents from William Morris to the Associated Booking Agency journeyed up to Harlem to see many Harper Apollo productions. Big stars like Betty Grable, Franchot Tone and Burgess Meredith who took seats in Harper's audience came to be inspired by the rich variety spectacles.

Leonard Harper's most faithful devotee was the up and coming *Variety* and *New York Daily News* columnist Ed Sullivan. Sullivan treasured Harper's works from way back and had been harvesting variety production show advice from Harper during his Connie's Inn nightclub days. Sullivan was eager to become a producer like Harper and he got his chops wet in a variety revue called *Dawn Patrol* in 1935 with Harper's inspiration.

Harper brought a revue out to the Folly Theatre in Brooklyn, N. Y. in1938. The show was titled *Hot Harlem* and it was a regurgitation of his 1932 Connie's Inn *Hot Harlem*. This new incarnation featured a number of variety acts such as Rubber Neck Holmes who dressed in a flaming red suit, the Six Whirlwinds-Lindy Hoppers, Rhythm Brown who tap danced while on roller skates and the trio Swan, Lee and Jackson. The band on deck was the Gary Lee Orchestra. The theatrical trade publication *Variety* described Harper's Brooklyn *Hot Harlem* as being a "Fairly well produced unit. It's entertainment of a sort but not powerful enough to carry it into higher scale spots. Producer is inclined to drag it out in spots, especially with dances. Twelve-girl line, the Harperettes, is capable enough, but is hampered by poor costuming. Standout of the line work is a Scotch number midway, done to a swingy 'Loch Lomond' piped by a male backstage via the public address system."

This dated version of *Hot Harlem* got just a mediocre reception but when you added all the problems that Harper was undergoing of late, his disgruntled chorus girls and the general discontent of most of the African-American variety acts in terms of compensation, future gigs and audience demands for headliners, it's not hard to understand why Harper at this point was periodically agonizing from mild to torrid states of occupational disconcertion.

Internally Harper was spiraling downward because he hadn't really cultivated anything but his theatrical life and that was forsaking him bit by bit. His wife Osceola for good reason gave the impression that she only cared about his take home pay while his mother Sarah who always had a place in her heart for him was aloof to him because he was incapable of delivering his daughter to her. His brother Gene and his former girlfriend Fannie and his daughter Jeanne, were now so far removed from his orbit that he had no socially inter-relational personal interactions away from his stages.

EV'RY SHOW'S GOTTA HAVE A FINALE

1939 was the year in which Harper began to experience firsthand the direct effects of his personal and professional downward tumbling along with many of his present and previous performers. Thomas "Fats" Waller was still able to deliver the musical goods on stage like the well-oiled musical utensil that he was but his performances were hampered because of too much alcohol consumption. At one point in his appearance Waller crawled out on the Apollo stage stark-naked except for the whopping curtain draped around his sweaty plump body.

Backstage Harper found his past Connie's Inn musical collaborator crying like a baby and whining about all of the money he owed out in back taxes, alimony and the loans he borrowed. Thomas Waller was also exasperated by the "clownish" image that he created for himself and questioned why nobody took him seriously. All the colored buffoon film parts with the constant rolling of his eyes while playing piano had taken its toll on the musical genius and he longed for some serious recognition.

Harper noticed as Ethel Waters' persona transfigured to that of the weighty maid/servant in maternal perpetuity singing with servitude wise-wisdom only a slave can emit while cleaning her boss's house or washing the master's family's dirty clothes. To make matters worse Ethel's husband/manager mishandled and robbed her performance payments as soon as Apollo owner Frank Schiffman remunerated her.

Duke Ellington was no longer the bug-eyed easily persuaded Harper boarder as he had become musical nobility and with all that notoriety and prosperity came, added accountabilities. Ellington at this juncture required the same quality in the performances of his band members that he had always expected of himself. His musical virtuosity would every so often lead to dispositional irascibilities when his performers were not up to par and didn't measure up to his musical standards.

Louis Armstrong's drawback at the time was that he hadn't evolved with the times sufficiently enough as a newfangled cultural consciousness had overcome Apollo audiences. A portion of Armstrong's act was to self-mimic his persona using his Southern origins while bursting slamming jazz rhythms out of his trumpet. One of Satchmo's prearranged stunts was to rush out on stage with his pants down to his ankles in an effort to telegraph to fired-up audiences that he was so full of smoking music that he had forgotten to put on his trousers. But once the laughing was over Armstrong got down to the business of sweet swinging sounds. The spinning of his eyes along with his syrupy hard whiskey invoked voice and the handkerchief were all part of his act that was gradually more difficult for politically alert black Apollo audiences to digest.

A publicity photograph and notice about Eddie Green's Sepia Arts Film Company and his motion picture *Dress Rehearsal* was arranged by Frank Schiffman. Harper and Apollo theatre manager Jimmy Marshall had little to do with the film except that it screened at the Apollo on September 30, 1939. *Dress Rehearsal* was a bonus special attraction to a Harper produced live Tiny Bradshaw showcase in the Apollo Theater. The use of three African-American men under the employ of Schiffman was a politically correct maneuver because Schiffman had recently been denunciated for offering contemptuously and insultingly low rental fees to screen films acted in or produced by Afro-Americans in his theatre. The difficult to release and low budgeted African-American film company titles were incapable of making returns when screened at the Apollo and the distributors charged Schiffman with trying to put them out of business.

The black film firms contacted the N.A.A.C.P. with their grievances but Schiffman succeeded in keeping the N.A.A.C.P. off of his back by flaunting his proof that he was a past president and the chief investor in Oscar Micheaux's Fayette Pictures Company. Frank Schiffman's strategic press releases, like the photograph featuring Harper and Marshall for the film *Dress Rehearsal,* was another technique he exploited to hush his detractors.

The N.A.A.C.P. held private meetings with the motion picture studio heads in an effort to try to convince them to be more, fair and balanced in their portrayal of people of the darker race. The N.A.A.C.P. meetings were closed door as they locked out the very talented actors that understood the topics and hindrances best. Actor Clarence Muse and his fellow African-American screen stars were just mere throwaway subjects of discussions. Bojangles, Stepin Fetchit, Louise Beavers, Paul Robeson and Hattie McDaniel were not brought into the N.A.A.C.P. deliberations or even asked to give their seasoned advice on how to best rid the industry of their racially destructive and stereotypical roles and hiring practices. The N.A.A.C.P. conferences with the Hollywood film studios went round and round in circles as the Hollywood lip service machine churned out long winded and inadequate results.

A few months after the 1940 N.A.A.C.P. motion picture get-togethers, the Twentieth Century-Fox Film Corporation snidely released their *Tin Pan Alley* movie. This same *Tin Pan Alley* casted white actors as jail cell convicts to have written the song *Honeysuckle Rose* from Harper's *Load Of Coal* revue. The slap in the face to the genuine Harper composer/collaborators Andy Razaf and Fats Waller was a racial snub not only because of the shameful prison setting of the white film characters but because of the lack of screen credit for the actual African-American men who wrote the hit tune. All of the other white authored songs signified in *Tin Pan Alley,* were correctly credited by their original authors.

HARPERETTES WALKED OUT OF THE APOLLO THEATRE

Harper's quandaries with his Chorus Line intensified during 1940 with the girls striking against the Apollo. Harper was in the middle of the crisis because even though the girls worked for him, as the Apollo's in-house staff producer he had a redundant allegiance to the owner/manager Schiffman who signed his paycheck. Harper needed those girls to shroud his Apollo shows during high spots and to bandage up the sluggish bumpy patches. Without the chorus line there would be substantial intervals of blank spaces within his theatrical productions. All of the other Apollo stage acts backed the chorus girls and unified with them in their walkout as Harper stood on the outside of this very troubling labor dispute.

Public support, along with other Apollo theatre performers who sympathized with the chorus line, forced Schiffman to agree to the terms demanded by the Actor's Equity, the American Guild of Vaudeville Artists and the Harlem Labor Union, all affiliated with the American

Federation of Labor. The girls then joined the American Guild of Variety Artists.

Once Schiffman resolved the labor dispute he set up another one of his well thought out publicity photographs, this time with five of the Apollo Chorus Girls peering over his shoulder triumphantly while his facial appearance concealed his suppressed resentment for having to sign the new work agreements and pay the girls more money. One way or another Frank was going to figure out how to cut or eliminate the chorus line altogether in order to continue making a profit at the Apollo. When and if Schiffman ever did get rid of his in-house chorus lines it would be akin to giving Leonard Harper his hug into Apollo theatrical oblivion. These newly agreed to legally binding contracts with the Apollo Chorus Dancers were costly and in the foreseeable future there was no getting around a tight surgical restructuring.

Besides having to upgrade the pay and work standards of the chorus dancers Schiffman was on the verge of coming in at a deficit at the Apollo anyway because some of the biggest Afro-American acts that played there were able to negotiate better deals for themselves with greater fees at major white theatres as they garnered unprecedented acceptance. These big league talents refused to return to the Apollo Theatre unless Schiffman could match the ducats. Changes in audience tastes had quickly gone overboard and manifested one night as Apollo patrons in the first ten rows jerked the seats into fragments demanding that the theatre feature only the main headlining acts. These fanatics no longer tolerated the distraction of having to sit thru Harper's dated variety filled formats of comedians, dancers, singers and skits before the headliners hit the stage.

At one noteworthy William Count Basie topped show audience members who were labeled "lindy-hopping jitterbugging hepcats" revolted and triggered an unruly brouhaha. The Apollo seats were impaired after these teenagers tugged off the arm rests and chucked them onto the stage until Basie came on to perform with his band. The opening variety acts waited backstage in dismay as a suffering Harper told them to calm down and that Schiffman would work things out.

Harper anxiously needed to find a production vehicle which could return him back to big time Broadway. With his new production of *On Strivers' Row* he assumed that he had a very good shot. *On Strivers' Row* would not be just another black Musical Comedy revue because it had a book with a plot and a strong connecting through-line with a story written by Abram Hill who had just co-founded the American Negro Theatre Company. *On Strivers' Row* previously had a profitable run with the American Negro Theatre and the Rose McClendon Players as a straight comedy drama before Harper got his hands on the, material. The thinking was that once he perked it up with strong singing and refashioned the piece with intelligently rhythmical foot work *On Strivers' Row* had the potential to be an inspirational blockbuster and Harper's path back to the "Great White Way."

Harper had a field day with setting up the scene of the 133rd Street Jitterbugs who while in the process of breaking up a snotty Harlem high society party shook their "pork rinds" till their butts vibrated off. Harper condensed *On Strivers' Row* to the standard revue size of just ninety minutes long. Harper had the pick of the litter because of all of the marvelous and exceedingly skillful African-American performers were out of work for long stints during this time.

Harper's confidence about the unlimited possibilities for his version of *On Strivers' Row* was due to the fact that three other African-American Musical Comedies were recently presented at the Apollo. One of them was *Tan Manhattan* with music by Eubie Blake and lyrics by Andy Razaf. *Tan Manhattan* had just been bought by the Shubert Brothers for a possible Broadway run. According to author Barry Singer in his book *Black And Blue-The Life And Lyrics Of Andy Razaf* "The supporting creative staff (of *Tan Manhattan*) was equally impressive. Addison Carey, second only to Leonard Harper as a Harlem revue producer, was chosen together with the great tap master Henry Le Tang, to choreograph *Tan Manhattan*."

On the adverse side of Harper's buoyant plans for a big Broadway reappearance with *On Strivers' Row* was the reality that "The Great

White Way" was governed by theatre bigwigs whose only intention was to extract and make use of just enough Afro-American flavor to mislead audiences into imagining that they were experiencing some sort of authentic Negro production without having to hire the actual behind the scenes above-the-line colored contributors. *On Strivers' Row* never ended up on Broadway just like its forerunner *Tan Manhattan* and after a fleeting tour in the wake of a week's run at the Apollo Harper's version of *On Strivers' Row* never opened up on any stage again.

From July until September 1941 for approximately seven weeks Frank Schiffman shut down the Apollo Theatre for restorations. The Apollo was a symbolic essential for the Harlem community because it was a reminder of their entertainment aptitude which ten years ago witnessed its legendary artistic Harlem Renaissance. Many popular Harlem nightclubs and theatres closed down but with the Apollo being open, the people of Harlem were able to remind themselves of the good old days of the Harlem Renaissance and look with pride to the home-grown stars that had risen up and become famous. The Apollo kept hope alive in the hearts and minds of many Harlemites who believed that better days were just around the boulevard.

Schiffman dismissed the girls in the chorus line along with everyone else while the Apollo shut down for renovations. No other club had the funds or was willing to hire the Apollo Chorus Girls during this period and they were left out in the cold without any income until the Apollo's fall opening. The girls were now card carrying members of the American Guild of Variety Artists the theatrical union which mandated that they were to be compensated at least at the minimum union wage.

Schiffman used this off time period to evaluate his production budget and examine just how much the A.G.V.A. union rate increases earmarked for the dancers had depleted his bottom line. He came to the conclusion that he had no choice but to release the Apollo Chorus line in order to afford to pay the big name acts. Schiffman planned to slowly phase out the dancers and hoped that audiences would never notice. Many of the filler and the sub-marginally talented variety acts that performed before and in between the great comedy, dance and solo acts would be the next to be booted out as devotees of big names like Ellington, Basie and Fitzgerald had become increasingly annoyed and on the verge of an audience rebellion as they tired of having to wait through the parade of filler acts before the big name celebrities performed.

When the Apollo Theatre re-opened for its gala premier Harper produced the production which featured the Ink Spots as headliners along with his usual cast of variety acts. Scores of Harlem big shots showed up for the resurrection of the theatre including the recently appointed first African-American Parole Commissioner Lieutenant Samuel Battles. Battles, was also the first New York City Police officer to receive a standing ovation from the proud uptown audience members. This revival of the Apollo meant the prospect of fresh new jobs and spanking new entertainment for lucky audiences. Hordes of people lined up and down 125th Street like sardines eager to enter the world's greatest showplace.

HARPER DID THE ELK'S RENDEZVOUS (1941-1942)

Harper continually kept up his longtime connections with the various Elk's Lodge halls in Harlem from the early 1920s into the early 1940s. He produced a show for the Elk's Convention in 1927 and he also staged a big 1927 Elk's Bathing Beauty Contest/Parade at the Manhattan Casino followed two years later with a 1929 *Hot Chocolates'* Elk's benefit for Elk's Lodge # 45 where he staged W. C. Handy, Peg Leg Bates and others. Therefore when Johnny Barone opened up his new Elk's Rendezvous nightclub it went without saying which producers name popped up and out front for the position of show stager. Harper's Elk's Rendezvous revues were petite in scale and budgeted with a shoe string and had an atmosphere that was more akin to a chummy cozy communal den than that of a swinging nightclub.

"The biggest little nightclub in New York" is what people started calling the Elk's rendezvous now that Harper was on board as its main producer.

Word that Harper was staging the revues brought long time Harlem nightlife devotees both black and white with occasional visitations from major Sepia and Caucasian celebrities back into the club. Harper's juicy set of dancing girls "The Rendezvouettes" were rather the remarkable attractions not only because they grooved but because their routines were so damn tight and sexy. "The Rendezvouettes" had to do without a generous wardrobe/costume budget and this meant that the outfits they donned were as skimpy as the law allowed pleasing many gentlemen customers in the audience. Regulars were dangling from the rafters as their eyes expanded from out of their foreheads while they tried to keep up with those shiny and desirable hard bodies bouncing and shaking to sudden rhythms.

Maurice Dancer wrote in his 1941 *Chicago Defender* press section titled *Broadway Invades Harlem via the Elks Rendezvous Hot Spot* that "Johnny Barone's new Elk's Rendezvous floor show is now on the lips of New York's café society for the new Leonard Harper production that has brought back memories of his Connie's Inn days when the veteran producer conceived and staged the town's smartest revues."

The regrettable sidebar to these Harper Elk's revues was that a great number of the main local stars were boxed into the same racial pigeonhole and professional corner that Harper was becoming increasingly imprisoned in and their work was restricted to the "no exit" small time boundaries of Seventh Avenue venues. These African-American talents were promising in their youth and for many of them their natural progression would have been to go Hollywood if they had not been of the sable hue. One prime example was Harper's Elk's Rendezvous female emcee the charming and irresistibly magnetic Edna Mae Harris. Harris was a woman who was chock full of theatrical skills as she could dance up a storm plus she bore impeccable comedic timing. As Edna Mae Harris performed in various Harper productions at the Apollo theatre she also found the time to star in the 1939-1940 films like *The Notorious Elinor Lee, Lying Lips* and *Paradise In Harlem*. During her stint as Mistress of Ceremonies for Harper at the Elk's Rendezvous she also appeared in the Sepia films titled *Murder On Lenox Ave.* and *X Marks The Spot*.

Another worthy case of a racially compartmentalized talent was Harper's sometime Elk's Rendezvous male host Ralph Cooper who also occupied his steady Wednesday Apollo Amateur Night gigs that were featured on the undercard of many Leonard Harper Apollo Theatre Showcases. Harper had heretofore casted Ralph Cooper and Eddie Rector in his 1926 Lafayette Theatre Harper uptown version of *Tan Town Topics*. Cooper was also introduced with his Kongo Knights in Harper's 1930 *Ballyhoo Revue* that was also staged at the Lafayette Theatre. Harper provided Cooper with the chance to work as his emcee in a few of his Elk's Rendezvous revues and it was to be Ralph's very first appearances at a local nightclub cafe.

Examples of some of the Harper amassed Elk's novelty acts that patrons gathered to see every week were the dainty languid wristed female impersonator James Wiley who purred in such a high pitched and assailable soprano voice that on a dime he/she could convert to sound like a bird with clipped wings, Johnny "Fifty-Second Street" Taylor the boogie-woogie pianist, Edna "Yak" Taylor who sang nearly in the vein of "Bessie Smith," Ruby Smith the actual blues singing daughter of Bessie Smith, Valda the burlesque strip-tease star who dramatically swerved her hips in a voodoo spell technique, Baby Selma the bantam tapster, Claudia McNeil the "Marion Anderson" of the Harlem nightclub scene, Myra Johnson previously with Thomas "Fats" Waller, Bobbie Caston formerly with Louis Armstrong, blackface comedian Dewey Brown, Viola Kemp contortionist-dancer, the Bye Sisters who were the African-American version of the "Andrew Sisters" or vice-versa and King Solomon the oddly skillful roller skater.

CHAPTER EIGHT
(1942 to 1943)

WANTED: GLAMOROUS GIRLS

It's 1942 and in his struggle to get back on Broadway with a big box office hit Harper opportunely allied with Belgium born producer Clifford C. Fischer. Clifford C. Fischer was considered the master at exploiting the opulent and unconventional French nightclub scene and showcasing it to inquiring American theatre audiences at his downtown New York French Casino nightclub. From the 1930s on Fischer marketed his radiant and risqué *Follies Bergere, Follies Parisienne, Follies De Femmes, French Casino Follies* and *Follies D' Amour* to stimulated Broadway, Miami, London and Chicago audiences. Fischer called his productions "Continental Entertainment" and to common unworldly American audiences it was like a cheap delightful French staycation.

    Harper also opened a brand new uptown dance studio called Suntan Studios during this time. He partnered with Fritz Pollard the retired football great who was America's first African-American National Football League coach. Pollard was intrigued by their business projects and both he and Harper had high hopes that many new entertainment opportunities would come to fruition from their Suntan Studio venture. Pollard possessed the first-rate business expertise needed to manage the studio space while Harper brought in the talent and artistic creativity. According to author John M. Carroll in his book titled *Fritz Pollard; Pioneer In Racial Advancement* "During the late 1930's he (Pollard) offered Harper the use of a block of vacant offices on the same floor as his *Independent News* operation on West 125th. Street near the Apollo Theatre to conduct tryouts and rehearsals for productions. Harper called his rehearsal rooms Suntan Studios. In his spare time, Pollard sometimes played piano during practice sessions and aided Harper in selecting talent for the productions." Harper introduced a charitable policy of never charging any of the underprivileged ghetto youth a fee to take his courses in entertainment training and development. In fact Harper employed many of the up and, coming juvenile singers, dancers and comedians from his Suntan Studios School to perform in some of his current revues.

Clifford C. Fischer and Harper teamed up and both producers were all systems go as they commenced to mount an interracial French/African-American Follies Revue for the International Casino, nightclub. High stepping African-American hoofers together with Caucasian showgirls was their plan and they believed they couldn't miss. Harper and Fischer proceeded to hold casting calls at Harper's new Suntan Studios and requested that all the girls be young, well formed, five feet nine or ten inches tall, and all racial, ethnic and national backgrounds were welcome. Harper believed that it would be better if the young ladies were fresh out of High School instead of seasoned chorus line dancers because they would be easier to train and he could mold their performances into being of the champagne grade showgirls that he necessitated. Prompted by Fischer's customary use of the showgirls in French numbers Harper obligated himself into guaranteeing that all the new hires would receive the biggest salaries ever paid in Harlem or on Broadway.

Fischer abruptly terminated his diversified casted French/African-American revue with Harper while they were in the middle of pre-production and deserted his new partner to mount the low budgeted and commercially lucrative Shubert Brothers co-production of *Priorities of 1942* featuring Hazel Scott. Fischer endeavored to replicate his *Priorities of 1942* achievement on Broadway during the same year with a musical called *Keep Em Laughing* starring Hildegarde, Zero Mostel and a family of dogs who deposited bricks (amongst other things), road around on scooters, and jumped on top of a miniature trapeze. *Keep Em Laughing* played to near empty audiences every night and had Fischer sobbing backstage because of his lost investment due to the dismal box office sales.

Harper who was left literally holding the bag when Fischer quit on him earlier in the year once again cautiously listened to Clifford's pipe dreams of bankrolling a Harper directed black and white French/African-American Follies revue that would tour major American cities. Harper was leery of Fischer's rekindled plans because he had already left him in the lurch. Harper continued on with his slowly collapsing work situation at the Apollo theatre and his limited production tasks in the small indistinct local Harlem nightclub's that he had been curbed and restricted to.

Harper and Pollard continued on with their extensive blueprints for Suntan Studios and the space initially became known as the favorite rehearsal hall for the likes of Ellington, Calloway, Holiday and other big names who had big bands.

After bombing on Broadway with *Keep Em Laughing* Clifford Fischer continued talking to Harper about his grand plans of exhibiting the black and white-French/African-American Follies showgirl revue. This time Harper was not only unenthusiastic but extremely skeptical of Fischer because of his leaving him high and dry in the recent past.

HARPER DID MURRAINS

On April 4th 1942 another new comfy and relaxed nightclub opened in Harlem it was called Murrains and it was located on the site of the nightclub formerly known as the Mimo Professional Club. Harper was engaged as Murrains in-house producer and Seventh Avenue radiated with the expectancy that the long gone days of the Harlem Renaissance might be returning. Murrains nightclub's historical significance arouse from the fact that it was the second major all African-American owned and managed nightspot in Harlem with Small's Paradise being the first. Murrain's cabaret was situated downstairs and there was an upstairs bar where Harper rehearsed his new chorus routines daily.

The Saturday night grand premier of Harper's Murrains opening generated the large crowds of committed nightlife devotees and Murrains Fountain Lounge was packed solid and overflowing with standing room only capacity crowd onlookers. Harper presented his floorshow revue with comedian Ralph Cooper along with his dancing partner Eddie Rector. Other acts included Miss. Rosebud Thompson the "Leaf Brown" African-American depiction of stripper Gypsy Rose Lee, Eight Harperette dancing cuties, a group of male demon jungle dancers and an army of vocalists who warbled with Christopher Columbus and his band superintending the musical chores.

Harper took full advantage of singer Setoris Morrow and the Smith Kids who sang West Indian Calypso folk songs while they deliberately incorrectly pronounced the dialect for laughs. The new Harper Murrains revue was described by local columnist Billy Rowe as being "sparkling with rhythm and music, with acts that are snappy and unusual". Former chorus girl Thelma Prince who danced for Leonard Harper at the Elk's Rendezvous, the Apollo Theatre and Murrain's said "When Mr. Harper made you put on your tap shoes he worked the shit out of you. He was a very clever man with his ideas and if he didn't know something he got someone who did. Like the time at the Apollo when he had us girls make music with regular bar glasses on stage, he hired somebody to show us how to play them."

While staging at Murrains, Harper passed off three white girls as black in his chorus of eight. But instead of triggering any ill-tempered disputes his tickled audiences argued amongst, themselves while struggling to identify which of the "black" girls were of the Caucasian persuasion. Well beyond the fifth week since its opening Murrains patrons still waited outside on long lines up and down Seventh Avenue to gain entrance, and Harper started to really trust that he had decisively begotten a new permanent base for his forthcoming production undertaking which would hopefully lead to a larger scaled Broadway return.

With the positive word of mouth from Murrains, Harper got another shot at Broadway but this time he wasn't hired as a producer/director but was put on salary as the dance choreographer/stage manager. It was for the new Ed Sullivan all African-American Musical Comedy titled *Harlem Cavalcade*. At the very least this new gig got Harper back into the swing of things on the Great White Way and nearer to his desire of revisiting his bygone triumphs and perhaps of conceiving wholly new extravaganzas. *Harlem Cavalcade* was *N. Y. Daily News* columnist turned producer Ed Sullivan's show and was billed as having the "World's Top Negro Entertainers". Sullivan had always been a fan of Harper's variety show revues from the old Connie's Inn days and Harper was responsible for many of the concepts later utilized by Sullivan on his vaudeville fitted national television show.

Harlem Cavalcade was to be part of a four man back to vaudeville movement. *Pittsburgh Courier* columnist Billy Rowe described the origins of *Harlem Cavalcade* and the men behind it as "plotting a new approach to theatrical greatness are Sullivan, Sissle, Vodery and Harper." *Harlem Cavalcade* was written by Noble Sissle as a means of entertaining the World War II troupes in training camps during this year of 1942 in which the United States and Russia along with the United Kingdom formed the Axis to defeat Adolf Hitler who was beginning to face a trouncing in his quest for world domination.

The *Harlem Cavalcade* revue chronicled the yarn of the upsurge of Colored theatricals thru the decade and boasted of having the largest African-American cast so far to be featured on Broadway. With the Shubert Brothers *French Follies* producer Clifford C. Fischer was on board as an additional partner and fractional financial sponsor of the *Harlem Cavalcade* production. Harper and Fischer continued to have discussions related to their cancelled interracially mixed black and white French/African-American Follies project for a Broadway run between rehearsal breaks backstage. The Harper, Fischer talks were ultimately futile as all future artistic notions took a backseat to the current project at hand.

※

STILL *CHOCK FULL OF RHYTHM*

Wishful thinking from the producers of *Harlem Cavalcade* induced them to make unsubstantiated statements to the press that they would be recruiting stars Theresa Harris and Dorothy Dandridge and put them under contract bringing both young ladies from Hollywood to be featured in their Broadway show. First of all Theresa Harris was on the west coast straining to break away from the restrictions of having to play maid servant roles after having been allowed to dance with Ginger Rogers in the 1933 film *Professional Sweetheart*. Dandridge on the other hand was on the threshold of attaining some co-starring credits in a few all African-American films which would sooner or later get her more screen time and notice. The closest thing to casting a star African-American Hollywood talent in *Harlem Cavalcade* was when the producers signed on Wini Johnson the fair skinned and combative "make-believe" wife of sluggish footed Stepin Fetchit. Wini brought along some excess luggage in the personage of her brother and "dancing partner" Bob Johnson.

Comic actor Tim Moore who was also cast in *Harlem Cavalcade* had a very long professional relationship with Harper. Tim Moore and Harper went all the way back to 1925 when Harper staged *Lucky Sambo*. Moore also clowned, it up Negro style in the 1931 Micheaux/Harper directed short film *Darktown Revue* which was shot simultaneously with the Micheaux/Harper directed talkie *The Exile*. For many years Tim Moore had Harper's Apollo theatre audiences in stiches. With the future arrival of television Tim Moore had America audiences giggling in their living rooms as the popular "Kingfish" character in the groundbreaking *Amos and Andy* television show.

Producer Ed Sullivan delivered a curtain speech during the opening night of *Harlem Cavalcade* in which he honored and voiced his admiration for black entertainers and he also dispensed a distinctive acknowledgement to bandleader Noble Sissle for his creative contributions behind the production. *Harlem Cavalcade* made use of microphones during certain scenes irritating suffering theatre audiences as they struggled to adjust their ears to the new unpolished theatrical application of a sound system. The disproportionately mixed sound setup intermittently blasted the vocals from the highest to the lowest levels of inaudibility and it might have been more advantageous if the producers had shelved their new microphones altogether.

The sound was not the only latest introduction in *Harlem Cavalcade* as Harper had devised a new dance craze called *Pushing the Sand* where he drilled his chorus line into covering the entire stage with beach sand while dancing on top of it. As Rowland Field reported in the *Newark Evening News* for his Broadway section "This lusty all-colored vaudeville revue which columnist Ed Sullivan has assembled is at its best when its many prancers go to town. As a dancing show it provides about every known brand of Harlem hoofing from extraordinary tapsters to strutting numbers by the chorus and from acrobatics to shuffles on a sand-covered stage. In between the various fast terpsichorean exercises there are a number of amusing comedy skits and some singing acts, but most of these are secondary to the dance specialists on the lively program."

A few of the reviews for *Harlem Cavalcade* were mildly sympathetic but nearly all of the critics were unable to give the show a flattering assessment. Most theatre critics and audience members found the first half of the musical as formless and tolerably distracting. But the second half of *Harlem Cavalcade* was viewed as slowly chugging along like a dry un-lubricated broken locomotive. By the second half ticket holders thought that they were in the company of a hollow over-long waste of time. *Harlem Cavalcade* came off as a very wearisome and bland piece of work with antiquated tunes. Even the newly composed tunes seemed deplorably outdated. The gags in *Harlem Cavalcade* were played out having all been seen before and the routines were dusty like an old trunk hidden in someone's attic for eons that should have never been reopened.

Sullivan and Sissle never had a clear vision of what *Harlem Cavalcade* was about. Was *Harlem Cavalcade* an African-American salute to the American World War II troops or was it a look back and sampling of ancient Afro-American Vaudeville? Critic Isadora Smith of the *Pittsburgh Courier* wrote in her review titled *Harlem Cavalcade Brings Life* the following "Put together in two parts, the show has a directness and whole-heartedness about it that could only come from those who have been kept off the main highway too long." Many of the other critics commonly knew that the production staff of *Harlem Cavalcade* had in fact been off the main thoroughfare for far too long and as a consequence they were out of touch in regards to nourishing their ever evolving audience's cravings. This was particularly ruinous news for Harper who had been fraught with the same order of predicaments uptown at the Apollo.

Harlem Cavalcade was intended to display and illuminate the moods of yesteryear but instead wound up as E. Billingsworth scribed in a 1942 *Encores and Echoes* clipping that *Harlem Cavalcade* was "merely a re-issue of ghost entertainment. About the best thing that could be said about it, is that it has a streamlined title. The jokes of its jesters pre-date the Victorian period." Even Noble Sissle's finale composition of *America Marches On* thick with nationalistic World War II gusto and homeland appeal couldn't salvage this theatrical catastrophe.

During the Broadway run of *Harlem Cavalcade* Harper brought his chorus line of sixteen girls called the "Harper Harlemaniacs" to the Cosmopolitan Opera House to perform at a benefit for the Harlem Children's Fresh Air Fund. The girls wore American army uniform costumes and toyed with the press while promoting *Harlem Cavalcade* but no amount of publicity and patriotic fervor could resuscitate this sinking ship of a production. *Harlem Cavalcade* featured a comedic graveyard scene titled *Midnight Sonata* which showcased standard Afro-American revue material utilizing two actors sitting by tombstones straining to get laughs. A few reviewers wittily articulated that the type of prehistoric performances demonstrated in *Harlem Cavalcade* should join the two humorless characters of the *Midnight Sonata* graveyard scene at the theatrical cemetery for its overall lack of imagination.

Although *Harlem Cavalcade* was botched because of its aged and insipid material that didn't shield the production or give it immunity from the menacing specter of racial compartmentalizing. The atrocity of racial pigeonholing reared its nasty head in certain negative reviews and comments. On May 4, 1942 John Mason Brown theatre critic for the *N. Y. World Telegram* stated of the *Harlem Cavalcade* dancers "Because all these good dancers who are hard to identify soon begin to seem much alike, in spite of all their differences, as so many *watermelon seeds*."

The press stated that "Harper is producing in six nite-clubs and has his dancing feet in the Ed Sullivan-Noble Sissle pie at the Ritz on Broadway" yet he still found the time to produce a charity show for the Harlem Children's Fresh Air Fund. Harper brought producer/columnist Ed Sullivan of *Harlem Cavalcade* to the event. The sold out fundraiser bequeathed all of its proceeds to be used for the acquisition of country property so that needy Harlem city children could experience the fun and fresh woodland air at the new summer camp.

The Broadway outing of Sullivan's Colored Musical Comedy cost the Shubert Brothers a loss of $20,000 after forty nine performances. In order to recoup some of these deficits Sullivan and the Shubert's elected to take *Harlem Cavalcade* on the road with the first stop being the Apollo Theatre. Cast changes weren't the only alterations as they attempted to recover their expenditures. The producers shrank, economized, skipped and speeded up every ingredient of the production with hopes of generating a return.

The Apollo Theatre was the first stop before *Harlem Cavalcade* with any luck might go on a tour of major cities. Apollo Theatre patrons enjoyed the show but found nothing new about it apart from that it reminded them that the days of Colored Musical Comedy, were over and done with. Because of the exceptional quality of Harper's past showcases and his singular choreographic work on *Harlem Cavalcade*, former Harper apprentice Ed Sullivan pursued his services to work on future productions soon after their failed *Harlem Cavalcade* closed.

EXILED ON SEVENTH AVENUE

The following is an excerpted description of Smalls Paradise in 1942 from: *The Autobiography of Malcolm X* by Malcolm X and Alex Haley "With Small's practically in the center of everything, waiting tables there was seventh Heaven seven times over. Even the little cellar places with only piano space had fabulous keyboard artists such as James P. Johnson and Jelly Roll Morton, and singers such as Ethel Waters. There *(Small's Paradise)*, I heard the old-timers reminisce about all those great times."

The Small's Paradise floorshow revues that Harper produced in 1942 were analogous to big familiar house parties with old friends who ruminated about the good old days within the milieu of the nightclub setting. These get-togethers were more nonchalant and laid-back than Harper's usual typical floorshow spectaculars of the past. Smalls' Paradise was packed with people who came to have a good time but were also aware that old father time was catching up with them and they were all getting on in age.

Arthritic ridden terpsichoreans and songsters well past their prime slowly rambled into Smalls' entrance and promptly snatched hold of their seats so as not to fall or lose their balance. Big stars dropped by to get a taste of the uptown flavor and a shot of soul for their debilitated adrenalines. According to the March 8, 1941 "Tavern Topics" column featured in the *N.Y. Amsterdam News,* screen actress Dorothy Lamour, movie star Ralph Bellamy, Bob Crosby (Bing's brother), actor Preston Foster and famous Hollywood director Eric Von Stroheim could every so often be seen having dinner, letting loose and relishing Harper's suitably intriguing miniature floorshows on any arbitrary night.

Some of the Smalls' Paradise talents who took to the stage had resolved within themselves the fact that they had progressed as far as they were ever going to get in their professional stage careers and they were never going to get on Broadway again or out to Hollywood. With no greater aspirations than generating a smile or two from an audience member these lifelong dedicated theatre professionals automatically lugged along with their love of performing as the only thing they had left. As the stage lights were, darkening for many of the once clever acts they unconsciously refused to give up and give in to the sands of time. The underlying quality that these players retained was that their absolute existence was demarcated not by purely human survival or God's decrees but by what song, costume, and dance number or comedic bit they could come up with to get a rise out of their audience and create enjoyment while they were able to.

Harper's six shapely coffee-colored cased chorine's clad in short-short striped zebra costumes had Small's patrons going crazy. Visitors like former Harper chorus line dancer Bessie Buchanan who later became New York State's first African-American Assemblywoman, and Parole Commissioner Sam Battles mingled with the likes of producer Clarence Robinson. Smalls' Paradise was one of the oldest nightclubs in New York City having operated for over twenty years and it was surprisingly still owned by Ed Smalls an African-American man.

The acts and titles were all interchangeable, for instance, *Harper's Wave Rhythm Frolics* could have been substituted for any number of his Small's Paradise revues. His super sexualized use of Hula and Bikini girls attired in meager Hawaiian outfits rocked whether they grooved on a sandy beach backdrop or while twisting their butts around light poles on a Parisian boulevard setting. Interspersed, intertwined, interwoven and sometimes monotonous and repetitive as they had come to be, the bottom line was that these Harper floorshows cooked and he always delivered top notch cabaret fare.

Horns attacking, sharp tapping feet, stylish and virtually undressed ample dancing girls shaking their trunk's as untamed strange foreign themed novelty acts vibrated on top of huge drums, some clowns with a few off-tongue elocution solos and you had the ingredients of a crafty

Harper show. It didn't matter if the Spanish dance team of Ramon and Chiquita lived just a few blocks away from Small's in Spanish Harlem the audience chose to imagine that they just disembarked from Monte Carlo or Bali. It also didn't matter if they were viewing Harper's Second Half or the First Half of the Twentieth, Thirtieth or Fortieth Edition of his *Smalls' Swings South Revue* let's just get on with the show.

In September 1942 Harper produced a stage show at the Roxy Theatre and during opening night Harper's Lindy Hopper's were coerced into becoming members of the American Guild of Variety Artists before they went out on stage. After enrolling in A.G.V.A. the Harper Lindy Hoppers collected salary upgrades of forty dollars weekly. Harper's Lindy Hopping dance captain received an A.G.V.A raise of fifty-five dollars. Harper's dancers at the Ubangi Club were the only uptown black chorus girls in a nightclub that were represented by A.G.A.V. and they were contracted to receive thirty-five dollars a week with an anticipated elevation in earnings to come shortly.

In October 1942 Harper went into rehearsal to stage a show for a new Harlem nite-spot called the RHUM-BOOGIE CAFE. The Rhum-Boggie Café was located on 131st. and Seventh Ave. at the site where the old Symphony Club used to be. All around showman and former owner of Harlem's Theatrical Grill, Dickie Wells was one of Rhum-Boggie's overseeing part-owners. Wells and Harper had the chore of interviewing and casting fresh chorus girls for Rhum-Boggie. Harper wanted Wells to sign Fats Waller and his Orchestra to open up the club and Waller was willing to perform as long as Harper was directing. Waller was prepared to come in for a five week stretch which would also include a live nationwide radio broadcast from the club.

The hastened imaginings of the Rhum-Boggie Café to be the next trendy Harlem nightspot dwindled away rapidly as the financiers ran out of funds and were unable to book name performers like "Fats" Waller who could have attracted huge opening night crowds. Without the significantly necessitated stars to lure in the masses the Rhum-Boggie Café had nothing to buzz about. Without a liquor license and after having suffered numerous bogus fire violations because the owners didn't have enough cash on hand to bribe crooked fire marshals the Rhum-Boggie nightclub just boggied into nonexistence. Harper was again left with a few more unfilled and unrealized dreams and left unaccompanied and isolated on another vacant stage floor.

1943 HARPER'S DEATH

January of 1943 brought Harper back down to the Times Square area's Hotel Edison where he was contracted to produce a revue titled the *Hotel Edison Revue*. The Hotel Edison sat right next to where he used to house his 1920s groundbreaking dance studio. The attractive young ladies that Harper gathered for his *Hotel Edison Revue* also took stabs at parts for the Twentieth Century Fox feature film *Stage Door Canteen* that Harper was also casting for. The publicity generated from these tryout sessions were used to improve the Twentieth Century Fox Film Company's tarnished image due to its long term and unremitting discriminatory negative portrayals of people of African descent. Harper was hired to do the African-American casting on two Hollywood studio motion pictures. Sol Lesser, one of the producers of *Stage Door Canteen* and part of a group of Hollywood executives who pledged a more even-handed treatment of blacks in future motion pictures, notified N.A.A.C.P. head Walter White that "Colored players are being used in the picture and in accurate portrayals of themselves."

Stage Door Canteen featured just about every big name star in Hollywood at the time from Katharine Hepburn, Ray Bolger, Merle Oberon, Helen Hayes, Johnny Weismuller, George Raft, Edgar Bergen with "Charlie" and Sam Jaffe. The musicians that were featured in the movie were Count Basie, Benny Goodman, Xavier Cugat and Ethel Waters. Harper was contracted to cast talent for the African-American scenes of the patriotic themed World War II film.

During the early part of 1943 Harper was briefly concerned that his dancers would run out of theatrical costume footwear due to the World War II rationing rules which limited Americans to only three pairs of shoes per-person a year. Good news came from Washington that the government agency O.P.A. the Office of Price Administration had agreed to allow exemptions for dancers if they could prove that they needed the extra shoes for their professional livelihood.

Harper resumed producing at Murrain's nightclub and rehearsed for a fresh new show titled *Sensations Of 1943*. He laboriously worked out hard driving new rhythm routines with his chorus girls. During a run thru Harper felt an uncomfortable pain in his, abdomen. It caused a strange bitter irritation in his heart. Harper told no one about the abnormal pains because he was so charged up about his recent weight loss and he didn't want anything like a health issue to hold up his new Murrain's nightclub floorshow premiere.

Harper had been confounded and stressed with anxiety and career asphyxia about his demoted position at the Apollo Theatre and of being limited into only producing at small uptown nightclubs. Harper questioned if all of his days at the famed Apollo theatre were over and brooded over whether he was about to receive the infamous hug from Schiffman that would doom him into theatrical anonymity.

On Thursday February 4th, 1943 during Leonard Harper's last dry run before the opening of his Murrain's *Sensations Of 1943* floorshow while demonstrating a sequence to his eight chorus girls he involuntarily tumbled. He jumped feverishly from off the floor as if he was flying just like he used to do during all those times of his youth down south when he was a Medicine tent show entertainer. Then he abruptly wobbled and was vertiginously reminded of his oldness and physical boundaries. He mistook his prevailingly discomfort for a bout of indigestion or a frequent minor stomach ache while he crawled to the nearest window for some fresh air.

Harper hoped that eating part of a sandwich and drinking a bicarbonate of soda would do the trick and make him feel better. He had a faint spell and collapsed onto the dance floor as all of his Murrain's Harperettes hurried to his side. The girls attempted to raise and revitalize him but their efforts were unsuccessful as he drifted further and further away.

Harper extended his hands to his eight dancers for one last time and as everything suddenly evaporated from his body he took his last gasps. Harper expired of a heart attack on his way to Harlem Hospital's emergency room. Leonard Harper died at eight o'clock pm which was forty minutes before the traditional start time of most of his nightclubs and floorshow revues.

A young Rev. Adam C. Powell, Jr. presided over Leonard Harper's Abyssinian Baptist church funeral and sermonized that God called Harper at age 44 because he devoted his life to entertainment and there was little difference between the church life and show business world because they both sought to serve humanity and make mankind's existence a little better. Apollo theatre owner Frank Schiffman conducted the arrangements and recited Bryant's "Thanatopsis." Flowers surrounded the casket as the most angelic, striking and delectable chorus and showgirls in the world added elegance as honorary enchanting flower bearers.

LEONARD HARPER
  (1899-1943)
His soul was in the theatre,
He loved its people too,
It seemed that ev'ry curtain call

To him, meant thrills a-new
He never wearied of his work,
His was a happy task,
A scene to set, a dance to stage

Was all that he would ask.

He was a true producer
Who fully gave his art,
To make show business better
And cheer the public heart.
His was a great performance,
Up 'til the final bow,
If there's a theatre in the sky
that's where you'll find him
now!

———Andy Razaf

THE AFTERMATH

The Sixth annual meeting of the Negro Actors Guild was attended by hundreds of its members and a moment of silence was held in Harper's memory after his funeral. Rev. Adam Clayton Powell Jr. the Assistant Pastor of the Abyssinian Baptist Church was also the Guild's Chaplain but he was unable to make this meeting so the moment of prayer was conducted by Asst. Pastor Reverend Ben Richardson. Some of the other members at this meeting were Rabbi Birstein, W. C. Handy the Guild's Treasurer, Fredi Washington the Recording Secretary, Canada Lee, Alberta Hunter and Lucky Roberts.

Fannie Pennington didn't attend Harper's funeral even though it was held at her house of worship the Abyssinian Baptist Church. Jeanne Harper his daughter was out of town during her father's transitional home going service but her grandfather Matthew Mark "Pop-Pop" Pennington being a devoted and forgiving servant of God attended and assisted in Harper's funeral and memorial ceremonies. Harper's spouse Osceola Blanks was truly remorseful and sorrowful about the unfair way in which she treated her husband during the final years before his death. Osceola's epiphany was the realization that her late husband was always firstly married to the theatre from his birth and that their marriage had always been a polygamous side-attraction to his preordained love for the stage, show business and his delight in pleasing audiences. After Harper's demise Osceola came to appreciate and fully understand her husband's lifelong amalgamation with the stage and it furnished her with the emotional closure that she needed during her time of grief.

Osceola and sister Berliana eventually moved in with each other and shared a spacious apartment in Harlem's famous Graham Court after Harper's burial. One of Osceola and Berliana's neighbors recalled that the sisters kept to themselves and never spoke of show business or Harper. The Blanks sisters loved to sew and continued to stitch fabric until their deaths.

Harper's mother Sarah Harper and his brother Gene Harper made a last ditch attempt to take care of his daughter Jeanne and move her out to Chicago but their custodial dreams evaporated after the death of their beloved Leonard Harper.

Llewellyn "Lew" Crawford, Harper's faithful assistant, made encroachments towards striding into his boss's old dancing shoes and he was appointed to take on Harper's duties by Fritz Pollard now the sole owner of Suntan Studios. Lew frenziedly struggled to persuade everybody that he was up to scratch in all of Harper's production endeavors. Crawford completed the production chores that Harper started at Murrains and put the finishing touches on Harper's Elk's Rendezvous Revue. Crawford had the support of Leighla Whipper the daughter of veteran movie actor Leigh Whipper who used to record Harper's delineations which he dictated to be communicated to his chorus girls.

Harper's last revue that he devised for the Elk's Rendezvous made no mention of him and instead attributed all the credit to Crawford hopping that he would follow and keep alive, Harper's money generating theatrical legacy. Only it didn't work. The new Harper Elk's Rendezvous production opened up on Friday February 12, 1943 and the lackluster response attested that the Harper gift had come and gone with his soul as his era of Afro-American Musical Comedy and fast nightclub floorshows had authoritatively perished forever with his passing.

The Harper Murrain's *Sensations Of 1943* revue that played a few weeks after his demise was decidedly a different story from the Elk's Rendezvous catastrophe. The Murrain's Cabaret was the location where Harper took his last dance steps and breath and it would have been obscene not to give him credit where it was lastly due. Harper's lethal Murrain's production was measured as dynamite and had a lineup featuring the homegrown warbling and dancing humorist Buddy Bowser who sang *Please Don't Ration Swing*. Jimmy Smith frolicked and tapped out rhythms and music with his feet on top of a contraption he invented called the Dancephone which was akin to a huge vibraphone. Norton and Norton the stunningly attractive classy ballroom dancers were on

Harper Murrain's *Sensations Of 1943* bill and they were sandwiched in between the talkative transvestite Dick Montgomery who did a striptease while singing in a falsetto voice. A few wonderfully amusing other side acts supplemented the floorshow for spice. Taft Jordan's orchestra backed up the fast footwork of Harper's eight dancing girls who moved and grooved it.

Drama Editor of the *N. Y. Amsterdam News* Dan Burley reported on the revue "What makes the new revue tick is the way it's put together. Begun by the late and lamented Leonard Harper, the show was completed by Llewellyn Crawford, protégé of the master producer, with the assistance of Jesse Stone composer of *WPA* and *Idaho*."

The Leonard Harper Theatre Workshop that continued on with his stage works which was discussed at his funeral astonishingly demonstrated to be unlike the same old vacuous dialogue of instantly neglected interment pledges made whenever a beloved individual succumbs to death. Harlem's *Amsterdam News* reporter Julius J. Adams wrote an article dated six years after Harper's death on September 10, 1949 titled "Pollard Inherited Sun Tan Studio After Producer Died" and said of Harper "He had established the Sun Tan Studio for the express purpose of developing young talent. Besides not charging the youngsters for helping them develop their talents, Harper would use as many of them in his shows as he possibly could. After Harper died a delegation of musicians, including Andy Kirk, J. C. Johnson and W. C. Handy called on Fritz and asked him if he would carry on the work at the Studio. Pollard agreed and then began one of the most interesting careers an ex-athlete ever had." Fritz Pollard preserved Harper's program of schooling and ripening young inner city talents for free. The studio operated a very remunerative casting and modeling agency while managing top name jazz acts to sustain the business and make a profit.

The casting of the Twentieth Century Fox film *Stormy Weather* utilizing Harper's co-staged 1933 hit floorshow revue title could have conceivably caused his heart to over pressure and stop. Just about anyone and everyone that Harper worked with was summoned out to

Hollywood to perform before the cameras in both *Cabin In The Sky* and *Stormy Weather*. Top talents like Ethel Waters, Louis Armstrong, Eddie "Rochester" Anderson, Bill Bailey, Lena Horne, Ada Brown, Benny Carter, Bojangles Robinson, Mae Johnson, "Fats" Waller, Cab Calloway, Mantan Moreland, the Nicholas Brothers and Duke Ellington, were all on the *Cabin In The Sky* and *Stormy Weather* payrolls en masse. Even Tondaleyo one of the Harper's young local discoveries was sucked into the Hollywood limelight. "Tonda" paid her own way out to the West coast for a *Stormy Weather* casting session look see. Possibly Harper's unsound arteries began to block when he got word that Busby Berkeley was commissioned to stage the *Shine* sequences in the Colored themed *Cabin In The Sky* film instead of him.

In a July 31, 1948 article featured in the *Chicago Defender* by Henry Brown titled "Sun Tan Studios Train Nation's New Starlets" Brown wrote "What Leonard Harper and the rest had started in the way of theatrical development was not to be abandoned with the untimely death of Harper, more than three years ago, but was carried on with the full co-operation of the big names in the profession. Acts are placed regularly through Joe Glasser, Wm. Morris Agency, 20th Century Fox, Dick Kollmar (Dorothy and Dick), Metro-Goldwyn-Mayer Agency and Vic Parnell of London. The rehearsal hall at the studio is a meeting place for the greats of the entertainment world. The Apollo Sun Tan studio has a rehearsal room for their stage talent."

HARPER APOLLO THEATRE SIGNATURE SHOWCASE
(HEADLINER) LISTINGS from 1935-1942

1935-HARPER APOLLO THEATRE SHOWCASE (Headliners) "HARLEM'S HIGH SPOT" "THE ONLY STAGE SHOW IN HARLEM"

Apollo Theatre May 3rd, Grand Inaugural Week Leonard Harper Stage Production Mrs. Louis Armstrong and her Kings of Rhythm Orchestra, Washboard Serenaders, Bessie Smith, King Louis II., Apollo Beauty Chorus

Apollo Theatre Friday, May 10th, Leonard Harper's *PEPPER POT* direct from French Casino—Follies Bergere Revue Leroy Smith and Orchestra, Apollo Beauty Chorus

Apollo Theatre Friday, May 17th, Jimmie Lunceford and Band Harper Revue Cast

Apollo Theatre Friday, May 24th, Don Redman and Band, Harper's Dancing Beauties

Apollo Theatre Friday, June 7th, Blanche ("Hi-De-Ho") Calloway and her Band in a Great Leonard Harper Show, Harper's Dancing Beauties-Who Dance as One

Apollo Theatre Friday, June 21st, Willie Bryant the Likeable Nitwit and his Broadcasting Band, Harper's Dancing Damsels

Apollo Theatre Friday, August 2nd, Harlem's Favorite Maestro back for Newer and Greater Triumphs Willie Bryant and a Great Leonard Harper Hit Revue, Harperettes

Apollo Theatre Friday, August 9th, Ted Koehler, Elida Webb and Leonard Harper present the greatest of all Night Club Revues *Cotton Club on Parade*, 25 Cotton Club Beauties

Apollo Theatre Friday August 23rd, Luis Russell and Band with Sonny Woods and Bobby Gaston in a Lavish Fast Stepping Leonard Harper Great Revue *Ladies Love Danger*, Sixteen Lovely Harperettes

Apollo Theatre Friday, September 6th, Ubangi Club Revue staged by Leonard Harper, Special Music by Andy Razaf and Paul Denniker with Mae Johnson

Apollo Theatre Friday, October 11th Willie Bryant and his Recording Band, America's Great and Beloved Juveniles Nicholas Bros. and an Excellent Leonard Harper Revue Cast, 12 Harperettes

Apollo Theatre Friday, October 25th, Tiny Bradshaw and His Really Sensational Band, 16 Leonard Harper Girls

Apollo Theatre Friday, November 8th, New Stars of Radio and Screen 4 Ink Spots Singing, Playing, Dancing Sensations, Chick Webb and Band with Ella Fitzgerald, Harper Beauty Chorus

Apollo Theatre Friday, November 15th, Don Redman *(The Farrell Family a white act of five flashed knives, came to blows wrestling, knocked out and whacked each other in a real red blooded fist fight on stage.)* 16 Girls Staged by Charlie Davis and Leonard Harper

Apollo Theatre Friday, November 22nd, An Unequalled Array of Stars in Leonard Harper's Greatest Show-Mills Blue Rhythm Band, Sixteen Lovely Harperettes

Apollo Theatre Friday, December 20th, *Leonard Harper's All-Star Revue*, N.B.C. Star Bob Howard, Queen Of The Blues Bessie Smith, A Star Grown Up Sunshine Sammy, 18 Harperettes

Apollo Theatre Friday, December 27th, Willie Bryant and Band and Leonard Harper's Great Holiday Revue, 16 Harperettes

1936-HARPER APOLLO THEATRE SHOWCASE (HEADLINERS) "THE WORLD'S GREATEST COLORED ATTRACTIONS APPEAR HERE ONLY"

Apollo Theatre January 10th, 4 Mills Brothers Radio's Greatest Sensation and a Leonard Harper Revue Cast of 50, 16 Harperettes

Apollo Theatre January 24th, Great Harper Show Noble Sissle and Band, Harper's Prize Chorus

Apollo Theatre February 7th, Teddy Hill and his Swing Band, 16 Harperettes

Apollo Theatre February 14th, Duke Ellington and his Famous Orchestra, Harper Revue Cast of 45

Apollo Theatre February 21st, Leonard Harper and Mildred Ray Present another, Great Show, Earl Hines and Band, Sixteen Harperettes

Apollo Theatre February 28th, Luis Russell, the Harperettes

Apollo Theatre March 6th, Louis Armstrong the King of them all and A Revue Cast of Fifty, 16 Harperettes

Apollo Theatre April 3rd, A Great Cast of 65 Colored and 65 White in a Spectacular Show by Leonard Harper and Mildred Ray Present *Brown and White Revue* with Willie (The Lion) Smith and Band, Special Added Attraction the Pardoned Killer! Lead Belly and 28 Beautiful Colored and White Girls. 14 Harperettes and 14 White Girls. *(Harper had a prison set built for Lead Belly who was dressed in a prison costume. Light skinned comedian Monte Hawley played the white Governor of Texas who pardoned Lead Belly because he sang so beautifully. Apollo Theatre audiences found his singing so repugnant that they said the back door alley cats ran away upon hearing his groans).*

Apollo Theatre April 10th, Cab Calloway (Hi-De-Hi-De-Ho) and his Cotton Club Band, 16 Harperettes

Apollo Theatre April 24th, Stars of "Porgy and Bess" Buck and Bubbles, 16 Harperettes

Apollo Theatre May 1st, Ink Spots, 16 Lovely Harperettes

Apollo Theatre June 5th, Earl Hines and his sensational Chicago Grand Terrace Band and Leonard Harper's Great Revue of New Stars *Six Feet of Rhythm,* 16 Harperettes

Apollo Theatre June 12th, Blanche Calloway and Band, 16 Lovely Harperettes

Apollo Theatre June 19th, Chick Webb and his N.B.C. Broadcasting Band with Ella Fitzgerald, 12 Lovely Harperettes

Apollo Theatre June 26th, Ethel Waters making her only theatre appearance away From Broadway, 16 Harperettes

Apollo Theatre July 17th, Leonard Harper & Coleridge Davis Present a Musical Comedy Hit *Sugar Cane* with Sunshine Sammy, 18 Boys & Girls

Apollo Theatre July 24th, Youthful Original Bama State Collegians, Erskine Hawkins, 16 Lovely Harperettes

Apollo Theatre July 31st, Luis Russell and his "Ole Man River" Band, Harperettes

Apollo Theatre August 14th, Cab Calloway "Hi-De-Ho" And His Cotton Club Orchestra Surrounded by Leonard Harper's Revue cast of 40, Harperettes, Cotton Club Boys

Apollo Theatre August 21st, Leonard Harper's *Creole Cocktail,* 16 Harperettes

Apollo Theatre August 28th, Claude Hopkins and Orchestra, the Harperettes

Apollo Theatre September 4th, Louis Armstrong and Band, 16 Lovely Harperettes

Apollo Theatre Sept. 11th, Duke Ellington and his Famous Band and Revue, 16 Harperettes

Apollo Theatre September 18th, Ethel Waters and a Show Worthy of America's Greatest Colored Star, 16 Harperettes

Apollo Theatre September 25th, Jimmy Lunceford and Band and Singers, 16 Harperettes

Apollo Theatre October 9th, Noble Sissle and his Band with Lena Horne, 16 Harperettes

Apollo Theatre October 23rd, the Sunset Royal Entertainers, the Sixteen Lovely Harperettes

Apollo Theatre October 30th, Lucky Millinder and Mills Blue Rhythm Band, 16 Harperettes

Apollo Theatre November 13th, Andy Kirk and Band and Leonard Harper's Great Revue, 16 Harperettes

Apollo Theatre November 27th, Mills Brothers, 16 Harperettes

Apollo Theatre December 11th, Leonard Harper's Musical Hit *League of Rhythm Revue*, 24 Boys and Girls

Apollo Theatre December 18th, Luis Russell, 16 Harperettes

Apollo Theatre December 25th, Claude Hopkins and Orchestra, 16 Harperettes *(Princess Pee Wee the midget from Ringling Bros and Barnum Bailey Circus shared the stage with fellow small person Prince Arthur. Pee Wee was spotted having sex with an average sized male performer in her dressing room and Apollo Theatre performers assumed that she was being raped because of her doll size. Princess Pee Wee's' lover was beaten backstage and chased out of the theatre.)*

Apollo Theatre (circa 1936) Willie Bryant, Dancing Girls are under the Leadership of Ristina Banks. Entire Revue Staged by Leonard Harper

1937-HARPER APOLLO THEATRE SHOWCASE (HEADLINERS)

Apollo Theatre January 8th, Willie Bryant and Band, 16 Dancing Harperettes

Apollo Theatre January 15th, Fats Waller and Band, 20 Harperettes

Apollo Theatre February 26th, Fletcher Henderson and a Fast Moving Leonard Harper Revue, the Harperettes

Apollo Theatre March 5th, Earl Hines and his Grand Terrace Orchestra and a Leonard Harper Great Revue Cast, the Sixteen Harperettes

Apollo Theatre March 12th, Buck & Bubbles, Jesse Stone a new Swing Sensation, 16 Harperettes

Apollo Theatre March 19th, Count Basie and Orchestra, the Harperettes

Apollo Theatre April 2nd, A cast composed exclusively of Musical Comedy Headliners Teddy Hill and Orchestra, Tip Tap Toe, the Sixteen Harperettes

Apollo Theatre April 9th, Chick Webb and Orchestra featuring Ella Fitzgerald, the Lovely Brown Harperettes

Apollo Theatre April 16th, Don Redman and Orchestra, 16 Harperettes

Apollo Theatre April 30th, Tiny Bradshaw, the Sixteen Harperettes

Apollo Theatre May 14th, Leonard Harper's Unbeatable Revue—Cast of 50, 4 Ink Spots, the Sixteen Lovely Dancing Harperettes

Apollo Theatre May 21st, a Great Star at his Greatest! A Revue to Be Proud Of!-Fats Waller, 16 Harperettes *(Harperettes danced in a horrifically terrifying ghost and otherworldly macabre skeleton number.)*

Apollo Theatre May 29th, the Record Breaker Louis Armstrong, Sixteen Lovely Dancing Harperettes

Apollo Theatre June 4th, Music Corp. of America—Managers of Benny Goodman and Most of America's Greatest Bands, Present Count Basie and Band Billie Hoilday

Apollo Theatre June 11th, Dynamic Original Lucky Millinder, Sixteen Lovely Harperettes in a Harper Revue

Apollo Theatre June 18th, Duke Ellington and his Famous Orchestra, 16 Harperettes

Apollo Theatre June 25th, Great Summer Show Don't Miss This One, Erskine Hawkins (Harlem Uproar Band) Stump & Stumpy, 16 Harperettes *(Harold "Stumpy" Cromer of the Stump Stumpy comedy/dance duo was disheartened at the style of contemporary Broadway dancing and choreography in musicals. After watching, a current performance a, displeased Stumpy asked "where did all the fast hoofing and fire-cracking footwork go. Harper wouldn't have, none of that! Harper wouldn't do that!")*

Apollo Theatre July 9th, Jimmie Lunceford, the Sixteen Lovely Harperettes

Apollo Theatre July 16th, *a Sensational New Band, Destined Soon to Take Its Place with the Greatest Orchestras* Edgar Hayes and Swing Band, 6 Cotton Club Boys, Harperettes

Apollo Theatre July 23rd, Major Bowes' The New Sensation New Colored Stars Revue, House Chorister Harperettes and others Produced by Leonard Harper

Apollo Theatre October 1st, Lucky Millinder, 16-Harperettes-16

Apollo Theatre October 15th, Luis Russell and Band, 16 Harperettes

Apollo Theatre November 5th, Count Basie and Band with Billie Holiday and James Rushing

Apollo Theatre December 31st, Leonard Harper presents a Peppery revue which will set the pace for great shows during 1938—Berry Brothers World's Greatest Dancing Trio, Dynamic Tiny Bradshaw and Band, the 16 Lovely Harperettes

Apollo Theatre (circa) Chick Webb and Swing Band and Ella Fitzgerald, 16 Beautiful Dancing Girls

1938-HARPER APOLLO THEATRE SHOWCASE (HEADLINERS)

Apollo Theatre January 7th, Chick Webb and Band with Ella Fitzgerald, Harperettes

Apollo Theatre January 14th, Noble Sissle and Orchestra, Ubangi Club Boys, Harperettes

Apollo Theatre January 21st, Duke Ellington and Orchestra, Leonard Harper Producer, Sixteen Brownskin Dancing Girls

Apollo Theatre January 28th, Claude Hopkins and Band, 16 Harperettes

Apollo Theatre February 3rd, We proudly present Hollywood's first outdoor screen triumph—with an All Colored Cast "Harlem On The Prairie" Leonard Harper's New *Faces and Figures of Swing* with a Splendid Cast of 50, Harperettes

Apollo Theatre February 11th, Don Redman, the Lovely Harperettes

Apollo Theatre February 15th, Earl Hines, the Harperettes

Apollo Theatre February 25th, Two outstanding attractions In A Grand Stage Show Count Basie and Swing Band with James Rushing, Louise Beavers in person, The Sixteen Lovely Harperettes (*The "Count" had eliminated Billie Holiday from his lineup because "it's easier to work without a girl singer". MCA officials confirmed that his reason given was the only one for dropping the vocalist.*)

Apollo Theatre March, Buck & Bubbles with Orchestra

Apollo Theatre March, Ethel Waters, Harper's Dancing Dolls

Apollo Theatre (Easter Week) Jimmie Lunceford, Harper's Brownskin Girls

Apollo Theatre April 1st, Cab Calloway (Hi-De-Ho) and his Cotton Club Orchestra, The Harperettes

Apollo Theatre April 22nd, Fats Waller and New Band, Sixteen Harperettes

Apollo Theatre April "Stuff" Smith and Band, Lovely Harperettes in Two Novel numbers and Intricate Tap Routines

Apollo Theatre May 6th, Major Bowes' New 1938 Colored Jubilee Revue, the Harperettes Seen In A Unique Introductory to the Revue

Apollo Theatre May 13th, Count Basie and Swing Band, Sixteen Harperettes

Apollo Theatre June 3rd, Chick Webb and Band with Ella Fitzgerald, 16 Harperettes

Apollo Theatre June, Willie Bryant and Band, Sixteen Harperettes Coached by Harper

Apollo Theatre June 24th, Tiny Bradshaw and Band, Harper Revue with the Famous Sixteen Harperettes

Apollo Theatre July 29th. All in One Great Show Mills Bros., the Harperettes

Apollo Theatre August 19th, Hot Lips Page and Band, Twelve Lovely Harperettes and Six Ubangi Boys

Apollo Theatre September 13th, Earl "Father" Hines and Orchestra, Harper's Dancing Boys and Girls

Apollo Theatre September Jimmie Lunceford, Sixteen Harperettes

Apollo Theatre September 23rd, Andy Kirk and Band, Sixteen Harper Apollo Dancing Cuties

Apollo Theatre October 14th, Lucky Millinder, Harper's Sixteen Dancing Beauties with Ristina Banks

Apollo Theatre December 9th, Leonard Harper & Joe & Johnson Join In Presenting 'Stuff' Smith and his Onyx Club, 16 Harperettes

Apollo Theatre December 16th, NBC's Pride Ovie Anderson, 16-Beautiful Harperettes

Apollo Theatre December 23rd the King of Them All Louis Armstrong and Band, the Harperettes

Apollo Theatre (circa 1938) Leonard Harper's elaborate *World's Fair Revue* with Harley Toots and his Rhythm Rascals Band, the Harperettes

Apollo Theatre (circa 1938) Bojangles-After three years in Hollywood since an appearance-Leonard Harper Stages a Specialty Written Revue for "The Mayor of Harlem" *(One of the features of this revue was a Dance-Off contest between Bojangles and the fabulous Harperettes chorus line.)*

Apollo Theatre (circa 1938) Four Star Shows with Willie Bryant, Al Cooper and his Savoy Sultans, Avis Andrews and Jackie Mabley, Leonard Harper and Mildred Ray Producers of the Revue

Apollo Theatre (circa 1938) Edgar Hayes and Orchestra, 16 Harperettes *(Harperettes featured in a smooth semi-comic' Snow Brown and the Seven Dwarfs number.)*

1939-HARPER APOLLO THEATRE SHOWCASE (HEADLINERS)

Apollo Theatre (circa 1939) Slim & Slam-"Flat Foot Floogie", Dancing Harperettes

Apollo Theatre January 21st, Earl "Father" Hines with Band, Harperettes

Apollo Theatre January 27th, Leonard Harper in association with Jimmy Johnson, Andy Razaf and J. C. Johnson, present a novel revue with Count Basie and Band, 16 Dancing Girls

Apollo Theatre March 1st, Fats Waller, [His Piano, His Organ, His Band], Revue Cast of 45. A Harper Production

Apollo Theatre March 17th, Nicholas Brothers and Don Redman's Band, Harperettes

Apollo Theatre April 8th, Count Basie and Band in *Leonard Harper's Easter Fantasy*

Apollo Theatre May 19th, Jimmie Lunceford and Band, Leonard Harper Producer, Brown Skin Dancing Girls

Apollo Theatre June 2nd, Willie Bryant and Band, Harperettes

Apollo Theatre June 9th, Louise Beavers in *"Reform School"*, Harperettes

Apollo Theatre August 5, Jimmy Lunceford and Band, Sixteen Pretty Dancing Girls

Apollo Theatre August 11th, Billie Holiday and "Boogie Woogie" Pianists, Mae Diggs and the 16 Harperettes

Apollo Theatre August 25th, the Seven Star band and the Four Star Revue-Leonard Harper-Presents Andy Kirk and Band

Apollo Theatre September 10th, Three Peter Sisters, 16 Lovely Harperettes

Apollo Theatre September 15th, Duke Ellington and his Famous Orchestra under Direction of Leonard Harper and Revue Cast, Dancing Chorus of Twenty Boys and Girls

Apollo Theatre September 22nd, Leonard Harper's *Red Hot Harlem*

Apollo Theatre September 30th, Tiny Bradshaw and Orchestra, the Sixteen Lovely Harperettes *(Special added attraction a screening of the all sepia movie "Dress Rehearsal" produced by and starring comedian Eddie Green and his Sepia Arts Film Company.)*

Apollo Theatre October 20th, the grandest eighty-five minutes of stage entertainment you'll ever see Buck & Bubbles, Teddy Hill and Band, Stump & Stumpy, Harper's Brown Skin Chorus

Apollo Theatre November 3rd, The Aristocrat of Swing from this year's run at Billy Rose's Diamond Horseshoe, Noble Sissle and Band, The Harperettes

Apollo Theatre November 10th, "Fats" Waller and Band

Apollo Theatre November 17th, Queen of Hi-De-Ho Blanche Calloway, Harper's Boys & Girls

Apollo Theatre (November—Thanksgiving Show) Edgar Hayes and Orchestra, Harper Chorus Line of Twelve Girls and Six Boys

Apollo Theatre December 25th, Cab Calloway and Band, Unit Assisted Under the direction of Harper

Apollo Theatre December 29th, Jimmie Lunceford and Band, Large Leonard Harper Revue Cast, Harper Stages Sixteen Pretty Dancing Girls

Apollo Theatre (circa 1939) Harry James (white) who had a wide following in Harlem at the time brings his trumpet uptown for the first time, Harper Revue Cast

Apollo Theatre (circa 1939) Trumpet player Bunny Berigan (white) comes North of Central Park to lead his orchestra in a week of swing as a Headliner with a very large Revue Staged by Leonard Harper, Harperettes

Apollo Theatre (circa 1939) Fats Waller All-Star Show, Harper's 16 Gorgeous Cuties

Apollo Theatre (circa 1939) Charles Barnet and Band, Harper's House Chorus Line

1940-HARPER APOLLO THEATRE SHOWCASE (HEADLINERS)

Apollo Theatre January 5th, Jumping with Andy Kirk, the 16 Harperettes

Apollo Theatre February 5th, Sister Tharpe, Coleman Hawkins and Band, the Deep River Boys, Production Staged by Harper and Sherman Dudley (*The Bible thumping, gospel guitar twanging Sister Rosetta Tharpe was boycotted by a few small uptight churches who accused her of performing in nightclubs and after hours spots and doing the work of the Devil. Sister Tharpe ignored the holier than thou squares and continued to spread the word of God while rocking and rolling.*)

Apollo Theatre February 16th, Earl (Father) Hines and Band, 16 Pretty Harper Trained Girls

Apollo Theatre March 1st, Lucky Millinder and Band, Apollo Brownskin Chorus (*The Apollo Chorus girls went on Strike for better labor conditions. Most of the Apollo theatre employees supported them and audiences refused to cross their picket lines until owner Frank Schiffman settled the dispute and negotiated a more amicable contract.*)

Apollo Theatre March 8th, Teddy Wilson and Band, 16 Lovely Apollo Girls-A Harper / Sherman Dudley Show

Apollo Theatre March (Easter Show) Ella Fitzgerald first time as head of her own Band and Jackie "Moms" Mabley, Sixteen Lovely Dancing Girls in Three New Harper/Sherman Dudley Ensembles (*Bandleader Chick Webb had died of Tuberculosis and Ella Fitzgerald took over his orchestra.*)

Apollo Theatre March 29th, Ralph Cooper in "Gang War" also cast of fifty favorites in the Musical Comedy *Harlem Showboat* by Leonard Harper and Sherman Dudley, Sixteen Dancing Beauties

Apollo Theatre April 26th, the Dynamic Maestro Tiny Bradshaw and Band and Revue, Lovely Brownskin Chorus

Apollo Theatre October 4th, Composer of "Tuxedo Junction" Erskine Hawkins and Band and a Great Leonard Harper Revue, Dancing Boys & Girls

Apollo Theatre October 18th, America's No.1 Swing Band Count Basie and Band, Sixteen of Americas Finest and Prettiest Dancers

Apollo Theatre November 1st, Mills Brothers, Claude Hopkins and Band, Harper's Chorus

Apollo Theatre November 8th, 'Fats' Waller and Band, Sixteen Brownskin Dancing Beauties

Apollo Theatre November 29th, the King of the Jitterbugs Tiny Bradshaw and Band

Apollo Theatre (Xmas Season Holiday Show) Erskine Butterfield "The Singing Vagabond of Keys", Apollo Dancing Girls in Beautiful Holiday Inspired Ensembles

Apollo Theatre December 27th, Her Royal Highness the First Lady of Swing-Ella Fitzgerald and All Star Orchestra

Apollo Theatre (circa 1940) Earl "Fatha" Hines and Orchestra

1941-HARPER APOLLO THEATRE SHOWCASE (HEADLINERS)

Apollo Theatre January 17th, Erskine Hawkins and Band, the Leonard Harper Chorus

Apollo Theatre January 24th, One of America's Favorite Trumpeters- Louis Prima and Band, Harper's Brownskin Chorus

Apollo Theatre February 14th, Les Hite and Orchestra

Apollo Theatre (Spring) Blanche Calloway and Band, Mary Bruce Dancing Boys & Girls in a Medley Staged by Harper and Mary Bruce

Apollo Theatre March 7th, A Sparkling, Spectacular Musical Comedy Based on Abram Hill's *On Strivers' Row* Produced under the Supervision of Leonard Harper

Apollo Theatre April 25th, Foremost Exponents of Swing Band and a Grand Boggie Woggie Revue Count Basie and Band, the Harprettes

(Apollo Theatre Temporarily Closes)

Apollo was closed from the last week of July until the first week of September for renovations. It was during this time that Frank Schiffman owner of the Apollo Theatre rethought the Harper variety show format and planned the removal of the newly unionized chorus line in favor of featuring and promoting headliner acts. Harper's utility as, the producer/director/stager, of these Apollo productions are drastically curtailed.

Apollo Theatre September 4th, Ink Spots **(After being closed for seven weeks the Apollo opens with a Summer Gala Reopening)**

Apollo Theatre September 12th, Ella Fitzgerald and Band, Harper's Ponies and Riders

Apollo Theatre (Fall) Eddie "Rochester" Anderson-the guy who made Jack Benny famous in a Leonard Harper Staged Revue with Babe Lawrence, A New Brownskin Chorus *(For many months the Apollo had been negotiating for Rochester but Jack Benny and CBS said "no" they couldn't spare him. But at long last Rochester returned to Harlem to head a revue staged by Leonard Harper.)*

Apollo Theatre December 13th, Its Friday the 13th... But Here's a Lucky Show! Composer Genius Duke Ellington and Band, a Gala Harper Revue "The Hep Cats Ball" and "A Handful Of Stars"

1942-HARPER APOLLO THEATRE SHOWCASE (HEADLINERS)

Apollo Theatre January 2nd, Leonard Harper's *Camp Caper's* with Claude Hopkins, the Tune Toppers, Willie Bryant and others

Apollo Theatre May 29th, From Broadway at $2.20 admission to Harlem's High Spot-Ed Sullivan Presents *Harlem Cavalcade* with the Greatest Stars and the Most Beautiful Girls ever assembled in one Show, Dances Staged by Leonard Harper

Apollo Theatre (circa 1942) Louis Armstrong and Orchestra and the Famous Leonard Harper Chorus

Apollo Theatre June 20th, Leonard Harper's *Chock Full of Rhythm Revue* with Claude Hopkins and Band, Harper's Beautiful Brownskin Chorus

(Harper's Final Show at the Apollo Theatre)

Apollo Theatre October 2nd, The Happy-Go-Lucky-Jive King Louis Prima and Band, Harper's Brownskin Beauty Chorus

AUTHORS NOTES

Abbreviation: UNPC/S—Unidentified Newspaper Clipping or Source

INTRODUCTION

p. vii *The Harlem Renaissance Dictionary for The Era* edited by Bruce Kellner, (Greenwood Publishing Group, Inc., 1984) mention
p. vii "Check all of the old": Edwina Evelyn of Salt & Pepper quote as verbalized to the author in her apartment.

CHAPTER ONE *(1888 TO 1923)*
THE EARLY YEARS: *MEDICINE SHOWS & SILENT MOVIES*

p. 1 "You talk…That's what my babe do": *"An Educated Coon Is Best of All"* Song by Scott Lawrence
p. 5 "Muse: And there were a couple": *Every Step a Struggle: Interviews with Seven Who Shaped the African-American Images in Movies Scarred By History* by Frank Manchel (New Academia Publishing), p. 257
p. 7 "And as my family": George Freeman quotes from *The Freeman Illustrated Colored Newspaper* (circa mid 1913)
P. 7 "Some of them": George Freeman quotes from *The Freeman Illustrated Colored Newspaper* (circa late 1913)

HARPER & BLANKS WITH LOVE

p. 16 "there is it's ceaseless activity": "Put And Take Is Lively" review *NY Times* Aug. 24, 1921

p. 16 "The show moves": Patterson James, 1921 UNPC/S

COLORED DARLINGS OF LONDON?

p. 24 "Plantation Title Not Prevented In London-Court Decides Against Cochran In Butt Injunction Matter", *Variety*, March 22, 1923 description of

p. 25 "The leading complainant, stirring up mischief": *Florence Mills: Harlem Jazz Queen* by Bill Egan (Rowan & Littlefield Pub., 2004), p.116

p. 25 "while the actors and actresses": "The Scandal of Negro Revues" by Hannen Swaffer *The Sunday Times/Daily Graphic London*, England March 6, 1923

p. 26 "so that niggers can act": "Negro Artists Not Wanted In London" *Baltimore Afro-American*, April 6, 1923

p. 32 "Within the show (*The Rainbow*)": Fynes Harte-Harrington No. 17 London The Empire, April 1923 *WordPress*.com

p. 33 "During their early period": *Astaire, The Man, The Dancer: The Life Of Fred Astaire* by Bob Thomas (St. Martin's Press, 1984), p. 45

p. 33 "outburst triggered some cries": *Florence Mills: Harlem Jazz Queen* by Bill Egan (Rowman & Littlefield Pub., 2004), p .81

p. 34 "scene, rendered by colored": *Plantation Days* review *The Illustrated London News*, April 14, 1923-622

p. 34 "The Negro "plantation" turn": "The Negro Turn" *Sunday Times of London* April 8, 1923

p. 34 "come under the Performing": *The Rainbow* review by H.G., (*London*) *Observer* Sunday April 8, 1923 (excerpted)

p. 35 "In spite of the adverse": "Colored Actor's Write of Prejudice in London" by Harper & Blanks, *Baltimore Afro-American*, May 11, 1923

HARPER MOVED TO HARLEM & DID THE LINCOLN THEATRE

CHAPTER TWO *(1923 TO THE EARLY 1930'S)*
HARPER DID CONNIE'S INN

p. 44 "Leonard Harper built a wall": dancer Ruby Dallas Young quote as verbalized to the author on a New York City bus.
p. 54 "Among the younger generation of": by Romeo L. Dougherty editor *New York Amsterdam News* April 20, 1923

HARPER DID THE LAFAYETTE THEATRE

p. 58 "There was much noise": <u>The Blacker the Berry</u> by Wallace Thurman (Dover Publications, 2008), p. 171
p. 58, 59 Leonard Harper's Lafayette Theatre Productions Title listing
p. 64 "Hollywood Sends Screen Star Home To Harlem, Muse Heads Harper Revue" *New York Amsterdam News*, March 1933 title mention

HARPER DID THE NEST CLUB
HARPER DID THE COTTON CLUB

p. 72 "Sonny says 'No, the first show'": "Stanley Crouch Jazz Interview with Sonny Greer" The Jazz Oral History Project- Institute of Jazz Studies Rutgers University/Smithsonian Institute, page. 66 to 68
p. 74 "It was an all-black show": "<u>That Vaudeville Style: A Conversation with Honi Coles, How Hope Started…,</u> by Mel Watkins AFP Alicia Patterson Foundation, 1979, Volume 2 # 6 Index p. 5

HARPER DID THE HOLLYWOOD INN/KENTUCKY CLUB

p. 82 "I was familiar with that kind": <u>Duke Ellington In Person: An Intimate Memoir</u> by Mercer Ellington with Stanley Dance, (Da Capo Press, 1988), p. 41

p. 83 "A man named Leonard Harper": <u>Sweet Man: The Real Duke Ellington</u> by Don George, (Penguin Group-USA, 1981), p. 45

HARPER DID SMALLS PARADISE

CHAPTER THREE *(1924 TO 1928)*
TAKE ME UP TO THE ONLY *HARLEM RENAISSANCE*

p. 87 "1. Harlem has attained": "Variety-Thinks Harlem Nite Clubs Have Broadway Skinned" *Baltimore Afro-American*, Oct. 26, 1929

p. 88 "The role of the chorus": <u>The Jazz Cadence Of American Culture</u> edited by Robert G. O'Meally (Columbia University Press, 1998), p. 285

p. 91 "Harper it was said": "Black Page Columnist" by J. A. Jackson, *Billboard* (circa early 1920s)

THE GREAT (WHITE) *LEONARD HARPER* WAY

p. 92 "Leonard Harper of Harper and Blanks have": "The Floor Show A Growing Feature" by J. A. Jackson *Billboard* (circa early 1920s)

p. 97 "like most producers, he": <u>Duke Ellington and his World: A Biography</u> by A. H. Lawrence (Taylor & Francis, Inc., 2003), p. 36

p. 100 "Cook points out that the Charleston": <u>The Wicked Waltz and Other Scandalous Dances: Outrage at Couple Dancing in the 19th And 20th Century</u> by Mark Knowles (Development and Dispersion of the-Charleston). (McFarland & Company), p. 147

p. 102 <u>Josephine: The Hungry Heart</u> by John Claude Baker and Chris Chase, mention (Rowman and Littlefield Publishers, 2001)

LEONARD HARPER & FLORENCE MILLS

p. 109 "the gods should send": "Sing a Song Of Sixpence" *Blackbirds of 1926* review by D. N. 1926 UNPC/S

p. 109 "Florence Mills is prancing": *Blackbirds of 1926* review, *New York Sun* first week of August 1926

LEONARD HARPER CHATTERED

p. 111, 112 "The only people who ever protested": "Man Who Built Reputation Because He Knew How To Pick Pretty, Shapely Chorus Girls, Takes Rap At Critics-"Hip- Movement" Dance Which Has Aroused Storm Of Protest–Has Trained Many Famous Choruses-Leonard Harper And Two Of His Pretty Chorines" by Floyd Calvin, *Pittsburg Courier* Jan. 15, 1927 p. A1

p. 112 "The average white chorus girl": *Variety* March 9, 1927 review of Harper's *4-11-44*

p. 113 "I first glimpsed": "Stage Mirror-LEONARD HARPER" by Eva A. Jessye *Baltimore Afro-American* August 20, 1927

HARPER DID THE SAVOY BALLROOM

p. 116 "Harper Revue Is Not So Hot-Savoy Presentation Below That Of Previous Effort By Producer" *New York Amsterdam News,* April 19, 1933 mention

p. 116, 117 "out of the ordinary": "Harper Revue Out At The Savoy-Local Dance Hall Returns To Policy Of Presenting Leading Bands" *New York Amsterdam News*, April 26, 1933

p. 117 "I was born and raised": Norma Miller (Queen of Swing Dancer) quote as verbalized to the author at the Schomburg Center for Research in Black Culture screening of "*The Savoy King*", October 2, 2012

HARPER DID NEW JERSEY

CHAPTER FOUR *(1928 TO 1929)*
HARPER'S *HOT CHOCOLATES'*
THE CONCEPT, THE CHALLENGE AND THE CHANCE

p. 125 "Connie's Inn new floor show": "Connie's New Music, Lyrics" review 1928 UNPC/S

p. 125 "Connie's Inn revue will try to follow": "Broadway Gets Darker": Connie's Inn Revue New York Show Talk by Maurice Dancer theatrical columnist (circa late 1928) UNPC/S

p. 125 "The new revue at Connie's Inn": "Hot Feet" review quote, *Pittsburg Courier* March 16, 1929

p. 125 "Ellington's fourth Cotton Club revue": <u>Beyond Category</u> by John Edward Hasse (Da Capo Press, 1995), p. 118

p. 126 "Early in the rehearsals": <u>Fats Waller</u> by Maurice Waller and Anthony Calabrese song conception-Edith Wilson-Black and Blue, (Cengage Gale, 1979), p. 86

p. 127 "Can you imagine hearing": <u>Hear me talking to ya: the story of jazz by the men who made it,</u> edited by Nat Shapiro and Nat Hentoff, Mezz Mezzrow (Dover Publications, 1966), p. 255

p. 129 <u>Black And Blue The Life And Lyrics Of Andy Razaf</u> by Barry Singer (Schirmer Books, 1992), mention

THREE TAN-SKINNED CREATORS

p. 134 "Quite a number of changes": "Hotter Chocolates" Backstage with Stage-Struck *Inter-State Tattler* June 14, 1929

p. 135 "That out of all of the many director/producers": Mrs. Alicia Razaf-Georgiade wife of Andy Razaf quote as verbalized to the author at her home in Las Vegas, Nevada

p. 139 "blacker than a rent collector's heart": Amanzie "Jazzlips" Richardson quote *N.Y. Evening Graphic* (circa 1929)

p. 140 "how high is up?": "Jazzlips Won't Leave His Attic Dressing Room" Jazzlips interview (circa 1929) UNPC/S

AN UNDYING BROADWAY INSCRIPTION

p. 142 "What she (Jota) did with her stomach": Souvenirs of Hot Chocolates' quote from the linear notes about Louise "Jota" Cook by Martin Williams on the original cast album Smithsonian Institution 1978

GRANT HARPER REID

p. 147 "The Negro is not merely": *Hot Chocolates'* advertisement on the road in Maryland, N.Y. January 27, 1930 of a *Herald Tribune* quote of a poster October 18, 1929—date of poster

p. 148 "the depression brought everybody down": Langston Hughes quote

p.149 "The Great Depression brought": *The Making Of A Ghetto/Negro New York 1890-1930* by Gilbert Osofsky quote (Harper Collins Publishers, 1971), p.186

p. 149 "most Negroes were out of vogue": Langston Hughes quote

CHAPTER FIVE *(1929 TO 1935)*
'HOT HARLEM' GOT FROSTY

p. 164 *Blacks In black and white: A Source Book On Black Films* by Henry Sampson (Rowman & Littlefield Publishers Inc. 1995) description of text

p. 165 "He (*Micheaux*) splurged on the": *Oscar Micheaux: The Great and Only: The Life of America's First Black Filmmaker* by Patrick McGilligan (Harper and Collins, 2008), p. 252-253

p. 166 "Leonard Harper's tap-dancing: *Oscar Micheaux: The Great and Only: The Life of America's First Black Filmmaker* by Patrick McGilligan (Harper and Collins, 2008) p. 253-254

p. 172 "Theatre Owner Talks To Garvey", Schiffman meets with Marcus Garvey in Jamaica referenced *New York Amsterdam News*, Feb. 3, 1932

HOLLYWOOD HERE WE COME—NOT!

p. 177 "We pass the Central, where Connie's": Harper's *Ace In The Hole Revue of 1932 of High Yaller Gals* reviewed for *Harlem By Night* by Maurice Dancer review Aug. 1932

p. 178 "the Immermans were frantically searching for a successor": "Connie's Inn Has New Revue", quote by theatre critic William Smith *Pittsburgh Courier Stage- Screen-Drama-Music* section Oct. 1, 1932

HARPER ROMANCED YOUNG FANNIE PENNINGTON

p. 180 "It was at one of those Baptizing Sunday's": Fannie Pennington quote as verbalized to the author (circa 1980s)

p. 181 "Papa took me to see Leonard's": Fannie Pennington quote (same source as above)

p. 181 "sometimes touted as the Negro": <u>Toms Coons Mulattoes, Mammies, & Bucks An Interpretive History of Blacks in American Films</u> by Donald Bogle (Continuum International Publishing Group-2001), p. 114

p. 181 "I met Harper in": Fannie Pennington's quote as verbalized to the author (circa 1980s)

p. 182 "he treated people nice": Fannie Pennington quote (same source as above)

p. 182 "Harper, I was fascinated by him": Fannie Pennington quote (same source as above)

HARPER "DUFFED" HARLEM FOR CHICAGO

p. 185 "Harper is so popular": "Downtown In Chicago", quote *Baltimore Afro-American* (circa early 1933)

p. 186 "is said to have sought": "Grand Terrace Café Shakes Up It's Cast-Big Shake Up In Grand Theatre / Valaida Snow Is Dropped In The New Deal" by Rob Roy quote *Chicago Defender* June 17, 1933 p. 5

p. 186 "Valaida Snow, singer": "Valaida Snow Now In The East For A Rest" quote *Chicago Defender* June 24, 1933

p. 188 "(Harper) took off by plane": "Going Backstage With the Scribe" quote *Chicago Defender* (circa 1933)

p. 188 Harper's *Get Lucky* mentioned by Billy Rowe, *Pittsburgh Courier* (circa 1933) description of revue.

RHYTHM FOR SALE

p. 190 "Harper pays less attention to his": anonymous quote, *Chicago Defender* March 1934

p. 190 "one of the finest revues": Harper's *Rhythm For Sale* quote by critic Earl J. Morris, Grand Town Day & Night, *Pittsburgh Courier* (circa 1933)

p. 191 "The greatest choreographer of my time": showman Leonard Reed's quote about Harper to Melba Huber, *Dance Universe Magazine* January 1, 2003

p. 191 "My first job with Leonard Harper was at the": quote by showman Leonard Reed as written to the author, November 17, 1998

p. 191 "Leonard Harper was a great producer": quote by dancer Margot S. Webb of Norton & Margot as written to the author, September 18, 1998

p. 193 "Truly, the Regal has": "Regal Theatre Goes Harlem And Patrons Wild Over Hit" quote by Rob Roy, *Chicago Defender*, May 19, 1934 p. 8

CHICAGO RHYTHM

p. 195 "Not even the 'Stormy Weather'": "Going Backstage With The Scribe" quote *Chicago Rhythm* a comparison to Harpers co-production of the *Stormy Weather-Cotton Club Revue*. *Chicago Defender* (circa 1935)

p. 196 "Grand Terrace's Show Is Musical Caviar, Says Roy" title quote review of Harper's *Grand Terrace Revue of 1935* by Rob Roy *Chicago Defender*, Feb. 16, 1935

p. 198 "I remember Leonard Harper very well": quote by Jack Schiffman, Frank Schiffman's son as written to the author, March 13, 1996

p. 198 "I remember a time when Leonard Harper could offer": "Grand Town-Day and Night" quote by Earl Morris, *Pittsburgh Courier*, August 22, 1935

CHAPTER SIX *(1935 TO 1937)*
UNSEEN PRODUCER/DIRECTOR

p. 203 "He was one of the greatest": quote from dancer Leroy Meyers of the Copasetics' as verbalized to the author on 122th. Street, Harlem (circa late 1980s) about Harper's work as the Apollo Theatre in-house producer
p. 204 <u>Uncle Tom's Cabin</u> by Harriet Beecher Stowe published in 1852 mention

HARPER DID THE UBANGI CLUB…TOO

p. 208 "I met Mr. Harper and started working": quote from dancer Cleo Hayes as verbalized to the author in front of her apartment building (circa mid 1980s)

FANNIE AND POCKET-SIZED HARRIET JEAN HARPER

p. 210 "For a time I left the church": Fannie Pennington's quote as verbalized to the author (circa 1980s)
p. 211 "Yeah we did two or three": Fannie Pennington's quote (same source as above)
p. 212 "when Joe Louis won a prize fight": Fannie Pennington's quote (same source as above)

MOTHER HARPER RELOCATED TO HARLEM
JEAN HARPER LEFT FOR DOWN SOUTH WHILE
FANNIE'S ON THE GO

p. 212 "at the age of two and a half years old": Jean Harper's quote as verbalized to the author (circa 1980s)
p. 213 "Leonard Harper is playing host to his mother": as reported in a gossip column Harper moves mom and niece into Harlem apartment from Chicago, (circa 1936) UNPC/S

p. 213 "There was a lady sitting in the": Jean Harper's quote as verbalized to the author. (circa 1980s)

p. 213 "Papa always taught in Sunday school": Fannie Pennington's quote as verbalized to the author (circa 1980s)

p. 214 "Sarah Harper was a nice lady": Fannie Pennington's quote as verbalized to the author. (circa 1980s)

p. 215 "and as he gave Jean": Betty Saunders quote as verbalized to the author (circa late 1980s)

p. 215 "I still joke": *And I Haven't Had A Bad Day Since: From the Streets of Harlem to the Halls of Congress* by Charles Rangel and Leon Wynter (St. Martin's Press, 2007), p. 108

p. 216 "Harper staged my group": Ludie Jones of the Lang Sisters, quote as verbalized to the author (circa 1980s)

THOSE FABULOUS HARPERETTES

p. 217 "Leonard Harper, the Flo Ziegfeld of Harlem": "Stars of Tomorrow-Twinkle Today" *Baltimore Afro-American*, March 21, 1936

p. 218 "Harper didn't talk to us chorus girls anymore": Jackie Lewis Parton former chorus girl quote as verbalized to the author at Co-Op City Bronx, NY. (circa early 1980s)

p. 219 "Perhaps we are too harsh on the Harperettes but the thrill is gone": quote by Alfred A. Duckett "Seeing The Show", *New York Age* first week of October 1936

THE WORLD FAMOUS APOLLO THEATRE...Y'ALL

CHAPTER SEVEN *(1937 TO 1942)*
HARPER DID THE DOWNTOWN HARLEM UPROAR HOUSE

p. 226 "If there were more to watch": "If There Were More To Watch, There Would Be More To Work" quote Ed Small's speaks on Small's Paradise (circa 1937) UNPC/S

p. 227 "A capacity crowd": "Small's Offers Speed, Rhythm In New Show" by St. Claire Bourne *N.Y. Amsterdam News*, October 2, 1937

p. 230 *Class Act: The Jazz Life Of Choreographer Cholly Atkins* by Cholly Atkins and Jacqui Malone (Columbia University Press, 2003) mention of book

p. 230 "prance fearlessly and": Theatre critic, quote by John Mason Brown about the Miller Brothers and Lois a description of the show *N.Y. World Telegram*, May 4, 1942

p. 230 "One of those times": *Class Act: The Jazz Life Of Choreographer Cholly Atkins* by Cholly Atkins and Jacqui Malone (Columbia University Press, 2003) p. 40-41

p. 230, 231 "I started working": *Unsung Heroes Of Rock 'N' Roll: The Birth Of Rock In The Wild Years Before Elvis* sub-chapter *He Who Controls The Rhythm* by Nick Tosches (Da Capo Press, 1999) p.14

p. 231, 232 "Most of them": *That Vaudeville Style: A Conversation From Honi Coles, Running With Ghosts*, by Mel Watkins (Alicia Patterson Foundation, 1979) Volume 2 # 6 Index p. 5

p. 233 "Fairly well produced": Harper's *Hot Harlem* review quote, *Variety* (circa 1938) (excerpted)

EV'RY SHOW'S GOTTA HAVE A FINALE
HARPERETTES WALKED OUT OF THE APOLLO THEATRE

p. 238 "The supporting creative staff": *Black And Blue-The Life And Lyrics Of Andy Razaf* by Barry Singer quote (Schirmer Books 1992) p. 310 description of staff of *Tan Manhattan*

HARPER DID THE ELK'S RENDEZVOUS (1941-1942)

p. 241 "Johnny Barone's new Elk's": "Broadway Invades Harlem Via The Elk's Rendezvous Hot Spot" quote by Maurice Dancer *Chicago Defender*, July 9, 1941 p. 21

CHAPTER EIGHT *(1942 TO 1943)*
WANTED: GLAMOROUS GIRLS

p. 243 "During the late 1930s": <u>Fritz Pollard: Pioneer In Racial Advancement</u> by John M. Carroll (University of Illinois Press 1992), p. 206

HARPER DID MURRAINS

p. 246 "sparkling with rhythm and music": Murrains nightclub review, quote by Billy Rowe *Pittsburgh Courier* (circa 1942)

p. 246 "When Mr. Harper made you put on": Thelma Price the former chorus girl quote, as verbalized to the author at the Apollo Theatre after the premiere of the movie *Been Rich All My Life* March 2006

p. 247 "plotting a new approach": *Harlem Cavalcade*, quote by Billy Rowe *Pittsburgh Courier*, spring of 1942

STILL *CHOCK FULL OF RHYTHM*

p. 249 "This lusty all-colored": Harlem Steps Out In Style quote by Rowland Field *Harlem Cavalcade* description *Newark Evening News-*Broadway Section May 2, 1942

p. 250 "Put together in two parts,": "Harlem Cavalcade Brings Life" by Isadora Smith *Pittsburgh Courier*, May 9, 1942 p. 21

p. 250 "merely a re-issue of ghost": "Encores and Echoes-Harlem Cavalcade" by E. Billingsworth May 1942 UNPC/S

p. 251 "Because all these good dancers": review quote by John Mason Brown *New York World Telegram*, May 4, 1942

EXILED ON SEVENTH AVENUE

p. 252 "With Small's practically": <u>The Autobiography of Malcolm X</u> by Malcolm X and Alex Haley (Random House Publishing Group, 1987), p. 80-83 (excerpted)

p. 252 "Tavern Topics" Small's Paradise mention, the big stars who came to Smalls Paradise during this period *New York Amsterdam News* March 8, 1941

1943 HARPER'S DEATH

p. 258 "His soul was in the theatre": LEONARD HARPER Poem by Andy Razaf read during Harper's funeral February 8, 1943

THE AFTERMATH

p. 261 "What makes the new revue tick": "Newest Murrain Revue Sensational" *Sensations Of 1943* review by drama editor Dan Burley a recounting of Harper's final nightclub revue at Murrains nightclub *New York Amsterdam News* February 27, 1943

p. 261 "He had established": "Pollard Inherited Sun Tan Studios After Producer Died" by Julius J. Adams *New York Amsterdam News*, Sept. 10, 1949

p. 262 "What Leonard Harper and the": "Sun Tan Studios Train Nation's New Starlets" by Henry Brown, *The Chicago Defender*, July 31, 1948 p. 13 (excerpted)

HARPER APOLLO THEATRE SIGNATURE SHOWCASE (HEADLINER) LISTINGS FROM 1935 TO 1942

PHOTOGRAPHS & ILLUSTRATIONS

Abbreviation: UNPC/S-Unidentified Newspaper Clipping or Source.

1. Book Cover Interior Nest Club. 1920s Courtesy Schomburg Center for Research in Black Culture Photographs and Prints Division N.Y. Public Library Otis C. Butler.
2. Harper & Blanks *The Smart Set Couple* United States Passport Photos. 1923.
3. Leonard Harper Press Photograph. 1924 UNPC/S
4. Leonard Harper System Broadway Dance Studio advertisement. 1924 UNPC/S
5. Interior The Nest Club. 1920s Courtesy Schomburg Center for Research in Black Culture Photographs and Prints Division N.Y. Public Library. Otis C. Butler.
6. Harper's *Tan Town Topics* advertisement. 1925 UNPC/S
7. Leonard Harper and the Famous Plantation Beauty Chorus in *Blackbirds of 1926* N.Y. Public Library Lincoln Center for the Performing Arts, White Studios. Billy Rose Theatre Collection.
8. Leonard Harper's *Pepper Pot Revue* featuring Bill (Bojangles) Robinson and the Harper Chorus Line. 1927. The Harperettes and Bojangles perform Dance-Offs and the chorus girls duplicated his patented tap steps phrase for phrase and pitter for patter. Audiences went wild.

9. Harper's *Club Kentucky* Revue advertisement. 1927 UNPC/S
10. Harper's *Hot Chocolates'* "Jungle Jamboree" scene featuring Baby Cox and Louise "Jota" Cook. 1929 N.Y. Public Library/Lincoln Center for the Performing Arts, White Studios. Billy Rose Theatre Collection.
11. Backstage at Harper's *Hot Chocolates'* with Louise "Jota" Cook 1929 with an inset of her likeness painted on *The Exile* movie poster 1931 N. Y. Public Library/Lincoln Center for the Performing Arts, White Studios. Billy Rose Theatre Collection.
12. Inside view of Harper's Floorshow at Connie's Inn. 1920s. Helen Armstead Johnson.
13. Harper's *Hot Feet* at Connie's Inn advertisement. 1929 UNPC/S
14. Leonard Harper leading the Hal Bakay Funeral Cortege with George Immerman (to his left) and Sam Wooding (far left) on 7th. Ave. Harlem across the street from Connie's Inn and the Lafayette Theatre. 1931 Inter-State Tattler.
15. Harper's Cosy Grill nightclub program. 1932 UNPC/S
16. Fannie Pennington at 21 years old in Asbury Park, New Jersey. 1935 Grant Harper Reid Collection
17. Harper's *League of Rhythm Revue* poster at the Apollo Theatre. 1936 UNPC/S
18. Leonard Harper in-house Apollo theatre producer looks on in Apollo theatre office as Eddie Green signs a motion picture deal. Jimmy Marshall manager of the Apollo accepts the contract. September 30, 1939. *Chicago Defender*.

BIBLIOGRAPHICAL LISTINGS

The Harlem Renaissance: A Historical Dictionary For The Era Edited by Bruce Kellner

Blacks In Blackface by Henry T. Sampson

Every Step a Struggle: Interviews with Seven Who Shaped the African-American Images in Movies-Scarred By History by Frank Manchel

Florence Mills; Harlem Jazz Queen by Bill Egan

Astaire, the Man, The Dancer: The Life of Fred Astaire by Bob Thomas

The Blacker The Berry by Wallace Thurman

Jazz Interview with Sonny Greer by Stanley Crouch for The Jazz Oral History Project On file at the Institute Of Jazz Studies, Rutgers University, State of New Jersey and the Smithsonian

"That Vaudeville Style; A Conversation With Honi Coles" by Mel Watkins APF (Alicia Patterson Foundation) Reporter Volume 2 #6 Index

Duke Ellington In Person: An Intimate Memoir by Mercer Ellington with Stanley Dance

Sweet Man: The Real Duke Ellington by Don George

Black And Blue The Life And Lyrics Of Andy Razaf by Barry Singer, Foreword by Bobby Short

Toms, Coons, Mulattoes, Mammies, & Bucks An Interpretive History of Blacks in America Films by Donald Bogle

The Jazz Cadence Of American Culture edited by Rob G. O'Meally

Duke Ellington And His World by A.H. Lawrence

The Wicked Waltz and Other Scandalous Dances: Outrage at Couple Dancing in the 19th. And Early 20th Century by Mark Knowles

Josephine: The Hungry Heart by Jean Claude Baker & Chris Chase

Beyond Category by Edward Hasse

Fats Waller by Maurice Waller and Anthony Calabrese

Hear me talkin' to ya; the story of jazz by the men who made it, by Nat Shapiro and Nat Hentoff

Harlem the Making Of A Ghetto/Negro New York, 1890-1930 by Gilbert Osofsky

Blacks in black and white: A Source Book On Black Films by Henry T. Sampson

Oscar Micheaux: The Great and Only: The Life Of America's First Black Filmmaker by Patrick McGilligan

The Conquest: The Story of a Negro Pioneer by Oscar Micheaux

And I Haven't Had A Bad Day Since: From The Streets of Harlem to the Halls of Congress by Charles B. Rangel with Leon Wynter

Class Act: The life of Choreographer Cholly Atkins by Cholly Atkins and Jacqui Malone

Unsung Heroes of Rock' n' Roll: the Birth of Rock In The Wild Years Before Elvis By Nick Tosches

Fritz Pollard; Pioneer in Racial Advancement by John Carroll

ACKNOWLEDGMENTS

Fannie Emma Pennington, Jean (Harriet Harper) Reid, Todd Winston Reid, Everett Winston Reid, Matthew Pennington, Calico, Doll Thomas, Margot S. Webb, Tondaleyo, Peg Leg Bates, Cleo Hayes, Leonard Reed, Edwina Evelyn, Ludie Jones, Bertie Lou Woods, Jackie Lewis Parton, Leroy Meyers, Ruby Dallas Young, Thelma Prince, Alicia Wilson Razaf-Georgiade, Norma Miller, Delilah Jackson, Betty Saunders, Stanley Crouch, Mel Watkins

The New York Public Library-The Schomburg Center For Research In Black Culture Manuscripts, Archives and Rare Books Division: Helen Armstead Johnson Collection-Foundation, General Research and Reference Division, The New York Public Library For the Performance Arts-Billy Rose Theatre Division, N.Y. Countee Cullen Library, N. Y. Mid-Manhattan Library, Reverend Calvin O. Butts III-Abyssinian Baptist Church Archives, Museum of The City of N. Y., City of N.Y. Municipal Archives-Records and Informational Services

Theatre Museum of London, National Museum of the Performing Arts, Westminster Reference Library of London-City of Westminster-England, Institute of Jazz Studies- Rutgers University the State of New Jersey, Louis Armstrong House & The Louis Armstrong Archives of Queens College, The Shubert Organization Archives, The Apollo Theatre Foundation, the Alicia Patterson Foundation

New York Daily Newspaper, The Freeman An Illustrated Colored Newspaper, New York Amsterdam News, New York Age, Theatrical World, Chicago Defender, Inter-State Tattler, Pittsburgh Courier,

Baltimore Afro American, Billboard, Variety, Dancer Universe Magazine, New York Clipper, The People's Voice, The ERA, The London Observer, The Illustrated London News, The Sunday Times (London), New York Sun, New York Evening Graphic, New York Daily Mirror, Christian Science Monitor (Boston), New York World Telegram, New York Post, New York Herald Tribune (London Bureau), Newark Evening News, After Dark the Nocturnal Adventures of Fynes Harte-Harrington/WordPress.com.

Edited by Nadine Khtikian

INDEX

Abyssinian Baptist Church, 180, 183, 213, 215, 257, 259
Ain't Misbehavin, 119, 126, 132, 134, 145, 146
Apollo Theatre Grand Inaugural Week, 205
Armstrong, Lillian, 140, 141, 205
Armstrong, Louis, 65, 106, 127, 130, 132, 133, 135, 140, 141, 145, 147, 164, 169, 170, 204, 205, 216, 220, 228, 234, 262
Astaire, Fred, 16, 33, 55, 96, 97
Atkins, Cholly, 230
Bailey, Bill, 207, 262
Baker, Josephine, 102
Balaban Brothers, 185
Basie, William "Count", 37, 220, 230, 237, 240, 255,
Berkeley, Busby, 97, 149, 262
Black And White Peroxide Vanishing Cream, 142
Black n Blue, 119, 128, 129, 144, 146
Blackbirds of 1926, 108-110
Blake, Eubie, 21, 22, 128, 164, 238

Blanks, Berliana, 10-12, 73, 105, 259
Blanks, Osceola, 10-19, 22, 25, 27, 31, 32, 41, 43, 45, 46, 49, 89, 91, 93, 111, 113, 147, 178, 182, 184, 193, 209, 213, 233, 259
Butt, Sir Alfred, 21, 24, 25, 28, 33, 35, 36
Calloway, Cab, 75, 114, 134, 188, 195, 220, 245, 262
Capone, Al, 71, 73, 184-186, 190, 199
Coles, Honi, 74, 215, 231
Colored Actors Write of Prejudice in London, 35
Cook, Louise "Jota", 142, 166, 167, 186
Cox, Baby, 138, 139, 177, 190
Crawford, Joan, 52, 81, 93
Crawford, Llewellyn, 206, 207, 214, 260, 261
Cromer, Harold "Stumpy", See: 1937 Apollo Theatre Listings June 25th., p. 269

Ellington, Duke, 37, 38, 46, 47, 72, 81-84, 86, 90, 91, 97, 114, 122, 125, 138, 145, 164, 180, 220, 228, 231, 234, 240, 245, 262
Ellington, Mercer, 82
Evelyn, Edwina, vii Introduction
Fetchit, Stepin, 220, 221, 232, 235, 248
Fischer, Clifford C., 243-245, 247
Friends of Josephine Baker Committee, 215
Garvey, Marcus, 172
Gershwin, George, 25, 27, 29, 32, 33, 86, 97, 102
Gilpin, Charles, 51, 52, 90
Grand Terrace Cafe, 184-199
Greer, Willian "Sonny", 72, 144
Handy, W. C., 73, 146, 240, 259, 261
Harlem Cavalcade, 247-252
Harper and Blanks, 11-18, 22, 29, 30, 32, 35, 37, 49, 89, 90
Harper, Gene, 1, 2, 45, 90, 187, 189, 233, 260
Harper, Harriet Jean, 187, 189, 193, 197, 204, 209-215, 233, 259
Harper, Sarah, 1, 2, 45, 90, 187, 189, 197, 210, 212-214, 233, 260
Harper, William, 1, 2, 66
Harper's Hollywood Follies, 78, 79, 94
Harper's Hot Chocolates', 106, 119-147, 163, 165-167, 169, 176-178, 181, 186, 203, 207, 210, 240
Harper's Lindy Hopper's 254
Harperettes, 62, 190, 193, 202-204, 217-219, 229, 233, 246, 257
Harris, Edna Mae, 241
Hayes, Cleo, 208
Hegamin, Lucille, 3
Hines, Earl, 186, 190, 192
Honeysuckle Rose, 135-137, 236
Hot Feet, 103, 124, 125, 129, 135, 146
Immerman Brothers (Connie & George), 43, 49, 52, 53, 75, 78, 101, 119, 121, 124, 139, 146, 169, 170, 178
Johnson, James Price ("J. P."), 18, 19, 22, 25, 29, 30, 86, 105, 121-123, 231, 252
Johnson, Jack, 14, 38, 70, 71
Jones, Ludie (The Lang Sisters), 216
Keeler, Ruby, 96, 103, 145
Keep Shufflin, 122-124, 181
Kentucky Club Revue, 38, 67, 68, 91, 117
La-Em-Strait Hair Products, 141
Lead Belly, See: 1936 Apollo Theatre Listings April 3rd p. 265
Leonard Harper Dance Studio, 96-101

Leonard Harper Theatre Workshop, 261
Leslie, Lew, 23, 24, 29, 75, 108, 109, 128, 130, 204
Load of Coal, 135, 136, 236
Luciano, Charles "Lucky", 79, 80, 106, 124
Lucky Sambo, 90, 105, 106, 248
Mad Dog Coll, 175, 176
Malcolm X, 252
Markham, Pigmeat, 62, 164, 193, 228, 231
Marx Brothers, 52, 96
McKinney, Nina Mae, 75, 76
Micheaux, Oscar, 164-169, 181, 248
Miller, Norma, 117
Mills, Florence, 23-25, 30, 31, 90, 93, 94, 107-111, 128
Miss. Colored New York, 173, 174
Moses Sisters, 76, 181, 188, 209
Muse, Clarence, 5, 6, 64, 65, 235
Myers, Leroy, 203
N.A.A.C.P., 144, 172, 194, 231, 235, 236, 255
Nicholas Brothers, 61, 65, 72, 75, 188, 190, 262
Nigger Problem Brought To London, 26
O'Neal, Jimmy, 18, 21, 36, 38, 73
On Strivers' Row, 231, 238, 239
Parton, Jackie Lewis, 218
Pennington, Fannie, 179-184, 188, 189, 204, 209-216, 233, 259
Pennington, Matthew Mark, 180, 187, 212, 213, 259
Pepper Pot Revue, 58, 86, 170, 171, 192
Plantation Days, 18-36, 38, 39, 43, 47, 54, 73, 93, 107, 121, 134, 163
Pollard, Daphne, 31, 93, 94
Pollard, Fritz, 243, 244, 260, 261
Powell, Adam Jr., 180, 183, 215, 257, 259
Prince, Thelma, 246
Princess Pee Wee, See: 1936 Apollo Theatre Listings December 25th p. 267
Pushing the Sand, 229, 249
Put and Take, 14-16, 92
Rangel, Charles, 215
Razaf, Andy, 86, 103, 120-122, 124-126, 128, 129, 131, 135-137, 146, 175, 182, 189, 206, 236, 258
Red Cap Follies, 64
Reed, Leonard, 191
Revusicals, 225
Rhum-Boggie Cafe, 254, 255
Richardson, "Jazzlips", 117, 130, 139, 140, 177
Roach, Hal, 61, 94, 118
Roberts, Lucketh "Lucky", 43, 91, 259

Robeson, Paul, 90, 235
Robinson, Bill "Bojangles", 46, 49, 58, 63, 76, 86, 88, 133, 163, 202, 207, 223, 235, 262
Robinson, Clarence, 57, 72, 74, 76, 105, 123, 193, 197, 201-203, 208, 253
Round N Round In Rhythm, 206, 216
Saunders, Betty, 215
Schiffman, Frank, 37, 56, 57, 65, 67, 68, 91, 108, 164, 165, 167-169, 193, 194, 197-199, 201-205, 220-222, 231, 232, 234-237, 239, 256, 257,
Schiffmam, Jack, 198
Schultz, Dutch, 49, 80, 123, 124, 128, 129, 139, 175
Scott, Mabel, 192, 206
Sensations Of 1943, 231, 256, 260, 261
Shubert Brothers, 16, 17, 30, 76, 92, 93, 101, 120, 238, 247, 251
Shuffle Along, 14, 18, 19, 21-23, 134
Sissle, Noble, 22, 195, 247, 249-251
Smith, Bessie, 14, 221, 242
Snow, Valaida, 186, 187, 191, 192, 195
Souvenirs of Hot Chocolates', 145
Stage Door Canteen, 255
Stone, Jesse, 231, 261
Sullivan, Ed, 52, 230, 232, 247, 249-252

"Sunshine", Sammy, 61, 62, 118, 190, 192, 206
Suntan Studios, 243, 244, 260, 261
Tan Town Topics, 101-103, 108, 124
Tharpe, Sister Rosetta, See: 1940 Apollo Theatre Listings February 5th p. 275
The Brown Skin Vamps, 99, 100
The Exile, 165-169, 248
The Leonard Harper Management Company, 59
The Leonard Harper System, 99
The Leonard Harper Theatre Workshop, 261
The McCormick Sisters, 142, 143, 181, 189, 210
The Red Rooster, 215
The Scar Of Shame, 143, 181
The Three Dixie Songbirds, 12, 45, 73, 105
Tondaleyo, 59, 262
Tough on Black Actors, 14
Tree of Hope, 42, 202, 223
Truckin, 228
Tucker, Earl "Snakehips", 48, 130, 171, 177, 227
Twentieth Century Fox, 65, 136, 137, 236, 255, 261
Two Clever Pics, 3
Ubangi Club Boys, 207, 208
Venable-Owens-Harper Trio, 8, 9
Victoria, Princess Alexandra, 54, 55

Vodery, Will, 30, 75, 102, 111, 195, 247
Waller, Thomas "Fats", 37, 49, 81, 103, 108, 120-127, 131-133, 135, 136, 145, 147, 164, 175, 180, 193, 206, 212, 228, 233, 234, 254, 262
Waters, Ethel, 21, 49, 72, 102, 133, 195, 234, 252, 255, 262
Webb, Margot, 191, 192, 195
West, Mae, 52, 69, 70, 88, 89, 190
White Tower Lodge, 211, 212
Williams, Mary Lou, 126, 127
Williams, Spencer, 14, 86, 103, 170, 171, 175
Wilson, Edith, 90, 108, 126, 128, 129, 133, 144
Wooding, Russell, 64, 127, 128, 171
Young, Ruby Dallas, 44
Ziegfeld, Florenz, 52, 60, 72, 91, 111, 217

Made in the USA
Charleston, SC
20 June 2013